# "GOD SAVE THIS
HONORABLE COURT!"

ALSO BY THE AUTHOR

*The Regulators:*
*Watchdog Agencies and the Public Interest*

# "GOD SAVE THIS HONORABLE COURT!"

*Louis M. Kohlmeier, Jr.*

CHARLES SCRIBNER'S SONS
NEW YORK

To Barbara
for infinite patience

# Contents

# Prologue

Nations, like the men whose communities they comprise, do not always live by the dictates of conscience. But nations that will endure cannot do so without a conscience and, as Earl Warren told Richard Nixon, "because you might not have looked into the matter," the conscience of the United States is in its Constitution and the keeper of its conscience is the Supreme Court of the United States.

Great Presidents do not need a written constitution. Abraham Lincoln told a doubting Secretary of the Treasury not to "bother with the Constitution . . . I have that sacred instrument here at the White House, and I am guarding it with great care." Lesser Presidents cannot do without a written Constitution.

The Constitution applies equally to the three separate and coordinate branches of government, the executive, the legislative, and the judicial. But there is no instant wisdom in the broad mandates of the Constitution that defines for each succeeding generation with its crises, domestic and foreign, the safe and proper balance between government authority and individual freedom. Presidents and congresses and courts therefore have clashed before in history over the meanings of the Constitution and now they clash with a new ferocity.

Yet it is the Supreme Court alone that holds the ultimate power to declare acts of Presidents or congresses null and void under our Constitution and thus to check excessive authority which is repression. It is the Court that bears the final responsibility for enforcing the Bill of Rights and ensuring individual freedom and human dignity. If the essential humanism of the Constitution is not to be found in the consciences of the members of the Supreme Court and in the wisdom of a Court that is independent of the political majoritarianism of the other two branches, then the nation can seek solutions for its crises only in constitutional amendment or, as it has once before in history, in consummate national violence.

This, then, is the danger of the new clash over the Constitution and this is the crisis of the Supreme Court.

CHAPTER I

# The Beginnings of a Battle

On Wednesday, July 14, 1965, the late afternoon sun was warm and inviting in London, not barbarously hot as it was in Washington. Adlai E. Stevenson, the United States Representative to the United Nations, was in London on a private visit, but he was staying at the American Embassy residence with Ambassador and Mrs. David K. E. Bruce. It was difficult to make a really private visit to London, as Stevenson would so much have liked. He had taped an interview for the British Broadcasting Corporation earlier in the day and had taken great care to say in just the right way that he stood with the President in support of the United States position in Vietnam. The night before there had been a party at the Embassy, quite pleasant, but Vietnam again had come up in the conversation. His role at the U.N. had become substantially more difficult in the past month since President Lyndon Johnson publicly had committed American servicemen in Vietnam to combat.

It was warm and bright outside the Embassy and the day was nearly over. Stevenson and Marietta Tree went for a walk. Mrs. Tree was an old friend and a fellow member of the U.S. Delegation to the U.N. They started walking along Grosvenor Street and were no more than fifty yards from the Embassy when Stevenson suddenly fell to the pavement. It was ten minutes past five o'clock and the streets were busy, but a doctor appeared within a minute or two. He could not revive Stevenson. An ambulance came to take Stevenson to St. George's Hospital near Hyde Park, where he was pronounced dead on arrival.

Adlai Stevenson's death of an apparent heart attack at the age of sixty-five was a surprise. He had looked fine at the party the night before. He had been U.S. Representative to the U.N. for four years. The Democratic candidate for President in 1952 and again in 1956, he had lost to Dwight Eisenhower both times. John Kennedy had beaten him for the Democratic nomination at the convention in 1960, and after Kennedy defeated Richard Nixon in the election, the President appointed him to the U.N., where he had stayed after Lyndon Johnson succeeded Kennedy. Stevenson, a quietly eloquent orator who was too much of an intellectual to win in the game he had played, really wanted to be Kennedy's Secretary of State, even more than to be President, he had told a friend. But it was suggested by the White House that he go to the United Nations instead of to the State Department and, agreeably as ever, he went. A lawyer, he most likely would have made a superb Supreme Court Justice, but Kennedy had not offered that either.

In Washington, President Johnson announced his regret over Stevenson's death and said he was dispatching "a delegation of distinguished Americans to London to bring back his body to America." The delegation, Johnson said, would be headed by Vice President Hubert Humphrey; the President had made him an experienced hand at funeral-going around the globe, as if there was nothing better for an eager Vice President to do. Stevenson was brought home to Illinois for burial, as Lincoln's body had been carried home.*

The death of Adlai Stevenson marked the beginning of a chain of events that led to a historic battle over the future of the Supreme Court which two Presidents—Johnson and Nixon—fought out with the United States Senate. At the time there was no apparent connection between Stevenson's death and the Court—in the public's mind anyway. For most men his death was an event to be mourned, or not, and forgotten. For the President it meant naming a new Representative to the United Nations. For Lyndon Johnson, as he privately pondered his course, it meant something more than simply the making of another appointment.

American representation at the United Nations was of importance to the Johnson Administration in the summer of 1965. The war in Southeast Asia was going badly, and the President had ordered regu-

*Stevenson was buried at Bloomington, Illinois.

lar bombings of Communist facilities in North Vietnam and then sent our military advisers into combat in South Vietnam. A large body of opinion in Europe as well as at home was against the President, and it was the U.N. Representative's task to help placate the Europeans and watch the Russians, in Southeast Asia and also in the unsettled Middle East. On the other hand, the U.N. post was not of overriding importance. Johnson was going to do what he had decided to do in Vietnam, despite European opinion. And, further, Stevenson at the U.N. had not truly been one of Johnson's men; he was Kennedy's man.

Johnson could have named to the U.N. position any one of a number of men. If he wanted an experienced diplomat, the State Department woods were full of them. There were those at Harvard who would grab at the opportunity, and Johnson's standing with Eastern intellectuals was such that he always could use another Ivy League prop. Or he could name one of his own men, meaning somebody he personally knew well and implicitly trusted, if that consideration outweighed diplomatic experience.

But Presidents do not name just anyone to anything. If the job is good enough to require presidential nomination and Senate confirmation, or even if it isn't, there always are plenty of job seekers among the party faithful. The higher the position the heavier is their pressure on the White House. Then, too, one always must consider the claims on the White House of people who, on request, have done favors for the President, such as senators who voted for legislation he wanted. And there were those from whom the President would want favors in the future. Many things to be considered, many men who would think the U.N. job a plum.

It did not take Lyndon Johnson long to make up his mind, and all those normal precedents that usually apply in the filling of high positions were of no use at all to the President. He told no one, not even those whose lives would be most directly involved, until he had all his moves lined up and was ready. Only then did he tell the principals—not one, but two—and neither liked the role Johnson had decided for him. But Lyndon Johnson vastly enjoyed and skillfully worked the power of the Presidency to manipulate men. Presidents may not be kings, but the badges of authority, the prestige of office —the White House itself, state visits of kings and potentates, Air Force One, all these things—vest in the Presidency a voice of great persuasiveness that none but the strongest men will deny. Lyndon Johnson, probably more than most Presidents, was most persuasive when he determined to be.

So the two men agreed, each with great and sincere reluctance for his own good reasons, and Johnson, with great satisfaction, made the announcements to assembled reporters and dignitaries.

First, on July 20, 1965, he stepped out of the Oval Office and into the White House rose garden to announce that he was nominating Arthur J. Goldberg, Associate Justice of the Supreme Court, to succeed Stevenson as Representative to the United Nations. "One week ago today," Johnson said solemnly, "we, and the world, lost Adlai Stevenson." He stressed the great honor and responsibility of the U.N. position, saying Goldberg "will speak not only for an Administration but he will speak for an entire Nation." Goldberg, having been confirmed quickly by the Senate, returned to the White House rose garden on July 26, where he was sworn in as U.N. Representative. Justice Hugo Black administered the oath as the President looked on, clearly pleased that Goldberg was leaving the Court and going to the United Nations.

Two days later at a White House press conference President Johnson made his other announcement. "I am happy today, here in the East Room," he said with obvious delight, "to announce that the distinguished American who was my first choice for the position now vacant on the Supreme Court has agreed to accept this call to this vital duty. I will very shortly, this afternoon, send to the Senate my nomination of the Honorable Abe Fortas to be an Associate Justice of the Supreme Court." Abe Fortas, who then was not the "Honorable" anything, said nothing.

The person and the Presidency of Lyndon Johnson were in some ways much like those of an earlier President, Andrew Jackson, who also had determined to place a man of his choice on the Supreme Court. Both were populists and both Democrats who were never able to communicate with Eastern Establishment intellectuals. Each came from poor, rural beginnings—Jackson from Tennessee and Johnson from Texas—and eventually each returned to the considerable real estate he had accumulated, Jackson to the Hermitage near Nashville and Johnson to the LBJ Ranch near Austin. As a young man, each was endowed with more than ordinary ambition, which took him to successively higher political office (Jackson detouring for a time to become a military hero in the War of 1812), and along the way each acquired substantial private wealth and a lasting respect for property rights. A major difference was that Jackson and his Supreme Court nominee, Chief Justice Roger Brooke Taney, did not regard slavery as a national evil. Johnson and his nominee, Abe Fortas, were not unsympathetic to blacks and poor whites. But each as President failed to perceive fully the deep currents underlying public dissatisfaction in his day. Both took a peculiarly personal view of the Presidency and of the uses of presidential power. Each was quick to anger at personal disloyalty and each was eager to reward personal devotion. As Taney served Jackson well and was rewarded, so Fortas served Johnson and, in the President's mind, deserved nothing less than the Supreme Court. Cronyism has earned an abiding place in American history.

Presidents from Washington through Nixon have approached their power to nominate members of the Supreme Court with varying attitudes. Executive or legislative power is distinctly different from judicial authority, and Presidents who have had little contact with the Court sometimes have regarded those appointments the way they looked upon a nomination to fill a Cabinet vacancy or any other high political position, in which the appointee serves at the pleasure and direction of the President. Most Presidents, however, seem to have put Supreme Court nominations on a loftier plane. John Quincy Adams wrote in his diary: "As the Supreme Judicial Court is the tribunal of last resort for the construction of the Constitution and the laws, the office of Chief Justice is a station of the highest trust, of the deepest responsibility, and of influence far more extensive than that of the President of the United States."[1] Whether a Chief Justice such as John Marshall or Earl Warren or an Associate Justice such as Oliver Wendell Holmes exerts a more extensive influence than the President on the nation depends on the men and the times. But members of the Court, who may serve for life, often have remained in office many years after the Presidents who appointed them have gone. Thus, in respectful recognition of the longevity of Justices and of their power to void as unconstitutional laws passed by Congress and presidential acts, most Presidents seem to have regarded Supreme Court nominations as the highest they can make. Where they find their men upon whom to bestow such honor, in the Senate, on lower courts, in the universities, among personal friends or elsewhere, is another matter.

Clearly, Lyndon Johnson viewed the Supreme Court as a lofty place, if not quite as celestial as John Quincy Adams saw it. Johnson's attitude stemmed from his earlier life. He first came to Washington in the early 1930s as a secretary to a Texas congressman, Richard M. Kleberg, and from that time on he was an active New Dealer who was as close as he could get to President Franklin D. Roosevelt. He won his own seat in the House of Representatives for the first time in 1937, the very time when the President was proposing to "pack" the Supreme Court. He had seen the Court exercise its power to rule New Deal legislation unconstitutional, he watched as President Roosevelt opened his assault on the Court, and he saw the Court change under the pressure of presidential and public opinion, even before FDR named a majority of its members.

Johnson as an aspiring politician also had more than a second-hand view of the Court. He had a personal opportunity to observe at first hand the power of the Supreme Court, or at least the power of a Justice. After serving in the House of Representatives in Washington for eleven years, in 1948 Johnson returned to Texas to run for a seat in the United States Senate. His most prominent opponent in the Democratic primary election was the state's former governor, Coke Stevenson. It was a close race, requiring a run-off election in which Johnson received 494,191 votes and Stevenson 494,104. The eighty-seven-vote difference in nearly a million votes cast resulted in denunciations on both sides, and lawsuits. Stevenson's lawyers moved the issue into a federal district court in Texas and obtained a temporary restraining order which prevented the Texas secretary of state from printing Johnson's name on the ballot for the November general election, until the court held further proceedings on Stevenson's vote fraud charges. Time was short. Johnson's lawyers flew to New Orleans, to appeal the restraining order to the United States Fifth Circuit Court of Appeals. An appeals court judge decided, despite the Johnson lawyers' plea for quick action, that a panel of appellate judges should hear the case and, in the interim, the restraining order would remain in effect. Thereupon the Johnson lawyers flew to Washington, where a young attorney named Abe Fortas took over. He took the matter to the next higher level of authority, which was Mr. Justice Black. Justice Black was the circuit judge for the Fifth Circuit. (Each member of the Supreme Court sits as appellate judge for one or more of the circuit courts of appeal.)

Fortas presented Johnson's case to Black, and the Justice signed an order staying the district court's temporary restraining order. Lyndon Johnson's name was then printed on the Texas ballot. On November 2, 1948, Johnson as the Democratic candidate, of course, handily defeated the Republican candidate and took his seat in the United States Senate. Had Justice Black, who was Franklin Roosevelt's first Supreme Court appointee, not signed the stay order, Johnson well might not have been elected to the Senate, or have become Senate Majority Leader and then Vice President and President. Many years later, after Lyndon Johnson had been in and out of the White House, the late Mr. Justice Black still had on the wall of his inner office in the Supreme Court Building a specially tinted and personally auto-graphed picture of Lyndon Johnson.

President Johnson for several good reasons, then, had great respect for the power and prestige of the Supreme Court. A vacancy on the Court was of the highest order of nomination he could make and the grandest of gifts he could give. When he announced the nomination of Abe Fortas, he was completely sincere in saying that Fortas "was my first choice for the position now vacant on the Supreme Court." He also said, "For many, many years, I have regarded Mr. Fortas as one of this nation's most able and most respected and most outstand-ing citizens, a scholar, a profound thinker, a lawyer of superior ability, a man of humane and deeply compassionate feelings toward his fellow man." That also was sincerely said, even if Johnson's native Texas verbiage made it sound less than sincere.

Fortas as a lawyer was indeed both a brilliant advocate and a compassionate defender. He practiced law at a large, old, highly polished desk in what once must have been the drawing room at the front of a Victorian red brick mansion which housed the Washington law firm of Arnold, Fortas & Porter. The firm long since had out-grown the mansion, spilling its more junior partners into four nearby office buildings. But the old red mansion at 1229 Nineteenth Street, a half-dozen blocks from the White House, remained the home of the firm and the preferred location of its senior members. Its large rooms were elegant still and downstairs there was a well-stocked bar, to which those invited would retire in the late afternoon. Suitable old mansions, preferably with large center halls and impressive stairways, are desired places of business for many big city law firms, for their reflected solidity and good taste, and firms that are forced into glass and steel skyscrapers often go to great expense to disguise their modern offices with winding staircases, somber wood paneling, and old English hunting prints. By these standards, the Victorian mansion of Arnold, Fortas & Porter was made even more impressive by its circular driveway in front, on which sometimes were parked black Cadillac limousines.

The suggestions of elegance, prestige, and power were not inappropriate. Arnold, Fortas & Porter was one of the largest and most successful law firms in Washington and, in the summer of 1965, Abe Fortas was its most eminent member. Fortas was born in Memphis, Tennessee, in 1910, the fifth child of a Jewish family that had no wealth. He went to work at the age of thirteen and made his way through Yale Law School and then came to Washington in 1934 to work for the New Deal. His mentors among New Dealers close to President Roosevelt included William O. Douglas at the Securities and Exchange Commission and Harold Ickes at the Department of the Interior, and in 1942 Fortas, at the age of thirty-two, rose to the position of Under Secretary of the Interior. Soon after the end of World War II, he left government to become one of the first of that considerable number of Washington lawyers who, having served the Roosevelt Administration, engaged in the private practice of a special kind of law, which consisted in no small part of leading big corporate clients and their lawyers through the legal mazes of the bureaucracy which the New Deal had spawned. Other generations of Washington lawyers, having served subsequent Democratic and Republican administrations, have followed, and now Washington has more lawyers per capita than any other city in America.

After World War II Fortas teamed up with Thurman Arnold, who, under Franklin Roosevelt, had headed the Justice Department's Antitrust Division, and with Paul A. Porter, whom President Truman had appointed head of the Office of Price Administration. Arnold, Fortas & Porter grew quickly and steadily. Its first client was the Coca-Cola Company, and by 1965 the roster of giant corporations it served included Pan American World Airways, Braniff Airways, and Federated Department Stores, as well as other equally desirable clients such as the Commonwealth of Puerto Rico and the National Retail Merchants Association. The three founding partners became rich, if not in the sense of accumulated wealth, then certainly in terms of an annual income of more than $150,000 each.[2] Mrs. Fortas, who in her

8

professional life uses the name Carolyn Agger, was a lawyer and the firm's expert on tax matters. With her additional income, the Fortases could well afford to drive their silver-colored Rolls-Royce, to live in a large, five-bedroom house in the Georgetown section of Washington, with a swimming pool outside and fine antiques inside, and to summer in another large house overlooking Long Island Sound in Westport, Connecticut.

If financial success may be taken as evidence of a lawyer's brilliance in advocacy, it does not necessarily illustrate the compassion which President Johnson attributed to Abe Fortas. That was another side of Fortas and of the firm of Arnold, Fortas & Porter. Nowadays, it is fashionable for large law firms to contribute a bit of their talent and time to the defense of black or young defendants whose causes are not popular and who cannot pay legal fees. Corporate clients who pay very well may, of course, indirectly help to subsidize this kind of compassion. But this firm, from the time of its founding, contributed a part of its considerable legal talents to the defense of indigents and others whose civil rights seemed to the firm to be endangered. Messrs. Arnold, Fortas, and Porter were liberal Democrats, but the reasons they accepted politically unpopular cases of clients who could not pay were explained also by the times. It was the era in which Washington was almost spellbound by fears of Communist subversion and Senator Joseph McCarthy of Wisconsin was the principal spellbinder. It was a time when Richard M. Nixon, as a young congressman from California, rose to national prominence predominantly as an investigator of the loyalty of Alger Hiss. The young Nixon was not a propagator of McCarthyism, but neither did he disassociate himself publicly from Senator McCarthy.

In those times, it took courage for a prominent law firm to step out in defense of the accused. The hostility of many lawyers to this kind of work in which Arnold, Fortas & Porter was engaged was demonstrated by an exchange between Paul Porter and another lawyer at a golf club.

"Paul," the other lawyer said, "I understand your firm is engaged in defending homosexuals and Communists."

"That's right," Porter answered. "What can we do for you?"[3]

Arnold, Fortas & Porter deserves some credit for the dissipation in the late 1950s and early 1960s of the internal security hysteria. For example, it won vindication in the courts for a group of Army employees at Fort Monmouth, New Jersey, whom McCarthy had accused of disloyalty. Fortas successfully defended Owen Lattimore, a Johns Hopkins University professor, against perjury charges that grew out of accusations that he was or had been a Communist sympathizer. Arnold and Porter won from the Supreme Court a decision that voided a loyalty board ruling against Dr. John F. Peters, who was a professor of medicine at Yale University and a part-time consultant to the government.[4] The lawyer who argued the Peters case for the government in the Supreme Court was an assistant attorney general named Warren Earl Burger.

Fortas also was accorded professional acclaim, by his liberal peers anyway, for two cases he argued and won as court-appointed counsel for indigent defendants in more ordinary types of criminal trials. In one, the *Durham* case, the Court of Appeals for the District of Columbia established a modern test for criminal insanity in the District of Columbia and the decision had wide effects throughout the nation.[5] The second was *Gideon* v. *Wainwright,* decided by the Supreme Court in 1963. Fortas's skillful advocacy before the Warren Court in that case established in law that indigents brought to trial in state courts on serious criminal charges have a constitutional right to court-appointed counsel.[6]

Abe Fortas was then an eminently successful Washington lawyer, professionally, financially, and socially. He was a welcome guest in some of Washington's best homes, with or without the violin he played with great talent. After Johnson became President, Fortas occupied a still higher place in Washington. He sometimes played his violin at White House social affairs, and he was a visitor there on many other occasions. How many none but Fortas and Johnson will ever know. Nor will it be known whether sometimes the black limousines in the circular driveway in front of 1229 Nineteenth Street delivered White House personages to the offices of Arnold, Fortas & Porter. For Abe Fortas served President Johnson as a personal confidant, sharing a relationship not unlike that which joined President Woodrow Wilson to Colonel Edward M. House, President Roosevelt to Harry Hopkins, or President Nixon to John Mitchell. A President, any President, seems to require a confidant whose judgment he respects, whose loyalty is beyond question, and whose ambitions are for the President alone. Lyndon Johnson's need of a wholly personal, totally loyal confessor was perhaps even greater than that of most other Presidents, and Abe Fortas filled that need.

In some ways Johnson and Fortas were not alike. Fortas was small in stature, precisely proper in his manner of dress, and quiet in his way of speaking, using profanity only selectively and then in an unoffensively effective sort of way. Lyndon Johnson was big, noisy, and did not use profanity selectively. It would have been absolutely unthinkable for Abe Fortas to pull up his shirt in public, as President Johnson did, to display the scar on his abdomen where his doctors had made an incision.

But in other and more significant ways Johnson and Fortas were alike. Each in his way was a man of overpowering ambition who had scrapped his way from poor beginnings in the South to a pinnacle of power in the national capital. Each had aimed for and attained personal wealth, although Johnson's attainment was considerably greater than Fortas's. Both respected and enjoyed power, and they could be resourceful and tough in exercising their respective kinds of power.

Johnson and Fortas had known one another since each had come to Washington in the 1930s as New Deal Democrats. They had been of particular service to one another at least since 1948 when Fortas helped Johnson to be elected to the Senate. Fortas served as personal counsel to Mr. and Mrs. Johnson for many years, and in November, 1963, Fortas was one of the few people who were at Johnson's side almost constantly in those hectic days that followed the assassination of John Kennedy. One of the chores Fortas performed for the Johnsons in those days was to draft the legal document by which Mrs. Johnson placed in trust with a pair of Texas friends her stock in the LBJ Company, which owned radio and television stations in Texas and which was the foundation of the Johnson family wealth.

An incident that grew out of the trusteeship of the LBJ Company stock illustrated the intimacy of the Johnsons and Fortas. After Johnson ascended to the Presidency, the LBJ Company became a politically sensitive matter. The company's investments in radio and television properties, which of course were regulated by the federal government, had grown rapidly in the same years during which Johnson's political stock was rising, first as a member of the House of Representatives and then as a member and Majority Leader of the Senate. The Johnsons had become millionaires as a result of the investments, and consequently, when Johnson became President, the press in Washington became more interested in the details of the accumulation of the family wealth.[7] But President and Mrs. Johnson refused to talk about the family business and the White House press office referred inquiries to the two Texans whom Mrs. Johnson had named trustees of her stock. But the trustees would not talk either. Instead, and without being asked by the press, Fortas called reporters to say that he would answer for the Johnsons and, from his desk in the Victorian mansion, he did answer.

The greatest reward Johnson could confer on his brilliant and compassionate friend of long standing would be to make him Chief Justice of the United States. But the President's first thought was that Fortas should be his Attorney General. When Robert Kennedy resigned as Attorney General in 1964, the position became available. Fortas, however, did not want it. He had held a high position in the executive branch many years earlier, and he convinced Johnson that he could better serve the President from his office than from the Justice Department. But when Stevenson died the President refused to be convinced that Justice Goldberg should not be moved to the United Nations and Fortas would not be the nominee who would fill the first Supreme Court vacancy available to this President.

The fact that neither Goldberg nor Fortas wanted the honors, which the President for different reasons sought to bestow on each, did not deter Johnson.

Goldberg had found the work of the Supreme Court and the companionship of the other Justices satisfying and sufficient. In his field, he also had been a most successful lawyer. His field was labor law, and he had been general counsel for the United Steelworkers of America and a principal architect of the merger of the American Federation of Labor with the Congress of Industrial Organizations. In 1961 he had joined John Kennedy's Cabinet as Secretary of Labor. The following year two vacancies occurred on the Supreme Court, and they were the only two appointments John Kennedy made to the Court. The first vacancy occurred in March, when Justice Charles E. Whittaker, a conservative and not particularly outstanding Eisenhower appointee, became disabled and could no longer serve. Kennedy named to the vacancy Byron R. White, who was deputy to Attorney General Robert Kennedy. In August, failing health forced the retirement of Justice Felix Frankfurter and President Kennedy nominated Goldberg.

Goldberg thus had become the fourth occupant of the "Jewish seat" on the Supreme Court. President Wilson had created the seat in 1916 by appointing Louis Brandeis to the Court. Goldberg's other predecessors in the seat were Benjamin Cardozo and Felix Frankfurter and his successor, as Lyndon Johnson would have it, would be Abe Fortas.

But Justice Goldberg did not want to leave and felt he should not leave the Supreme Court. In the White House rose garden on July 20, 1965, Johnson conceded that Goldberg had agreed to resign from the Court and go to the Unitd Nations "at the insistence of the President." When Goldberg stepped before the microphones in the rose garden to reply, he said "Thank you" to Johnson and then added, with audible sadness, "I shall not, Mr. President, conceal the pain with which I leave the Court after three years of service. It has been the richest and most satisfying period of my career."

A few of its members in history have taken temporary leave of the Supreme Court to undertake presidential assignments, as Chief Justices John Jay and Oliver Ellsworth did to be ambassadors and as Justice Robert H. Jackson did much later to serve President Truman at the Nuremberg trials in Germany after World War II. But Justices' acceptance of such presidential assignments, even though temporary, have been severely criticized and permanent departures from the Court for allegedly higher office have been almost unheard of. The Constitution in conferring lifetime tenure on members of the Supreme Court assumes they will neither seek nor accept more.

Goldberg sought no more. He left the Supreme Court at Johnson's urgent request, apparently hoping that after a suitable period of time at the United Nations the President would reappoint him to the Court to resume his service there. But Goldberg extracted from Johnson no firm promise that he would be returned to the Court, and Johnson did not return him.*

Fortas's reasons for not wanting to go to the Court have not become crystal clear with the passage of time. His respect for the power of the Supreme Court was never in doubt. Perhaps he was satisfied where

*Goldberg's role at the United Nations was apparently as frustrating as Stevenson had found his under Johnson. Goldberg was increasingly cut off from the power centers in Washington, and he resigned from the U.N. position in April, 1968. Thereafter he practiced law in New York City as a partner in the firm of Paul, Weiss, Goldberg, Rifkind, Wharton & Garrison. In 1970 Goldberg was the unenthusiastic and unsuccessful Democratic candidate for governor of New York. He maintained silence concerning the Supreme Court until the Spring of 1971, when, as the conservative Burger Court was emerging, he warned that history and tradition counsel "against the future overruling of the Warren Court's libertarian decisions." Goldberg, writing in the New York *Times,* "On the Supreme Court," April 12, 1971, page 37, and April 13, 1971, page 37.

he was. Perhaps his reasons related to personal matters, financial or other. Perhaps his ability to assess his own future and that of the Court and the nation was more acute than the vision of Lyndon Johnson. In any event, Fortas, like Goldberg, in the end was unable to defeat Johnson's determination and flattery. In the East Room, where Johnson announced the Fortas nomination two days after Goldberg was off the Court, the President said: "Mr. Fortas has, as you know, told me on numerous occasions in the last twenty months, that he would not be an applicant or candidate, or would not accept any appointment to any public office. This is, I guess, as it should be, for in this instance the job has sought the man. Mr. Fortas agrees that the duty and the opportunity of service on the highest court of this great country, is not a call that any citizen can reject."

The Senate almost perfunctorily confirmed Johnson's nomination of Fortas to sit on the Supreme Court. The Judiciary Committee held a hearing that lasted less than three hours. Senator Albert Gore introduced the nominee to the committee, because Gore represented Fortas's home state of Tennessee and because Gore was a liberal Democrat who was pleased to make the introduction. The American Bar Association's standing committee on federal judiciary told the committee it found the nomination "highly acceptable." Fortas's friends from Coca-Cola, Federated Department Stores, and elsewhere attested to his worthiness. The only opposition was voiced by two witnesses whose testimony harked back to the discredited McCarthy era. One suggested to the committee that Fortas at one time might have "belonged to a committee with a lot of Communists on it." The other witness brought up Fortas's defense of Owen Lattimore. The Judiciary Committee, although a bastion of Senate conservatism, without undue hesitation recommended approval of the Fortas nomination.

When the nomination reached the Senate floor on August 11, 1965, only three senators rose to speak against it. The three, all conservative Republicans, were Carl T. Curtis of Nebraska, Strom Thurmond of South Carolina, and John J. Williams of Delaware. Senator Curtis charged that Fortas had "put the United States last" when, during the 1964 presidential election campaign, Fortas had gone to newspaper editors in Washington to ask them to withhold news of the arrest of White House aide Walter Jenkins on a morals charge. But the opposition was insignificant and the Senate confirmed the Fortas nomination by voice vote.

On Monday morning, October 4, 1965, the Supreme Court opened its new term and as Chief Justice Earl Warren led the seven other incumbent Justices to their seats behind the long bench in the marble courtroom, the marshal of the Court sounded his traditional chant:
"Oyez! Oyez!! Oyez!!!

"All persons having business before the Honorable, the Supreme Court of the United States, are admonished to draw near and give their attention, for the Court is now sitting.

"God save the United States and this Honorable Court!" And, with President Johnson seated in the courtroom, Abe Fortas raised his right hand and swore to defend the Constitution and the Court and the marshal escorted him to his seat at the bench.

Thus did Lyndon Johnson by his will create an event that was the first in a chain, the end of which Johnson thought he could see but which, as it turned out, he could not.

But 1965 was a deceptive year. The year before Johnson had secured his own right to the Presidency with an overwhelming victory at the polls. He was renowned in Congress as a President of legislative mastery, and in placing Abe Fortas on the Supreme Court he was fulfilling a personal desire and, incidentally, preserving the libertarianism of the Warren Court. But the euphoria of 1965 was a prelude to crisis, for Johnson and for the Supreme Court.

# CHAPTER 2

# The Nature of the Court

The Supreme Court is a quiet, even a mystical place. It is possibly the only place in Washington or anywhere else where the President comes and says nothing—or usually says nothing. The quiet is such that the Court's marble temple is not wired for instantaneous television transmissions, as are the White House and the Capitol. The Court speaks only through its opinions and not through press releases. The relative unpretentiousness of its emblems of authority is such that the Court has but one black Cadillac limousine, which is assigned to the Chief Justice and shared by him with the Associate Justices as necessity demands.

Admittedly, the Supreme Court has been changing since President Nixon came to its chamber.

The traditional quiet, the unpretentiousness and the dignity are entirely appropriate to the role of the Supreme Court in American government. There are essentially three kinds of power a government can exercise over or on behalf of its people. In the United States, the power of the sword belongs to the President, the power of the purse to Congress, and the power of the law to the Court. The power of the law is most basically a moral power which commands obedience to the extent the governed believe the law to be justly and equally applied.

Almost all civilized nations, including the most totalitarian, have supreme courts. However, a supreme court is not particularly vital to the people in nations where it is merely the court of last resort in the interpretation of laws that are written by the elected or appointed governors who hold the powers of the sword and the purse. The

Supreme Court of the United States is uniquely vital to the people because it is not merely the court of last resort for the interpretation of laws enacted by Congress and signed by the President. The Supreme Court participates in the making of the law, and it is a third co-equal branch of government because America has a written Constitution and the Supreme Court also is the final interpreter of the Constitution and its amendments, including the Bill of Rights. The Constitution separates and limits the powers of each of the three branches of the central government, it reserves to the states the powers not allocated to the central government, and it commands that the central government and, through the Fourteenth Amendment, the states not tread on the rights which the Bill of Rights reserved to the people. The Constitution is the supreme law of the land, and the Court is the final interpreter of the Constitution.

The Supreme Court is, then, the ultimate protector of individual liberty and of the mutual covenant which is the Constitution. Paul A. Freund, of Harvard, in writing about civil disobedience among citizen demonstrators who lack an effective voice in government, has said:

> Fidelity to law is an obligation based on reciprocity, on the right of participation. The mutual covenant, unhistorical as it may be as a ground of political obligation, reflects a long and vital philosophic tradition going back at least to the Old Testament and coming down through the Mayflower Compact. . . .
>
> Participation in the political community implies more than the mere right to vote. It implies equality of access to administrative and decision-making posts, including places on the police force, in the probation service, on the judiciary, and generally in those positions through which the community exerts force against recalcitrant members.[1]

The Court's role as final arbiter of the Constitution is checked by the constitutional proviso that the Court can rule only on cases and controversies brought before it. The limitation is not without force, but in fact all of America comes before the long mahogany bench. Americans seem forever to be rediscovering with fascination Alexis de Tocqueville's observation of more than a century ago that in the United States there is almost no major political issue which sooner or later is not converted into a legal question and taken to court. In our constitutional democracy, it could hardly be otherwise. Rapists, murderers, and thieves come regularly before the Supreme Court to plead for their rights, and so do General Motors Corporation and the Communist Party of the U.S.A. But in recent history particularly, the Court's major decisions have not evolved from the pleadings of individual parties. The major cases and controversies, while still styled as individual pleadings, have in fact been decided with the adversary participation of the principal organizations that speak for the various divisions in American society, including the National Association for the Advancement of Colored People and the NAACP Legal Defense and Education Fund, the National Association of Manufacturers, and the American Civil Liberties Union, as well as the Department of Justice, the Federal Bureau of Investigation, and the various states. The Court thus decides broad issues of law and order, of affluence and indigence, of conservation and industrialization, that organized Americans often present to the other branches of government and that the other branches often could resolve.

There is then no reason for dismay in the fact that the Supreme Court in American history has been damned as well as praised or that great struggles have been waged and are being waged again for control of the Court. A tension among the three branches of government is inevitable and the Constitution assumes only that no one of the three will gain dominance over the others. At any time in history any branch might lead, although none should race too far ahead or fall too far behind.

Certainly the rights and privileges which the Constitution guarantees the people are more likely to be fulfilled when Congress moves toward resolution of major issues on which the nation is divided and still more will be accomplished if the President shares a leadership role with Congress. The rights of black citizens to voting quality, for example, are much more likely to be significantly obtained through Congress and the President than through the Supreme Court alone. Congress has the money and the President controls the law enforcement machinery. But, more important, these are the branches which react to and influence the will and desire of the majority of the public, which in the end must agree to abide by the law, whether written by Congress and signed by the President or written by the Court.

In popular political rhetoric, the Court is practicing "judicial restraint," or "strict constructionism," when it declines a role of leadership and it is practicing "judicial activism," or "loose constructionism," when it assumes leadership ahead of the other two branches in the resolution of the nation's social, economic, and political problems. But such labels are false and misleading, despite their contemporary usage in Washington.

The Supreme Court fails the Constitution and the nation when its members take a restrained and subordinate view of their role in government. At such times in history when the Court has fallen into lockstep with the other branches, it has risked becoming a mere rubber stamp, particularly for the President.

But what popularly is called judicial activism also can lead to national disaster, as when the Court has used its power as final arbiter of the Constitution to obstruct or defeat the legitimate leadership of the other two branches in the resolution of large social, economic, and political problems. On such occasions the Court has rendered upon itself what Charles Evans Hughes termed self-inflicted wounds.

The most illustrious hours in the Court's history have come when it has asserted positive leadership, as it did in the early days of the Republic under Chief Justice John Marshall and in more recent times under Chief Justice Earl Warren. After the vicious attacks on the Marshall Court and on the Warren Court subsided, the other branches and the nation followed the Court's lead.

Clearly, then, when the majoritarian branches will not or cannot respond to the legitimate claims of citizens to rights and privileges which are theirs, the Constitution demands that the Court exercise leadership. For where great issues and large numbers of citizens are involved, if the Court as the government branch of last resort turns away those who are denied their rights and privileges, then the moral force of the law will give way to lawlessness and the mutual covenant may be broken.

The Constitution and its Bill of Rights are brief documents that set forth powers and privileges only in broadest terms. Their breadth has permitted them to survive as the nature of America's problems has changed over nearly two hundred years and it is the reason why the Court is a powerful and stormy place, its quiet notwithstanding. Celestial guidance is unavailable to give specific meaning to the Constitution and the Bill of Rights in each succeeding generation, so the Justices must choose their independent course with reference only to their own consciences and to the essential morality which underlies the documents. "The first requisite for one who sits in judgment on legislative acts is that he be a philosopher," Professor Freund has written. The second, he added, "is that he be not too philosophical."[2]

When the Court has erred, Congress with the concurrence of three-fourths of the states can amend the Constitution. But generally when it has rendered its self-inflicted wounds, the Court, without correction by constitutional amendment or by the arrival of a new majority, has reversed itself before it was too late.

Until the present time the Court has erred only once on a great and divisive issue and the mutual covenant was broken. It was *the* American issue, which more than any other was with this nation on the day its Constitution was adopted and is with us still. The issue, of course, was and is the rights and privileges of black Americans, and on this issue the covenant once was broken when the Supreme Court was overruled by civil war.

In the first years of the Republic political power was about evenly divided between slave states and those which had abolished or were in the process of ending slavery. Congress did nothing to disturb the situation, and could hardly have acted on a matter of such gravity had it wanted to, for it was far from certain how much of their autonomy the states had given up to the federal government under the new Constitution. In those early years the Supreme Court did not have much to do because nobody brought much of anything to it. President Washington sent the first Chief Justice, John Jay, off on a diplomatic mission to England. It was not until John Marshall was appointed in 1801 that Presidents ceased using Chief Justices for ambassadorial assignments abroad, and it was still a few years more before the Marshall Court boldly established the precedents which have guided the exercise of government power ever since. In 1803 in *Marbury* v. *Madison,* for the first time holding an Act of Congress unconstitutional, the Court established the supremacy of the Constitution over any other conflicting law.[3] In 1819, in *McCulloch* v. *Maryland,* the Court upheld from state challenge the power of Congress to charter the Bank of the United States, even though the Constitution did not specifically give Congress that power, and for the first time held that Congress may make all laws "necessary and proper . . . which are not prohibited . . . on which the welfare of a nation essentially depends."[4] And it was in 1824 in *Gibbons* v. *Ogden,* in a classic interpretation of the power the Constitution delegated to Congress to regulate commerce, where the Court laid down the doctrine that when a

law of Congress and a law of a state collide, state law must fall.[5]

The slavery issue soon came before Congress, the President, and the Supreme Court, in various forms.

The Congress that sat under the old Articles of Confederation, which preceded the Constitution, had adopted in 1787 the Northwest Ordinance, covering the westward land lying north of the Ohio and east of the Mississippi rivers, and with it adopted an attached compact with settlers in the territory stating, "There shall be neither slavery nor involuntary servitude in said territory." In 1803 the Louisiana Purchase was signed and Congress did nothing to change the legal status of slavery, which had been permitted in the Louisiana territory under French law. As Ohio, Louisiana, and other states carved out of these Northwest and Louisiana territories were ready to come into the Union, they entered alternately as free or slave states and the national political balance on the issue was thus maintained. In 1819 there were twenty-two states in the Union, eleven of them slave states and eleven free states. But Missouri, a border state, threatened to tip the balance and its entry was debated for months in Congress. The result was the Missouri Compromise of 1820. Missouri entered the Union as a slave state and Maine entered as a free state, but, most importantly, slavery was "forever" prohibited in the vast territory lying north of a line 36° 30′ latitude.

For some years after 1820, slavery was not a burning political issue. As more states entered the Union, the balance was more or less maintained and new compromises were hammered out in Congress. By a compromise in 1850, for instance, Southerners in Congress accepted the abolition of the slave trade in the District of Columbia and Northerners swallowed the Fugitive Slave Act, which made it far easier for slave owners to obtain the return of blacks who had escaped to the North. Through these years, Southerners agitated for repeal of the Missouri Compromise and in 1854 Congress passed the Kansas-Nebraska Act which in effect did repeal the 1820 compromise, by giving to the people of the states to be carved from these two territories the right to determine whether they would enter the Union as slave or free states. Abolitionist William Lloyd Garrison burned a copy of the Constitution, and John Brown, madman as well as abolitionist, raided the Federal arsenal at Harpers Ferry. Still there remained hope that men such as Henry Clay and Daniel Webster, so long as they lived, would succeed in forging new compromises and with them buy time. Time for the realization of some scheme by which Congress would solve the slavery problem, under law, by abolishing slavery. One possibility, long discussed by reasonable men, was a plan under which the federal government would compensate Southern slave owners in exchange for abolition of racial servitude.

In Congress and out, the slavery issue was debated in terms of constitutional rights versus states' rights. During the thirty-four years John Marshall presided over it, the Supreme Court put down firm bridges over which Congress might have passed to a settlement of the issue, under law. Chief Justice Marshall strongly supported the concept of federal supremacy over the states and eloquently upheld the right of Congress to exercise broadly the powers allocated to it by the Constitution. He wrote, in one famous decision of the Court, "Powerful minds, taking, as postulates, that the powers expressly granted to the government of the Union, are to be contracted into the narrowest possible compass, and that the original powers of the states are retained, may, by a course of well digested reasoning, explain away the constitution of our country, and leave it, a magnificent structure, indeed, to look at, but totally unfit for use."[6] And, in another, he wrote, "The sound construction of the constitution must allow to the national legislature that discretion, which will enable that body to perform the high duties assigned to it, in the manner most beneficial to the people. Let the end be legitimate, let it be within the scope of the constitution, and all means which are appropriate are constitutional."[7]

The constitutional doctrines that rang forth from the Marshall Court frightened and angered the Chief Justice's fellow Virginians, even though the Supreme Court in his lifetime did not rule directly on the issue of whether black slavery violated the Constitution and its Bill of Rights. Yet, John Marshall came close to the issue. The case of *Gibbons* v. *Ogden,* decided in 1824, concerned steamboats, not slaves, but the Chief Justice's opinion used the occasion to assert that, while Congress in 1803 had passed a law allowing the states to decide whether they would permit the continued importation of slaves, that law "constitutes an exception to the power of Congress to regulate commerce."[8] Marshall's assertion caused alarm in the South. Five years later, in 1829, the Supreme Court decided its first case in which the question of slavery was involved. The question was whether a slave, drowned in a steamboat accident, was freight, for which the steamboat company would be liable, or was a passenger, for whom it presumably would not be liable without further legal action. "In the nature of things," the Chief Justice ruled, "and in his character, he resembles a passenger, not a package of goods. It would seem reasonable, therefore, that the responsibility of the carrier should be measured by the law which is applicable to passengers, rather than the carriage of common goods."[9]

Chief Justice Marshall died in office in 1835, at the age of seventy-nine, and President Andrew Jackson, serving his second term, would name his successor. Slavery at that time was not a consuming political issue, and it had not moved on to the court of last resort. The nomination and confirmation of Marshall's successor therefore did not turn directly and inevitably on the issue of slavery. Marshall's strong support of federal supremacy and the implications his doctrines held for the slavery question of course had made the Supreme Court extremely controversial. The nomination of his successor therefore marked one of the first great political struggles for control of the future of the Supreme Court. But the struggle seems not to have been waged in terms of the constitutional philosophy of the nominee so much as over partisan politics and cronyism.

Jackson's choice as the new Chief Justice was Roger B. Taney, a plain man who had made his mark not in the law but in politics. The rough and tumble of Jacksonian Democracy had great crowd appeal and with it began a first era of anti-intellectualism, populism, and politics in Washington. Taney was a Marylander who had been an early supporter of Jackson for the presidency. In 1831 he became Jackson's Attorney General. Later he took a leading role in the President's battle against the Bank of the United States, and for this the Senate refused to confirm his nomination to be Secretary of the Treasury. Jackson's defiant reaction was to nominate Taney to be an Associate Justice of the Supreme Court. The Senate by a close vote postponed action indefinitely, which was tantamount to rejection of the nomination. When Chief Justice Marshall died, Jackson once more dared the Senate, by nominating Taney to be Chief Justice. Another vacancy having occurred, the President at almost the same time nominated Philip P. Barbour of Virginia to be an Associate Justice. The Whigs in the Senate objected strongly to both men and delayed action for nearly three months, hoping Jackson would withdraw the nominations. But Jackson refused to budge and finally, after an executive session of the Senate in which no records were kept, Taney and Barbour were confirmed on March 16, 1836. Of the new Chief Justice, a New York newspaper editorialized, "The pure ermine of the Supreme Court is sullied by the appointment of a political hack."

Chief Justice Taney was not a political hack, but neither did he possess the qualities of mind and spirit or the firm belief in constitutional supremacy that made John Marshall great. Taney remained Chief Justice for twenty-eight years which proved ultimately the most violent in the nation's history and, as such, the most disastrous for the Constitution and the Court.

The monumental constitutional bridges built by the Marshall Court were not immediately burned by the Taney Court. Indeed, so fundamental were they to the national pursuit of happiness and prosperity that subsequent courts in later years broadened them to carry an ever heavier weight of federal legislation. But great principles, constitutional or other, are not built in absolutely steady progression. The language of the Constitution is so broad and the facts of each case and controversy so different that the Court can change direction without explicitly overturning prior decisions, if it so desires.

Marshall did not deny all power to the states and Taney did not reject totally the concept of federal supremacy. But Taney placed a higher value on states' rights than had Marshall, and Taney changed the Court as Southerners hoped and Northerners feared he would. His first important opinion, delivered the year after he became Chief Justice, suggested that change was in the wind. The opinion upheld the authority of Massachusetts to permit construction of a second bridge across the Charles River at Boston and thus to break the monopoly of the owner of the first bridge which the state had franchised.[10] Property rights are to be "sacredly guarded," Taney wrote, but "we must not forget that the community also has rights." The case did not pit state authority against federal power and it remains famous not as a definition of states' rights but of the superiority of public over private rights. Nonetheless, it suggested the new Chief Justice's attitude toward states' rights, as well as his populism.

Four years later the Supreme Court decided another case which was further evidence that Taney did not hold the federal government in the highest esteem. Federal versus state power again was not directly involved, but slavery was.

24

The Spanish schooner *Amistad* had cleared Havana, Cuba, on June 27, 1839, with a cargo of fifty-four blacks who had been brought recently from Africa by Spanish slave traders. Out of Havana, the slaves rose and seized the ship, killing the Spanish captain and the cook and sparing the lives of two other white Spaniards aboard so that they could navigate the vessel for the coast of Africa. But the Spaniards changed course and steered for the United States. On the morning of August 26, the *Amistad* was discovered off Montauk Point, Long Island, by the U.S. brig *Washington*. The Navy crew boarded and took possession of the schooner and sailed her into New London, Connecticut. The blacks were taken to jails in New London and Hartford, under custody of a United States marshal.

Claims and counterclaims then were filed in the federal district court in Connecticut for the schooner and its crew. The commander of the Navy brig filed for a share of the salvage value and certain local Connecticut residents also claimed a share. The two Spaniards who had navigated the Amistad northward filed claims to the slaves. The U.S. attorney for Connecticut, William S. Holabird, filed on behalf of the Spanish government a claim which had been presented to the American government by Spain's minister to the United States. The official Spanish claim asserted that the *Amistad* and her slave cargo were the property of Spanish subjects and that the United States was obligated by its 1819 treaty with Spain to restore them to their owners. And, finally, two white New England abolitionists, who were among a growing band of early civil rights lawyers in the North, took it upon themselves to represent the jailed blacks. The two white lawyers filed, on behalf of the blacks, answers to the various claims in which they asserted that the U.S. government had no right to intervene in the case and insisted that the blacks, having arrived in the free state of Connecticut, now were free men.

The district court ruled that, since the blacks were "born free" and kidnapped in Africa in violation of laws of Spain prohibiting its subjects from engaging in the slave trade, they were to be delivered to the U.S. President, to be transported back to Africa. The U.S. government and the abolitionist lawyers, on behalf of the blacks, both appealed and the circuit court affirmed the district court's decision.

Before the Supreme Court the controversy was shorn of its nonessential features. On one side was the federal government, represented by Henry D. Gilpin, Attorney General in the Van Buren administration, wanting to turn the blacks over to Spain, which presumably would try them for piracy. On the other side were the blacks, whose case for freedom now was being argued by abolitionist lawyer Roger Sherman Baldwin of Connecticut and by former President John Quincy Adams, now seventy-four years of age and a vigorous abolitionist member of the House of Representatives. The case had drawn wide national attention and the Supreme Court listened to arguments for eight days. On March 9, 1841, the Court handed down its decision.[11] It held that the United States was not obliged by treaty to return the blacks to Spain, because slavery was illegal under Spanish law and the slaves were thus not the lawful property of Spanish subjects. The Court reversed the lower courts' decision that the blacks be turned over to the President. Inasmuch as the voyage of the *Amistad* violated no U.S. laws proscribing the slave trade, the blacks were simply "declared to be free" by the Court. Eventually they were returned by the United States to Africa.

In the *Amistad* case, then, the Taney Court rejected the Attorney General's argument that the Court must be bound by the terms of the U.S. treaty with Spain. But the decision made no new constitutional law directly bearing on the slavery controversy in America, and perhaps it was significant that the opinion of the Court was written by Justice Joseph Story rather than Chief Justice Taney. Taney did not dissent to the *Amistad* decision and, as a personal matter, he did not condone slavery. As a young man, he had released the slaves he had inherited. But, as time would show, Taney did not preach what he practiced when states' rights came into direct and unavoidable conflict with the human rights of blacks and the authority of the federal government to secure those rights.

Its decision in the *Amistad* case notwithstanding, the Taney Court came more and more to be regarded as pro-slavery long before it finally confronted, directly and unavoidably, the ultimate constitutional question. In one decision, for example, it upheld the interest of Mississippi in an issue involving payment for slaves imported from another state. In another it upheld the constitutionality of the Fugitive Slave Act, the South's gain in the compromise of 1850. And finally, in 1857, at a time when the slavery question was waxing in the political arena and igniting incidents of violence in various parts of the nation, the Court came to the ultimate question and renounced John Marshall's doctrine of federal supremacy, thus thwarting Congress and the possibility of peaceful compromise without constitutional amendments. It was when the Chief Justice was eighty years old, and decades after he had freed his own slaves, that the Taney Court decided the Dred Scott case.

Dred Scott was a slave, owned by one John Emerson, an Army surgeon who was stationed at St. Louis. Missouri, under the Compromise of 1820, was a slave state. Dr. Emerson, accompanied by Dred Scott, in 1834 commenced a journey which took him first to a post in Rock Island, Illinois, and then to Fort Snelling in what later became the state of Minnesota. Illinois was a free state under the Northwest Territory Ordinance of 1787 and the Minnesota territory was free under the Compromise of 1820. In 1838, Dr. Emerson returned to Jefferson Barracks near St. Louis, still owning as his slaves Dred Scott and Harriet, whom Dred had married with Emerson's permission at Fort Snelling, as well as the two daughters, Eliza and Lizzie, who had been born to Dred and Harriet Scott. Not long after their return to Jefferson Barracks, Dr. Emerson died. In 1846, Scott sued Emerson's widow in a Missouri court, claiming that their sojourn on free soil made him and his wife and daughters free. The state supreme court held in 1852 that under Missouri law he and his family remained slaves.

The following year Scott's case was filed in federal court and started on its way to the Supreme Court, which decided it in 1857. It is unclear what or who motivated Scott in 1846 to begin the action in the state court. He was an obscure, apparently good-natured slave who would not have filed the original suit unaided.

Once in federal court, Scott's case clearly became an abolitionist cause. Attorney General Gilpin, in arguing the *Amistad* case before the Supreme Court, had pointed out that the case had not been brought by slaves, but "the question of freedom or slavery was brought at the instance of persons who took up the cause of the slaves." Similarly, Scott's case in federal court was aided and abetted by an early breed of civil rights lawyers and abolitionists in St. Louis. It was planned to be a constitutional test case. By 1852, when the Missouri supreme court decided Scott's case, the Emerson widow had remarried. Her new husband was a strong abolitionist member of the House of Representatives from Massachusetts, C. C. Chaffee. Mrs. Chaffee arranged a fictitious sale of Scott, his wife and children to her brother, John F. A. Sanford, who resided in New York. The purpose

27

of the "sale" was to establish that the parties to the case resided in different states and thus to create federal court jurisdiction on the basis of diversity of state citizenship.

The plans thus having been carefully laid, the abolitionist lawyers filed suit in 1853 in federal court in St. Louis. Scott's suit claimed again that, because he and his family had been removed to free soil, they could not be owned in slavery. The issue was best put by Chief Justice Taney when the case was decided by the Supreme Court:

"The question is simply this: Can a negro, whose ancestors were imported into this country, and sold as slaves, become a member of the political community formed and brought into existence by the Constitution of the United States, and as such become entitled to all the rights, and privileges, and immunities, guaranteed by that instrument to the citizen?"

The federal court in St. Louis ruled against Scott on May 15, 1854, and the case began to attract national interest as one more stage on which the issue of slavery was being debated with growing heat and emotion. There were growing numbers of seizures by U.S. marshals, under the Fugitive Slave Act, of runaway slaves in the North. There was, in St. Louis itself, the old courthouse where Dred Scott's first case had been tried and on the steps of which black men, women, and children were auctioned off. Ahead, as Dred Scott's federal case was making its way to the Supreme Court, was the Kansas-Nebraska Act, with which Congress left the slavery question to popular sovereignty and brought on a massacre in "bleeding Kansas." There was consternation in Congress when Representative Preston R. Brooks of South Carolina responded to a vicious antislavery speech by Senator Charles Sumner of Massachusetts, titled "The Crime Against Kansas," by beating Sumner over the head with a cane as he sat helplessly at his desk in the Senate chamber. There was the emergence of Abraham Lincoln of Illinois as a voice that spoke against slavery, but without viciousness or any intention of abruptly abolishing slavery as it existed in the South.

The Supreme Court heard argument on the Dred Scott case in February and again in December of 1856. In the interval, James Buchanan of Pennsylvania was elected President and the Dred Scott case engaged Congress, where Northerners, fearing what might come, introduced legislation to reorganize the Court. Buchanan took office March 4, 1857, and in his Inaugural Address spoke of the case before the Court. "In common with all good citizens, I shall cheerfully submit to the Court's decision," he said, adding that the issue of slavery in the territories and new states "will be speedily and finally settled" by the Court.

The Court three days later inflicted its wound upon itself and the nation. Each justice wrote a separate opinion. A clear majority, headed by Chief Justice Taney, concluded that the status of a slave was fixed by the law of the state in which the question was raised and that Dred Scott under Missouri law therefore remained a slave.[12]

The Court could have stopped there. But six of the justices, led by Taney, concurred in the further holding that, inasmuch as slavery was for the states to decide, blacks could not be U.S. citizens and Congress was without power to exclude slavery from any state or territory. By this ruling the Court held unconstitutional the Missouri Compromise, even though it had been nullified by Congress three years earlier. Worse, far worse, the Court's ruling foreclosed future legislative compromise, without constitutional amendment. In his opinion, Taney said, "No word can be found in the Constitution which gives Congress a greater power over slave property, or which entitles property of that kind to less protection, than property of any other description."

The Chief Justice then went forward alone in his opinion to complete for his time the destruction of the Supreme Court as a symbol of equal justice under law. Searching the Constitution for meanings that could not under Marshall's statement of its purpose be there, Taney referred to colonial sentiment in the century that preceded the Declaration of Independence and the Constitution, saying that Negroes "had been regarded as beings of an inferior order, and altogether unfit to associate with the white race, either in social or political relations; and so far inferior, they had no rights which the white man was bound to respect." Whatever Taney was searching for, the words were racist and were taken to be his own.

The Court's repudiation of the humanism on which the Constitution must finally rest was in turn repudiated by the Civil War four years later and then by the Thirteenth, Fourteenth, and Fifteenth Amendments to the Constitution. The Court could not alone have prevented war. If no more it could have remained neutral. Instead it ruled for slavery, foreclosing political compromise and itself becoming a cause of war.*

*For a discussion of the relationship of the Supreme Court's decision to the war that followed, see Samuel Eliot Morison, *The Oxford History of the American People* (New York: Oxford University Press, 1965), pp. 593–600.

CHAPTER 3

# The Abiding Issue

It was four years short of a century from the time the Taney Court decided the Dred Scott case until the Warren Court was formed. It was the Supreme Court which before and again after the Civil War most brutally turned away the Negro in America. The blacks waited nearly a century before they finally found some measure of satisfaction in the Constitution and the Court.

No issue has plagued the conscience of America longer, led to more violence, or been a bigger wart on her Constitution than racial justice. If the survival of the nation through Civil War, race riots, and internal strife is tribute to the resilience of the Constitution, it is also impressive evidence of the patience of blacks.

Their forbearance is difficult for a white man in America to understand. Slavery was ended by war in which blacks as well as whites died, and the Constitution was amended to give Negroes the civil rights the Taney Court had said they could not have. For a moment after the war, Negroes began to collect what the Constitution said was theirs, but only for a moment. The promises remained empty for nearly a century and Negroes still have not gained rights fully equal to those of white citizens. Those leaders white and black who spoke most eloquently and stood most resolutely for equal rights have been assassinated: Abraham Lincoln, John F. Kennedy, Martin Luther King, Robert Kennedy.

The law cannot change men's minds. It cannot erase prejudice, fear, and hatred from white minds or insecurity, anxiety, and fear from black minds. But law, if it is the law, as that word is understood in a constitutional democracy, can control men's actions and help to lead to a change in men's minds. This is what Abraham Lincoln meant when he declared the Dred Scott decision to be "wrong," saying the law cannot make men equal but equality of rights is the essence of a free society, "constantly looked to, constantly labored for, and even though never perfectly attained, constantly approximated."*

Lincoln spoke those words before the Civil War. Today, in large part because of the Warren Court's moral leadership, more legal rights have been accorded the black minority than a century ago. But equality with the white majority still is not approximated, even closely. Today Negroes have more and expect more; and if, or when, in some tomorrow black aspirations, expectations, and pretentions rise to a level which whites can fully understand, a new accommodation must be had or the violence of a century ago may be repeated. This apparently is what President Eisenhower had in mind when, on sending federal troops into Little Rock, Arkansas, to quell the mobs that opposed a federal court's school desegregation order, he said his action was required by the oath he had taken to support the Constitution and "failure to act would be tantamount to acquiescence in anarchy and the dissolution of the Union."

Mr. Eisenhower made the statement after Senator Richard Russell of Georgia had likened the President to Adolf Hitler for dispatching troops to Little Rock. There subsequently were news reports from Washington to the effect that the President had remarked privately that his appointment of Earl Warren as Chief Justice was the worst mistake he had ever made. If the remark was made it did not represent Dwight Eisenhower's public attitude toward civil rights or the Warren Court, and it was the President's public stance that was crucial. Because President Eisenhower sent troops to Little Rock, and because he and Presidents Kennedy and Johnson after him possessed the political courage to support the Warren Court's leadership in civil rights, a start toward racial accommodation was begun. But it was a long, long time in coming.

So deeply had the Supreme Court wounded itself with the Dred Scott decision that the Court in a sense did not recover its place as the third co-ordinate branch of the federal government from Taney to Warren. One usually does not think of the Court in the name of its Chief Justice except when a strong man has sat in that chair, and

*In a speech at Springfield, Illinois, June 27, 1857.

31

in the period that covered most of the last half of the nineteenth century and ran well into the first half of the twentieth, the names best known and honored are those of strong men who became famous as dissenters rather than as leaders of a court majority. Foremost are the names of the first John Marshall Harlan, Oliver Wendell Holmes, Louis D. Brandeis, and Benjamin N. Cardozo. Dissent may be more productive of philosophic discourse than is concurrence, and these dissenters rank high as philosophers in America and their dissents often became the law of the land at a later date.

So gross was the Taney Court's abuse of trust that President Lincoln early in the Civil War ignored a writ issued by the Chief Justice challenging the constitutional authority of the President to allow military tribunals to try civilians. Taney died in 1864, when the war was three years old, and Lincoln appointed Salmon P. Chase to succeed him, probably in order to get rid of Chase, who had been a troublesome member of the President's Cabinet.

The Court played no significant part in the events of the Civil War or the Reconstruction Era which followed. When Lincoln announced his Emancipation Proclamation in September, 1862, it was more a tactical gesture than a fact. It freed the slaves in the Confederate States, where it could not reach, but not in the border states which remained loyal to the Union; he timed the proclamation, which went to the heart of the reason for the war, to take advantage of the Union victory at Antietam, to reinforce morale in the North, and to gain support among European nations which might otherwise have given substantial help to the Confederacy. The President relied on his constitutional power as commander in chief of the army and navy to issue the proclamation, and it would have been a good constitutional question to ask whether he was acting within his constitutional authority or whether the power to free slaves rested only with Congress. The question was never answered, and there was no need to answer it. In February, 1865, after General William Tecumseh Sherman marched through Georgia to the sea and the South was defeated militarily, Congress proposed the Thirteenth Amendment saying, "Neither slavery nor involuntary servitude . . . shall exist within the United States. . . ." A few months later Lee surrendered at Appomattox Courthouse in Virginia, ending the war. In June, 1866, Congress approved the Fourteenth Amendment, conferring United States and state citizenship on blacks and saying, "No State . . . shall abridge the privileges . . . of citizens . . . nor shall any state deprive any person of life, liberty, or property, without due process of law. . . ." It was followed three years later by the Fifteenth Amendment, saying, "The right . . . to vote shall not be denied or abridged . . . on account of race, color, or previous condition of servitude." Each amendment was ratified by the required number of states, and by those in the South as a requisite to readmission into the Union.

A century later, it often is forgotten that, in the several years immediately after the war, many thousands of Negroes in the South exercised their new right to vote. A number of blacks, many of them educated men who had been freed long before the war, served in state legislatures, on the courts, and in Congress. One, Hiram R. Revels, was elected in 1870 to the Mississippi seat in the United States Senate once held by Jefferson Davis. For the moment, Southern whites seemed to be accepting the demise of slavery and the blacks were being helped by the federal government to exercise their voting rights, to secure fair wages from their former owners, and where necessary to obtain food, clothing, and medical care.

But the willingness of the North to promote and of the South to accept change soon were brought to an end by a complex of factors over which historians still disagree. The North's willingness to forego malice toward the South was reflected in Lincoln's reconstruction policies, but Lincoln was assassinated and his successor who adhered to those policies, President Andrew Johnson, was impeached and nearly convicted by Congress. Congress for a time imposed military rule which the South deeply resented. The South resented perhaps even more and feared the political emergence of Negroes, who outnumbered whites in some parts of the South. There were race riots. Hundreds of blacks were killed in Memphis and New Orleans. The Ku Klux Klan and similar white supremacy gangs were organized to terrorize and murder Negroes.

The initial reaction of Southern states and cities to abolition and to Negroes' exercise of their rights as free men was the enactment of "black codes" which prohibited Negroes from carrying guns or having whiskey, barred them from working in trades without getting a license, restricted their street movements, and in many other ways kept blacks in their place. The black codes were repealed by the Union's military governors in the South and by Congress, which in 1866 passed the first Civil Rights Act, to give Negroes the same rights as white men "to make and enforce contracts, to sue, be parties and give evidence, to inherit, purchase, lease, sell, hold and convey real and personal property . . . and be subject to like punishment, pains and penalties and to none other, any law, statue, ordinance, regulation or custom to the contrary notwithstanding."

The South found other means. The states turned to voting standards and poll taxes that effectively disenfranchised Negroes, to zoning laws which effectively restricted areas in which they might live, and to the "separate but equal" idea of segregating the races with "Jim Crow" laws. The laws separated blacks from whites in railroad cars and on trolleys and buses, in schools and hospitals, at restaurants and hotels, and barber shops, rest rooms, water fountains, and virtually everywhere else. The facilities for blacks were separate but rarely equal.

Congress in 1875 passed another Civil Rights Act to enforce the Fourteenth Amendment against the Jim Crow laws. It was "an Act to protect all citizens in their civil and legal rights," outlawing racial discrimination in hotels and inns, on public conveyances, in theaters and other places of public amusement.

With Taney long gone and the Supreme Court's elevation of states' rights brought down by the Civil War, it would be thought that the Court finally now would acknowledge John Marshall's dictum that the Constitution to endure must be adapted to the various crises of human affairs. The opportunity for the Court to redeem itself came as Negroes and civil rights lawyers brought a number of cases and controversies before the court. In one group of cases, blacks, citing the 1875 Civil Rights Act, challenged their exclusion from a hotel restaurant in Topeka, an opera house in New York, and the dress circle of a theater in San Francisco.

In the Civil Rights Cases decided in 1883, the Supreme Court threw out the 1875 Act as unconstitutional.[1] Eight justices decided that the act "steps into the domain of local jurisprudence" and if a private corporation or businessman wanted to discriminate against blacks there was nothing Congress could do about it. The Fourteenth Amendment gave Congress power only over discrimination practiced by a state, the majority ruled. Justice Harlan dissented in a strong, thirty-six-page opinion asserting that corporations and businesses served public functions and were subject to the limitations which the Amendment placed on states.

34

The Court finished its evisceration of the Fourteenth Amendment a dozen years later. Homer Adolph Plessy, a Negro, had boarded a train in New Orleans and seated himself in a car for whites. The conductor ordered him to move to a Jim Crow car, as required by Louisiana law. He refused and was arrested. Albion Tourgee, a gifted novelist and lawyer, argued Plessy's case but failed to convince a majority of the justices.[2] The Court in 1896 upheld the constitutionality of Jim Crow laws under the Fourteenth Amendment and adopted the "separate but equal" idea as doctrine. It was a fallacy for blacks to assume "that the enforced separation of the two races stamps the colored race with a badge of inferiority," the Court said. "If this be so, it is solely because the colored race chooses to put that construction on it."

Justice Harlan dissented:

> The present decision will not only stimulate aggressions, more or less brutal and irritating, upon the admitted rights of colored citizens, but will encourage the belief that it is possible, by means of state enactments, to defeat the beneficent purposes which the people of the United States had in view when they adopted the recent amendments of the Constitution. Sixty millions of whites are in no danger from the presence here of eight million blacks. The destinies of the two races, in this country, are indissolubly linked together, and the interests of both require that the common government of all shall not permit the seeds of race hate to be planted under the sanction of law. In my opinion, the judgment this day rendered will, in time, prove to be quite as pernicious as the decision made by this tribunal in the Dred Scott case.

Harlan's prescience soon became obvious enough. The Court's decision stimulated agressions, both brutal and irritating, on blacks, although it did not, or has not yet, proved as pernicious as the decision in the Dred Scott case.

Between 1889 and 1918 more than 2,500 Negroes died in lynchings and riots, some of the worst of which were in Illinois, Ohio, and Indiana. Brutality, it would seem, was stimulated by the abolition of slavery. Segregation of schools and housing became the law not only in the South but in border states as well and segregation became the practice in parts of the North. In Washington, the seat of government, federal offices, restaurants, and rest rooms were segregated. And in practice public facilities were separate but not equal. By 1915 South

Carolina was spending $23.76 for the education of an average white child in a public school and $2.91 for the average black child.

Blacks, then, had appealed to the court of last resort for the equal justice under law which they thought had been won with the Civil War. The Court had put them in their place, and then the Court and the country turned to other interests. Clearly, the turning of the Court that began under Chief Justice Taney continued for many, many years. The issues changed, but the Court for three decades into the twentieth century remained remarkably consistent in unwisely and unrealistically thwarting John Marshall's doctrines and elevating property rights on occasion to a place in the Constitution superior even to states' rights.

Congress in 1890 passed and President Benjamin Harrison signed the Sherman Act, the country's first federal antitrust law, to bar monopolies and price-fixing and to countervail the great concentrations of industrial power which were being assembled by John D. Rockefeller, J. P. Morgan, James J. Hill, and other men who were the new aristocracy, born of the rapid industrialization which began after the Civil War. Economic freedom always has been regarded as a necessary counterpart of political freedom in the United States, and Congress, in exercising its constitutional power to regulate commerce, was attempting to insure that private trusts and monopolies would not infringe on the competitive equality of others. But the Supreme Court, over Justice Harlan's dissent, rejected the first significant antitrust case brought before it by the Justice Department by refusing to hold the Sugar Trust in violation because, it said, the Sherman Act could apply only to "commerce" and the Sugar Trust was engaged in "manufacturing."[3] In other antitrust cases, against Standard Oil Company of New Jersey and American Tobacco Company, the Court, still over Justice Harlan's dissent, developed what was called the "rule of reason," meaning that only "unreasonable" restraints of trade were illegal and the rest were legal.[4] The Court did not throw out all of the government's antitrust suits, but it injected into the Sherman Act a lasting weakness and uncertainty which many years later led John Kenneth Galbraith to assert, accurately, that antitrust enforcement was a "charade."

Congress enacted the first federal income tax, a 2 per cent tax on incomes over $4,000, and some of the nation's most prominent citizens saw in it the seeds of anarchy and communism. The Supreme

36

Court in 1895 held it unconstitutional, reasoning that the Constitution required a tax on income to be apportioned according to population.[5] Justice Harlan's dissent said the Court's ruling was "a surrender of the taxing power to the moneyed class," and the decision was overruled in 1913 by the ratification of the Sixteenth Amendment.

The Court in 1905 struck down, as "unnecessary and arbitrary" and thus a violation of the Fourteenth Amendment, a New York State law which said bakers were not to work more than sixty hours a week. Justice Harlan dissented, as did Justice Oliver Wendell Holmes, who observed that laws might be "novel and even shocking" and still be constitutional. The first President Roosevelt had appointed Holmes in 1902; Harlan died in 1911. The two, so different in background, did not always vote together. Harlan, a Kentuckian and former slave owner, was a convivial man with a bald head and a big nose who was said by a friend to go to bed with "one hand on the Constitution and the other on the Bible." Holmes once described him as "the last of the tobacco-spittin' judges." Holmes, descended of Boston and Harvard, was a scholarly man whose appearance became more distinguished as his huge mustache and full head of hair turned white. But both Harlan and Holmes had served in the Union army in the Civil War and on the Court they shared a philosophical kinship, even though they sometimes disagreed, particularly when Holmes did not see the Sherman Act as a great blessing.

The repressive laws which Congress enacted and President Wilson enforced during World War I were exceeded, if ever, as instances of panic persuasion, only by the government herding of U.S. citizens of Japanese ancestry into detention camps during World War II. In 1917 Congress passed the Espionage Act, intended mainly to punish interference with the draft, and in 1918 a Sedition Act, which was broad enough to jail almost anyone critical of the war or government. There were some 2,000 prosecutions under the 1917 law and Justice Holmes, writing for a unanimous Court, held the law did not violate the First Amendment guarantees of free speech and press. But Holmes dissented when the Court upheld the 1918 law, sending to prison leafleteers who urged the "workers of the world" to support the Russian Revolution, and when it upheld a New York State criminal anarchy law, jailing U.S. Communist Benjamin Gitlow for circulating his "Left Wing Manifesto." Justices Holmes and Brandeis both dissented in the two cases, with Holmes seeing no national danger in "these poor and puny anonymities." President Wilson had named Louis D. Brandeis to the Court in 1916. He took Justice Harlan's place as Holmes's frequent co-dissenter and often there was a threesome with Harlan Fiske Stone, whom President Coolidge named in 1925.

In the Court's "Gay '20s," the majority overthrew minimum wage laws of three states and a law Congress passed to fix minimum wages for women in the District of Columbia. To the latter decision, which seemed to flow from the Nineteenth Amendment giving women equal voting and other legal rights with men, Justice Holmes replied in dissent: "It will need more than the Nineteenth Amendment to convince me that there are no differences between men and women."

A Harvard professor named Felix Frankfurter in 1930 wrote: "Since 1920 the Court has invalidated more legislation than in fifty years preceding." A Court so dedicated to a dead past and so enthralled with the property rights of moneyed classes and corporations, even where these clashed with states' rights, could stand only so long as most whites were prosperous, most blacks weren't rioting, and the occupants of the White House were preoccupied with wars abroad or were simply passive men. When those conditions no longer held the Court could not stand for long, and it did not.

When Justice Holmes retired in 1932 at the age of ninety, President Hoover named Benjamin N. Cardozo. "Mr. Hoover performed what was probably the most popular act of his presidency," Professor Freund has said.[6] Cardozo succeeded to the seat and the dissenting role which had been occupied by Justice Holmes. Brandeis, Stone, and Cardozo each was the product of an Eastern school (Harvard, Amherst, and Columbia, respectively) and each was prominent in the law before his appointment.

In the first three months of Franklin Roosevelt's Presidency, Congress enacted fifteen major laws which vastly expanded federal authority to deal with the Great Depression. The excesses of the affluent '20s had come tumbling down. The stock market crashed, many banks failed, farm prices tumbled, and nearly twenty million people were on relief. The Supreme Court, which happened to be moving into its new marble temple at the time, was not as insensitive to the world around it as sometimes is said. It began to change quite soon, and change was far advanced before President Roosevelt was able to name a majority. Of course, the Court read the election returns and heard President Roosevelt's criticism of it, and some of the Justices were moved and some were not. But this is no cynical commentary on those who were moved; those who were moved did not abandon their independence of judgment to political expediency, and surely to change is better than to be insensitive to the end as Chief Justice Taney once had been.

The change was beginning to become apparent in 1934, when the Court handed down a 5-to-4 decision upholding a New York State law which fixed milk prices to prevent them from falling more. Among those fifteen emergency New Deal measures enacted in 1933, the Court upheld passage of the Federal Securities Act and creation of the Tennessee Valley Authority. The majority sustained the policy of reducing the dollar's value in gold.

But six of the "nine old men" held unconstitutional, as an invasion of states' rights, the Agricultural Adjustment Act. Stone, Brandeis, and Cardozo joined in a strong dissent saying, "Courts are not the only agency that must be assumed to have capacity to govern." In a 5-to-4 decision the majority voided as unconstitutional Congress's attempt to strengthen wages and prices in the soft coal industry, saying these were "local evils."

In perhaps its best remembered anti–New Deal decision, the Court held unconstitutional a key portion of the National Industrial Recovery Act.[7] But that decision in 1935 was unanimous. Congress with that law went too far in delegating to the President the power to fix wages and prices in concert with industry, and in suspending in a wholesale fashion the antitrust laws for businesses which co-operated with the President. Many New Dealers came to share the unanimous Court's conclusion that the 1933 law went too far. Many also feared that the NRA was becoming an administrative monster. When the Court struck it down, the National Recovery Administration's blue eagle was not a disastrous loss. Congress incorporated its best features in the National Labor Relations Act, which delegated the issue of unfair labor practices to an independent board instead of to the President, and the Supreme Court in a 5-to-4 decision in 1937 upheld that delegation.

The four holdouts changed least, and President Roosevelt proposed to Congress a "court-packing" plan to increase the Court's membership to as many as fifteen Justices. But Congress wanted no part of so direct an assault on the Court and it is doubtful that the President was entirely serious. In any event, deaths and retirements gave FDR seven vacancies to fill from 1937 through 1941 and he named Hugo L.

Black, Stanley Reed, Felix Frankfurter, William O. Douglas, Frank Murphy, Robert H. Jackson, and James F. Byrnes. Cardozo died in 1938, Brandeis retired in 1939, and Roosevelt elevated Harlan Fiske Stone to Chief Justice where he remained until his death in 1946.

The Court that FDR made concentrated first on the economic issues of its times, overruling the Court's 1922 decision which held child labor laws a matter of exclusive state concern and upholding much more new federal legislation. At times the majority seemed to be ruling with less than a wholly independent mind, as in 1944 when it upheld the government's detention of Japanese-Americans over the objection of three dissenting Justices who asserted the detention camps were "a clear violation of constitutional rights" and "utterly revolting among a free people."[8] But with time the Court that Franklin Roosevelt had made, and that President Truman continued, so far as the ideology of his appointees was concerned, seemed to regain its independence. The Court, for instance, in 1952 told President Truman he had no constitutional authority to seize the nation's steel mills, even in wartime when they were faced with a strike that would halt production.[9] It was an era when no great leader of a majority and no great dissenter emerged. No great leader did in fact come forth, to make Justice Harlan's half-century-old dissents the law, until the advent of Earl Warren.

CHAPTER 4

# The Warren Court Leads

The ancient issue of white discrimination and black rights began to
revisit the Supreme Court and the Constitution in the late 1930s. Why
then? Perhaps because the Great Depression had degraded black
masses even more than white. Perhaps also because a handful of
Negroes had overcome discrimination, in the sports and entertainment worlds anyway. Jesse Owens won four gold medals in the 1936
Olympics in spite of Hitler's snubs of this non-Aryan. Because increasing numbers of Negroes were migrating to Northern cities where
at least they were free to organize and where, with the help of some
whites, they had begun to contest discrimination in the South and
North. The National Association for the Advancement of Colored
People and the National Urban League had been formed two decades
earlier and these initial ventures in black self-help now were beginning
to gain the strength of numbers and of self-assurance. Because certainly of a national climate inspired in Washington where Franklin
Roosevelt, now in his second term, had led massively successful assaults on old citadels of state and private power. And because the
Supreme Court was coming around.

Even before the 1930s, the constitutional issue had begun to return
to the Court, in sporadic bursts with long periods of silence between.
In 1917 the Court held unconstitutional a Louisville, Kentucky, ordinance which barred blacks and whites from moving into homes on
city blocks occupied predominantly by members of the other race. In
1927 Justice Holmes held for a majority of the Court that states
violated the Fourteenth Amendment by preventing Negroes from
voting in primary elections. During these years, when the Court

invalidated a great deal of state and federal legislation dealing with social and economic problems, it did not invariably uphold Negro claims to racial equality. But neither did the Court which President Franklin Roosevelt attacked, for voiding early New Deal legislation, invariably reject blacks' claims.

During the 1930s the periods of black silence grew shorter as more cases involving the issue of racial equality reached the Court. In 1935, in a case from Alabama, the Court voided as unconstitutional the trials of eight young Negroes because qualified blacks had been excluded from the juries which found the eight guilty of rape. In 1938 the Court held that Missouri acted unconstitutionally when it told Negroes applying for entry to the Missouri Law School that it would pay their tuition at an out-of-state law school. Missouri must provide legal education for blacks itself, the Court held. These were decisions handed down during the years that the Court was beginning to change under pressure exerted by President Roosevelt. But the Court that FDR made did not become famous for its civil rights libertarianism.

After World War II, blacks were silent no more in asserting their constitutional rights. War is a leveler of men and a creator of great expectations for the peace to come. But more, great wars abroad that are popular at home must be moral crusades against an evil foe. After the Japanese attack on Pearl Harbor, World War II became all of that, and it left deep impressions on many blacks and some whites in postwar America. Before the war was over President Roosevelt began to desegregate government offices and rest rooms in Washington and he named the first Negro to the rank of general in the Army. President Truman in 1948 issued an executive order to end segregation in the armed forces. The late Ralph Bunche became Under Secretary of the United Nations, and Private First Class William Thompson in the Korean War became the first black soldier since the Spanish-American War to win the Congressional Medal of Honor.

Negroes home from the wars took not to the streets to assert racial equality in America, but to the courts to establish, for themselves and their children, their right to an equal education.

Before World War II, blacks had begun to test their new organizational strengths against the Missouri Law School and other institutions of higher learning. They won their most important victory after the war, when the Supreme Court in 1950 held that Texas did not meet the separate but equal standard in establishing a new law school for blacks. In argument before the Court, eleven Southern and border states argued along with Texas that a new, separate law school could provide Negroes with an education equal to that provided whites by an older, established law school. The Supreme Court unanimously rejected the states' argument, ruling that the new school could not provide educational equality because the older University of Texas Law School "possesses to a far greater degree those qualities which are incapable of objective measurement," including "reputation of faculty, experience of the administration, standing in the community, traditions and prestige."[1]

The 1950 decision eroded the separate but equal doctrine which the Court had established in 1896. But none of the decisions won by blacks against institutions of higher learning, before or after World War II, overturned the old doctrine. It was only after expectations had been raised by the war and after these preliminary victories were won in the Court that blacks mounted a direct assault on the doctrine and did so with a massive challenge of racial discrimination at the elementary and high school levels. By 1952 there were cases at the Supreme Court seeking the desegregation of public schools in South Carolina, Kansas, Delaware, Virginia, and the District of Columbia. The Court in December of that year heard argument on the cases from South Carolina, Kansas, Delaware, and Virginia, but seemed unable to take the final step that would reverse the 1896 doctrine. The Court's term ended in June, 1953, with no decision. On September 8, while the Court still was in recess for the summer, Chief Justice Frederick M. Vinson, who had been appointed by President Truman in 1946, died suddenly. Earl Warren, President Eisenhower's first appointee to the Court, took his oath as the new Chief Justice on October 5, when the new term opened.

Fifteen years later, on July 5, 1968, Earl Warren looked back. Shedding judicial aloofness, he came down now from the place above the noisy crowd; he held a press conference. It was in the East Conference Room of the Supreme Court Building, a spacious room with wood-paneled walls, fireplaces, and handsome crystal and brass chandeliers that make it gracious and warm in contrast to the stark white marble of much of the rest of the building. The Rembrandt Peale painting of Chief Justice Marshall hangs over one of the fireplaces.

Chief Justice Warren was asked to rank the Court's major decisions of his time in order of their significance. The most important, he said, were not the school desegregation decisions but the one man, one vote decisions which told the states to restore equal voting rights to those to whom voting equality had been denied. Second were the school decisions. Third were the decisions in the area of the rights of those accused of criminal offenses.

For each of these decisions the Warren Court was roundly denounced by some and stoutly defended by others, and the controversy it created was greater than at any time since the Marshall Court. But there was an underlying philosophy which bound much of the Warren Court's work: a philosophy which held that, when the other branches of Government are not capable of responding to the rightful demands and grievances of the people, it is the proper role of the Court to exercise leadership and initiate social change. Abe Fortas has stated: "Our law and law courts have often been the theatre in which social conflict is acted out and its issues resolved. With the advent of the Warren Court this role was progressively expanded."[2] The Warren Court opened its doors and those of the federal court system to indigent persons and non-propertied classes who earlier had been thrown out by the courts and whose petitions to the executive and legislative branches were unavailing. In opening its doors and thus expanding its horizon to cases and controversies which in another day would not have been accepted, the Court engaged in "no real invasion of state authority," Professor Freund has written. "What the Court has done is to insist on procedural observances by both federal and state agencies, and on the standards of fair play which are implicit in the concept of due process of law."[3]

Blacks as a class of course benefited most because they had been denied most. But by no means was the Warren Court's insistence on procedural fairness and standards of fair play for blacks alone. Under the Warren Court's doctrines, it and lower federal courts have told highway planners that they must hear citizens who do not want their homes torn down to make way for another superhighway. The courts have told utility companies they cannot erect huge new power plants on broad rivers without listening to the objections of conservationists. They have told a federal agency it cannot renew a broadcasting station's license without considering the objections of the people who are the station's listeners. And the Warren Court conferred on citizens "who assert only the status of federal taxpayers" the right to enter a

44

federal court to challenge the constitutionality of certain Federal spending programs.[4]

These are potent privileges, for whites and blacks, and bureaucrats, legislators and Presidents may shudder at where they might lead. This, then, is the harmonizing theme that underlies so much of the Warren Court's work: its attempt to move toward a more open, more free society and to renew the essential premise of the mutual covenant, the right to participation in government in exchange for fidelity to law. This is why Earl Warren said that the one man, one vote cases were "the most basic decided in my time." If the electoral process was more truly representative of all the people, there would be less need for judicial intervention. The Supreme Court did not seek, for instance, the school desegregation issue, but took it when it came. Justice Robert H. Jackson, during argument before the Court on the school desegregation cases, observed that it "is perfectly clear under the Fourteenth Amendment that Congress is given the power and duty to enforce the Amendment by legislation," adding, "the reason this case is here was that action couldn't be obtained from Congress."[5]

The Founding Fathers built into the Constitution what have been called fruitful tensions among the three branches of the federal government. If the tensions have been fruitful, in advancing the people's pursuit of happiness while at the same time preserving their freedom, they also at times in history have been spectacular when one branch is locked in a power struggle with another. When the Warren Court stated what the law of the land must be in the one man, one vote, the school desegregation, and the criminal rights cases, it was asserting the supremacy of judicial authority more strongly than the Court had asserted itself since the days of Chief Justice Marshall. The political controversy that surrounded the Warren Court on all sides was commensurate with its assertion of supremacy. That the Warren Court followed paths which were logical extensions of decisions arrived at before Earl Warren became Chief Justice served only to make Warren more controversial, for the Court earlier hesitated to take those final steps which would bring it into real and immediate conflict with the other two branches. In taking those steps, the Warren Court seized the initiative in formulating solutions to pressing national problems which Congress and the White House had chosen largely to ignore. And the Court's great and historic assertion of constitutional supremacy led eventually to jugular political combat over the future of the Supreme Court, after Earl Warren.

The school cases came first in the chronology of the Warren Court. The deliberations among the members of the Court always have been tightly guarded secrets, but there is reason to believe that after the Court heard argument on the school cases in December, 1952, some of the justices were not willing to reverse the separate but equal doctrine. To ascribe to Earl Warren alone the Court's subsequent unanimity in reversing the doctrine may be to credit the new Chief Justice's persuasive powers too highly. Nevertheless, after Warren arrived, the Court in December, 1953, heard the cases from South Carolina, Kansas, Delaware, and Virginia reargued and on May 17, 1954, the new Chief Justice delivered the unanimous opinion of the Court.

The decision, more forceful and historic for its unanimity, reversed the separate but equal doctrine adopted in 1896 and established as the law of the land the position which had been taken by the late dissenting Justice Harlan. Chief Justice Warren's opinion held that separate schools for black children are inherently unequal and therefore state laws which required racial segregation in education are unconstitutional. "In the field of public education the doctrine of 'separate but equal' has no place," the Warren opinion declared.⁶ It continued: "In these days, it is doubtful that any child may reasonably be expected to succeed in life if he is denied the opportunity of an education." Separate schools, even if they are equal in physical facilities, deprive black children of equal educational opportunities, he said. "To separate them from others of similar age and qualifications solely because of their race generates a feeling of inferiority as to their status in the community that may affect their hearts and minds in a way unlikely ever to be undone."

The 1954 decision is known as *Brown* v. *Board of Education*, taking its name from the Kansas case which was begun when Oliver Brown of Topeka sued the city school board on behalf of his eight-year-old daughter, Linda Carol. The South Carolina, Delaware, and Virginia cases were decided with the Kansas case and eventually the Court's decision required the desegregation of elementary and high schools in twenty-one Southern, Southwestern, and border states where segregation existed by reason of state law.

The Court in 1954 did not say how or when the states must desegregate their schools. It studied the matter and when it decided in 1955 it did not order immediate desegregation or fix dates in the future. Recognizing the practical problems ahead, it took a conciliatory attitude toward the South, saying that lower federal courts in supervising desegregation in their areas must require "a prompt and reasonable start toward full compliance," and school districts must proceed "with all deliberate speed."[7]

The school decisions rested on that part of the Fourteenth Amendment which says that states shall not deny to any person "equal protection" of the laws. The one man, one vote decisions flowed primarily from the same "equal protection" portion of the Amendment, which had been proposed by Congress in 1866 and ratified by the states two years later. The criminal rights decisions were based on the portion of the Amendment stating that no state "shall . . . deprive any person of life, liberty, or property, without due process of law."

The Warren Court's decisions enforcing the right of all qualified citizens to vote began in 1962. The Fifteenth Amendment, proposed in 1869 and ratified in 1870, stated: "The right of citizens . . . to vote shall not be denied or abridged by . . . any State, on account of race, color or previous condition of servitude," but in the South blacks had been denied voting rights by a great variety of subterfuges such as the poll tax, the white primary and, as Anthony Lewis makes clear in *Portrait of a Decade,* his book about the first ten years of the Warren Court, by white violence and black fear.[8] In the one-party South, the Democratic primaries were the only meaningful elections and Negroes by state law and party rule were excluded from voting on the theory that primaries were private party matters. The Supreme Court, in a series of decisions that began with the Holmes opinion in 1927, held the white primaries and similar devices to be unconstitutional. The Twenty-fourth Amendment, ratified in 1964, proscribed the poll tax in federal elections. The Warren Court in 1966 finally banished the poll tax, to which four Southern states still clung in state elections, even though it prevented poor whites as well as blacks from voting.[9]

The one man, one vote decisions were still more basic to the concept of political participation and self-government. In a most fundamental and practical sense, the decisions were related to the real and growing problems of the nation's cities, which increasingly have been abandoned by middle-class whites and left to poor whites and blacks. Many states, North and South, long had denied to city voters representation equal with that of rural voters, by the simple device of failing to reapportion seats in state legislatures and in Congress as population patterns changed. With this device, voters in rural electoral districts maintained a disproportionately large share of political power and the inequality of the situation became more glaring as urban electoral districts housed more and more relatively less affluent voters. The Tennessee legislature, for example, had not reapportioned districts since 1901, even though the state constitution required that legislative districts be redrawn every ten years so that each legislator represented an approximately equal number of people. In Connecticut about 10 per cent of the people could elect a majority of the state representatives. In Vermont in 1950 one state representative represented forty-nine people and another represented 33,000. In Colorado the state legislature in 1955 apportioned educational funds by giving Denver with 90,000 school children $2.3 million and giving a semi-rural school district with 18,000 children $2.4 million.

The Supreme Court, beginning in 1946, had several opportunities to speak to the issue and declined them. Justice Felix Frankfurter, the Harvard professor whom President Franklin Roosevelt named to the Court in 1939 to succeed Cardozo and who remained until 1962, said in 1946: "Courts ought not to enter this political thicket."[10] But the Warren Court entered in 1962, ruling in the case of *Baker* v. *Carr* (from Tennessee) that the Fourteenth Amendment's guarantee of "equal protection of the laws" gives each citizen the right to equal representation in a state legislature and malapportionment is a "debasement of their votes."[11] Justice William J. Brennan, appointed by President Eisenhower in 1956, wrote the majority opinion. By the end of 1962, citizens in thirty states had brought suits in federal courts seeking reapportionment of state legislatures. In cases decided in 1964 and later, the Supreme Court applied the one man, one vote formula to both houses of state legislatures, saying that differences in population apportionment among legislative districts could not rest on geographic, historic, or economic grounds alone, and it extended the doctrine to congressional districts and eventually to some local election districts. Justice Frankfurter, until he retired, dissented as the Warren Court went marching into the political thicket. A new Justice, John M. Harlan, grandson of the famous dissenter of a different kind, appointed by President Eisenhower in 1955, dissented in the voting rights cases on the ground of states' rights. Another dissenter to the extension of the one man, one vote doctrine to congressional districts was Justice Potter Stewart, a 1958 Eisenhower appointee.

The Warren Court's criminal rights decisions, third in order of development, illustrate again the Warren Court's concern with the equality of all men. Men who are wealthy or prominent do not often find themselves in a criminal court, assuming their gains are not ill gotten, and when they do they demand their lawyers or their mouthpieces. The criminal courts are better known to the poor, the young, and the black, who are most likely not to know their right to counsel (if they can afford a lawyer), their right to remain silent, and the other rights afforded them by the Constitution.

The criminal rights decisions also illustrate the great validity of the Constitution as a statement of principles and the great invalidity of any assumption that the principles mean other than what men say they mean. The first ten Amendments, ratified in 1791, are known as the Bill of Rights because they stand against repression by enumerating not only freedoms of religion, speech and press but also "the right . . . to be secure . . . against unreasonable searches and seizures"; the right not to be held for a "capital, or other infamous crime" except on indictment of a grand jury, and the right not to be tried twice for the same crime or to bear witness against oneself; the right to "a speedy and public trial, by an impartial jury [and] to be confronted with the witnesses against him"; and the right not to be oppressed by "excessive bail . . . [or] cruel and unusual punishments." The Supreme Court is the particular guardian of these rights, which always have applied to federal prosecutions and trials. But most criminal punishment in this country traditionally has been exacted under state law in state courts, and it still is, although the enactment by Congress of more federal criminal statutes and the growth of the Federal Bureau of Investigation in the fairly recent past is bending tradition. Yet, there still remain very large constitutional questions about the extent to which the Bill of Rights as a whole applies to the states, and the settled view until the Warren Court was that the criminal rights amendments did not apply to the states, except in the most notorious of circumstances.

In that background the Warren Court, with less unanimity than in the voting or school decisions, proceeded to address itself to the issue of the powers of state and local police and prosecutors versus the rights of accused individuals. Applying the Fourteenth Amendment's command that no state "shall . . . deprive any person of life, liberty, or property, without due process of law," the Court in the 1960s applied a number of the specific guarantees of the Bill of Rights to the states and thereby undertook a sweeping reform of state criminal procedure. In the famous case of *Gideon* v. *Wainwright,* argued before the Court by Abe Fortas as Court-appointed counsel, the Court held that poor persons must be supplied with a lawyer at state expense in serious criminal cases.[12] In other decisions, it held that indigents also must be supplied with lawyers for appeal and with court transcripts at public expense. It barred from state courts, as well as federal, "evidence secured by official lawlessness" such as the entry of a house by police without a warrant. On the well-grounded theory that too often suspects are intimidated and worse in police stations, the Court extended to state prosecutions privileges against self-incrimination and, in the *Escobedo* and *Miranda* decisions, it built protections around the use in courts of confessions obtained by police.[13]

Revolutions begun by the judicial branch are most likely to succeed when they are launched by a Court that is strongly led and unanimous. But Court-directed revolutions can never succeed completely and permanently until and unless the other two branches and ultimately the majority of the people follow the Court's leadership and accept its moral suasion. By these standards, then, the Warren Court's decisions striking down racial discrimination promised to be the most enduring of its works.

Certainly, as those decisions ordering an end to discrimination began to unfold, Presidents, Congresses, and the nation started to fall in behind the Court's leadership, but slowly, reluctantly, and with reservations. After the Court in 1954 held separate schools for whites and blacks illegal, border states including Kansas, cities such as Baltimore, and several hundred school districts in many parts of the country voluntarily moved to integrate their schools. President Eisenhower directed that school segregation be ended in the District of Columbia.

Presidents Eisenhower, Kennedy, and Johnson sought from Congress progressively broader civil rights laws. Their commitments did not come easily, and each, with the possible exception of President Kennedy, avoided an overly broad commitment to the cause of civil rights. Nonetheless, Congress in 1957 passed the first Civil Rights Act since 1875, with the support of Republican Dwight Eisenhower and the help of the Senate Democratic Majority Leader, Lyndon B. John-son. Its main provision allowed the Justice Department to bring suits on behalf of Negroes who were denied the right to vote in federal elections. In 1960, Congress passed another Civil Rights Act, to aug-ment the 1957 law by providing for federal voting referees to register Negroes where local election officials refused.

Congress passed several more laws which, like the 1957 and 1960 Acts, relieved blacks of the sole responsibility to seek their own relief in court and brought to their assistance the administrative machinery of the federal government by placing on the Justice Department a responsibility for initiating suits. President Kennedy sent to Congress in 1963 a proposal for the most significant civil rights legislation that had been passed since the years immediately after the Civil War. It advocated a federal law to bar the exclusion of Negroes from restau-rants, hotels, theaters, and other places of public accommodation; to permit the Justice Department to bring suits to force the desegrega-tion of public accommodations as well as schools; and to outlaw racial discrimination by employers and labor unions. President Kennedy did not secure its enactment. After his assassination and after the Senate invoked cloture to halt a filibuster, the Senate passed the bill. Presi-dent Johnson signed it into law as the Civil Rights Act of 1964. In 1968 President Johnson obtained from Congress another significant Civil Rights Act, which outlawed racial discrimination in the sale and rental of private housing and allowed the Justice Department to bring suits against landlords and real estate agents. Theoretically at least, the 1968 law opened a way for blacks to escape urban slums for the green grass of suburbia.

These legislative gains and presidential commitments after the Court's crucial 1954 decision were not won simply because Congress and the White House were falling in behind the Warren Court. They were won also because blacks in the South, often aided by young people from the North, pressed their demands for equality on local officials in many Southern cities and towns.

Late in 1955, Mrs. Rosa Parks, a black woman, sat in the front section of a public bus in Montgomery, Alabama, which by custom was reserved for whites. She was arrested and the Montgomery bus boycott began, under the leadership of two Negro ministers, Martin Luther King, Jr., and Ralph D. Abernathy. Dr. King and a hundred other bus boycotters were arrested and the turmoil continued for a year until the Supreme Court in 1956 declared it unconstitutional for Montgomery to segregate bus passengers. The tactic of nonviolent direct action, coupled with federal court action, spread across the South under its principal advocate, Dr. King, to lunch-counter, theater, and other sit-ins, and it was against this background that the first Civil Rights Act was proposed in 1956 and enacted in 1957.

Organized, nonviolent resistance to local discrimination and parallel and court actions by blacks often were met with white opposition and arrests. Fifteen days after Congress passed the Civil Rights Act of 1957, President Eisenhower sent federal troops into Little Rock, Arkansas, to quell white mob resistance to a lower federal court order under which nine black children were to enter Central High School with 2,000 white students. This kind of "disgraceful" action, as Mr. Eisenhower called it, strengthened the blacks' cause. In the 1960 presidential campaign, unlike four years earlier, both national party platforms endorsed new federal legislation to assist school desegregation, although, as Anthony Lewis wrote, GOP Candidate Nixon in 1960 did not speak out boldly on the issue as he campaigned in the South that fall.[14]

"Freedom rides" rolled across the South in 1961, organized by the Congress of Racial Equality from its base in Washington, to desegregate intercity buses and terminals. There were many arrests and a few bus burnings, and only then and at the request of the Kennedy Administration did the Interstate Commerce Commission, created in 1887, order bus companies and railroads to desegregate transportation facilities in the South. In May, 1961, the "freedom riders" arrived in Montgomery, Alabama, and were met with violence. President Kennedy sent 400 armed U.S. marshals and deputies to Montgomery, under the supervision of Deputy Attorney General Byron White, to restore order.

Tension continued to mount, as in Albany, Georgia, where Dr. King was jailed again, and in Cambridge, Maryland, where blacks with shotguns were met by National Guardsmen with rifles and blood was let on both sides. In 1962 President Kennedy sent troops to Oxford, Mississippi, under the supervision of Robert Kennedy's new Deputy Attorney General, Nicholas deB. Katzenbach, to integrate the state's university by securing the admission of one black man, James Meredith.

In Mississippi in 1963 NAACP leader Medgar Evers was murdered in the doorway of his home. In Birmingham, Alabama, a Negro movement led by Dr. King to integrate nonviolently public accommodations throughout the city was answered with police dogs, fire hoses, and then a bomb blast at the Sixteenth Street Baptist Church, killing four young black girls who were attending Sunday School. On May 21, 1963, a federal district court judge ordered the University of Alabama to admit two Negroes and Governor George Wallace rose to national prominence with the defiant declaration, "I will be present to bar the entrance of any Negro." He was physically present "in the schoolhouse door," as he had promised, and was moved aside by soldiers sent in by President Kennedy and by an equally resolute Nicholas Katzenbach. The following day, June 11, 1963, the President made a national television address asking each American to "examine his conscience" and recalling the plea for racial tolerance made by Justice Harlan "at the turn of the century." Eight days later, the President sent to Congress what became, after the massive March on Washington by 200,000 Americans, white and black, and after the assassination of John Kennedy, the Civil Rights Act of 1964.

The next great advance in civil rights legislation came after the assassination of Martin Luther King, Jr., and the black uprisings that spread all across the nation in the hours after his death.

Dr. King, thirty-nine years old, was assassinated in Memphis, Tennessee, on April 4, 1968. Within hours blacks took to the streets in Washington to riot, burn, and loot, and whites fled the central city area in alarm and dismay. Within days the racial violence erupted in 125 cities in twenty-nine states. President Johnson quickly broadcast on national radio and television a statement in which he said, "America is shocked and saddened by the brutal slaying of Dr. Martin Luther King. I ask every citizen to reject the blind violence that has struck Dr. King, who lived by nonviolence." Shortly thereafter the President urgently requested Congress to enact the civil rights bill he had requested two years earlier and Congress on April 10, six days after King's slaying, finished action on the Civil Rights Act of 1968 which, in addition to its open-housing provisions, contained an anti-riot section.

As black and white violence flashed over those years, sporadically but with growing intensity, the Warren Court in its quiet place hewed to its constitutional line. Blacks, emboldened in the courts as on the streets, brought many new legal challenges to advance their fight for equal justice under law and one of the cases they brought asserted the novel theory that the Civil Rights Act of 1866 was not a dead letter.

The 1866 law said that all citizens "shall have the same right as is enjoyed by white citizens to inherit, purchase, lease, sell, hold and convey real and personal property." A century after its enactment by Congress, it was assumed by almost everybody that the statute did no more than to grant blacks the legal capacity to buy and sell property. But blacks decided to test the law to see whether its provisions, which on their face were more sweeping than the Civil Rights Act Congress had passed in April, 1968, had real meaning. In June, 1968, the Warren Court, acting on a suit brought by a St. Louis Negro, resurrected the 1866 law by ruling in the case of *Jones* v. *Mayer* that a black man was entitled to sue for damages a real estate developer who refused to sell him a house in a white suburb.[15] The Court subsequently decided that under the 1866 Act a damage suit also could be brought against a suburban neighborhood swimming club for its refusal to admit an otherwise qualified black family.[16]

In the school desegregation decisions, the legislative reapportionment rulings, the criminal rights rulings and others, the Warren Court overturned constitutional precedent. It often acted where Congress or the states could have legislated, but where these arms of government under majoritarian control had not acted.

But the majoritarian branches of the federal government followed the Warren Court's essential moral leadership and eventually the Southern states also followed, even if the other branches and the states followed at a distance and then under the stress of nonviolent black pressures. Congress enacted civil rights legislation for the first time since the Civil War era. Presidents Eisenhower, Kennedy, and Johnson, fulfilling the oaths they had taken at their inaugurations to uphold the Constitution, courageously employed United States marshals and troops to enforce the desegregation decisions of the Supreme Court or of lower federal courts which were carrying out the Warren Court's mandates.

Civil rights laws, whether made by Congress or the Court, perhaps more than other kinds of laws must depend for their ultimate fulfillment on the good faith of the majority of the people, white and black. The law, constitutional or statutory, in the school, reapportionment, and even the criminal areas was dealing with ingrained patterns of human behavior involving millions of people in hundreds of communities far from Washington. The Supreme Court's decisions could never directly reach all of the people and the laws passed by Congress could reach them only with painful slowness.

Yet, the moral suasion initiated by the Warren Court spread like waves in every direction and in some measure touched every man, woman, and child, white and black. Blacks' rights, legal and otherwise, were rolled forward and whites' prejudices were rolled back from where they had been in 1953. Blacks, for the first time since the Civil War era, realistically became eligible for public office in the local, state, and national governments. Negroes became known more often as Afro-Americans, putting them theoretically on a par at least with Japanese-Americans and other hyphenated Americans. In the entertainment world, Amos 'n' Andy were out and Bill Cosby was in. Blacks demanded and won from universities in the North special black study programs and they began to rewrite American history as it concerned the Afro-American.

It is tempting to conclude then that the Warren Court led a lasting revolution in America. But it was a revolution that always had to be seen in perspective and that is not yet completed.

By 1964 only about one per cent of the three million black children in the eleven states of the Old South were in desegregated schools. By 1969 the figure was up only to 6 per cent. School segregation in cities of the North, which resulted from housing patterns that in turn reflected the white flight to the suburbs rather than racial separation by state law as had existed in the South, presented a question the nation and the Court had not yet faced. Racial equality for blacks in housing and in employment opportunities also was largely unfulfilled. The new civil rights laws enacted by Congress had given the Justice Department the power to sue on behalf of blacks to improve housing and employment opportunities, but the department had exercised its discretion by filing suits not by the hundreds but in quantities that could be termed tokenism, given the long history of racial inequality in America and the magnitude of the problem in the late 1960s.

The revolution inaugurated by the Warren Court was, then, neither final nor complete, and it could not be made so unless it was sustained by a continuation of moral leadership as enlightened as that which had been brought to the Court by Earl Warren and as courageous at least as that which had been brought to the Presidency by Dwight Eisenhower, John Kennedy, and Lyndon Johnson.

CHAPTER 5

# The Black Seat

If the Constitution and its Bill of Rights are read side by side with a history of the Negro in America, it becomes perfectly obvious that the tortuous inconsistencies between the two are intolerable. When the Supreme Court ruled in 1954 that black boys and girls could no longer be prevented by state law from attending schools with white children, it hardly could have done otherwise. So glaring were the inconsistencies that the other two branches of the federal government, and presumably the majority of the American people which they represented, accepted the morality of the Court's ruling and then expanded on it with new Civil Rights Acts.

Yet, there was some amount of opposition, not large perhaps but vengeful, from the moment Chief Justice Warren on May 17, 1954, announced the decision of the Court in the school desegregation cases and it remains questionable whether the majoritarian branches would have passed the new Civil Rights Acts if blacks had not reinforced their cause with sit-ins, freedom rides, and indeed even with riots. Decades of Negro history, written by a white majoritarian hand, would not be wiped out with a mere Supreme Court decision. To the contrary, the vengeful opposition would grow as the Warren Court's libertarianism expanded. America never has lacked opportunistic politicians who are willing and able to forgo true leadership for a chance to forge a reactionary majority by putting latent angers and fears into words. In time, the growing opposition to the Warren Court would find its voice.

Reaction to and defiance of the 1954 decision arose immediately in the South. White Citizens Councils were organized to co-ordinate local opposition and white academies were opened so that white children would not have to attend school with blacks. "Impeach Earl Warren" placards sprouted throughout the South. In 1955, the year the Supreme Court handed down the second part of its school desegregation decision, three blacks were lynched in Mississippi, marking the first such murders in the nation since 1951. In 1956, more than a hundred members of the House and Senate in Washington issued the Southern Manifesto, which declared that the "unwarranted decision of the Supreme Court now is bearing fruit." It ended with a promise to "use all lawful means to bring about a reversal of this decision which is contrary to the Constitution." Lyndon Johnson of Texas was one of only three Southern senators who refused to sign the manifesto.

As the Warren Court's libertarianism manifested itself in the one man, one vote rulings, the criminal rights decisions, the rulings rejecting the loyalty oath mania of the McCarthy era, and in other areas of the law, the opposition spread outside the South. In 1958 at a meeting in Pasadena, California, thirty-six of the chief justices of the state supreme courts voted in favor of a resolution that was highly critical of the Warren Court. Many bills were introduced in Congress to curb the Court's powers. For example, Senator William E. Jenner, Republican of Indiana, sponsored a bill that would have forbidden the Supreme Court to review any cases involving congressional committees, federal employe security rules, state laws on subversion, local school board regulations on subversion, and state requirements for admission to the bar. Police and prosecutors in various parts of the nation joined in attacking the Warren Court for allegedly hampering their efforts to capture and convict those guilty of crimes. Other measures were introduced in Congress to mitigate the effects of the Court's one man, one vote and its criminal rights decisions.

But the Warren Court remained steadfast and Congress and the White House fended off the attacks on the Court, for as long as Earl Warren remained Chief Justice and the White House was occupied by Eisenhower, Kennedy, and Johnson. The Court's decisions on issues other than school desegregation often were less than unanimous, and the lack of unanimity encouraged Congress to enact several measures that were intended to undo in part some of the Court's criminal rights decisions. But the Eisenhower Administration opposed the Jenner bill in 1958, and this and subsequent attempts to seriously undermine the Warren Court's libertarianism were not successful.

57

Until 1968 the Court, Congress, and the White House were moving together, particularly toward the enlargement of rights and privileges of blacks. Since 1968, the moral leadership·of the Court has been placed in jeopardy and the momentum which carried civil rights forward in Congress and the White House has been slowed if not lost altogether. The pattern of black progress, consisting of court actions and nonviolent demonstrations which were followed by new civil rights legislation, has been broken. Violence often has taken the place of nonviolence and repressive laws have taken the place of legislative advance. It is impossible to say precisely when opposition to the Warren Court began to overtake reluctant acceptance of the Court's leadership. But certainly there were signs of growing opposition in 1967 when President Johnson, who had named Abe Fortas to the Court in 1965, came upon his second opportunity to nominate an Associate Justice.

Inasmuch as impeachment of a Justice and amendment of the Constitution both are, by intention of the Founding Fathers, terribly laborious methods of seeking political revenge against the Supreme Court, the President's nomination of new members of the Court and the tone of Senate confirmation proceedings ordinarily are the most practical means of judging whether the revenge seekers are gaining or losing ground. Perhaps the first real test of the majoritarian branches' feelings toward the Warren Court came in 1959, when President Eisenhower nominated Potter Stewart. (Eisenhower had given Stewart a recess appointment in 1958.) Stewart's support of the Warren Court's racial desegregation decisions was well known and the Senate delayed from January 17 until May 5 before it voted on his nomination. He was confirmed by a roll-call vote, of 70 to 17. All of the seventeen dissenters were Southern Democrats. The next nominations were those of Byron White and Arthur Goldberg, both made by President Kennedy in 1962. They were confirmed by voice vote, without a roll call. President Johnson's nomination of Abe Fortas in 1965 was also confirmed by voice vote. There were, in the Senate's consideration of each of these nominations, political considerations unrelated to the Warren Court. But the Court's libertarianism also was involved in each of the confirmation proceedings, because Southern senators were dedicated to a reversal of the Warren Court's decisions by "all lawful means." The means certainly included opposition to confirmation of new, liberal Justices. But the South's time to rise again had not yet arrived. The majority of senators still were willing to move civil rights forward, in Congress and on the Court.

In part because President Johnson personally believed in racial equality, he seems never to have recognized fully the depth of Southern resentment in Congress against the Warren Court or the strength of Southern determination to overturn the Court's decisions, given the opportunity. He nominated liberal thinkers to the Court, but it was not their libertarianism that recommended them to Johnson. His approach to Supreme Court vacancies had little to do with ideology, and much to do with the peculiarities of Lyndon Johnson. He succeeded in placing two of his nominees on the Court, but neither of the vacancies he filled came to the White House unanticipated. Normally Court vacancies cannot be well antitipated because the Constitution confers on Justices lifetime tenure, and the independence tenure breeds. Consequently, vacancies often in history have been created by unexpected death or illness and rarely have come about because of resignation at a President's wish. But Johnson was not a patient man, willing to wait for ordinary vacancies. He tried to make his opportunities and in so doing forged a second link in the chain which unknowingly led to the battle for control of the Court.

As Johnson "promoted" Justice Goldberg to the United Nations, so did he move other men as on a great chessboard. Johnson of course had more reason than most Presidents to move men, although the reason did not extend to the Supreme Court. It extended only to the White House staff and the Cabinet. Johnson had inherited the Administration of his predecessor. For a variety of personal and political reasons, he wanted and needed men of his choice, but continuity and public opinion precluded hasty changes immediately following the Kennedy assassination. So the Kennedy Cabinet remained almost intact through the remainder of the term to which Kennedy had been elected in 1960, although the White House staff began to change more quickly when Johnson became President. After Johnson on November 3, 1964, was elected President in his own right, the Cabinet began to change, and the only Kennedy man who remained with Johnson through January, 1969, was Secretary of State Dean Rusk, a faithful defender of Johnson's Vietnam policies.

The one member of John Kennedy's Cabinet who did not stay with Johnson even through the November 1964 election was Robert F. Kennedy, the late President's Attorney General and brother. Robert

Kennedy resigned on September 3, 1964, to run as the Democratic candidate for United States senator from the state of New York. It might have been politically wise for Johnson to have kept Kennedy in the Cabinet, for Kennedy's election to the Senate in November was the beginning of a new Kennedy presidential campaign machine which could be steered with great skill and enthusiasm to run down Johnson in 1968. But Johnson could not control Kennedy and there were great gulfs of emotion and personality that separated the two. Also, there was a certain gain for the President in Kennedy's departure from the Justice Department.

The Department of Justice is politically the most sensitive of the great departments of the executive branch and therefore the personal trustworthiness of the Attorney General is most important to the President. The Department always has been important because it controls litigation before the Supreme Court to which all government departments and agencies are parties. But in recent years the Justice Department has acquired an additional importance as a focal point of Administration policy on contemporarily crucial political issues, including civil rights, criminal rights, and law and order. This added role stemmed in part from decisions of the Warren Court and the presidential burden of enforcing those decisions. But it also stemmed from enactment of the new civil rights acts since 1957. The Department under those acts was charged with a central role in enforcing the voting, educational, housing, and job rights of black citizens. While other departments which administer federal grant programs do not have large influence over policy matters, because Congress fixes the amounts of the spending, the Justice Department has great discretion in deciding the quantity and quality of civil rights lawsuits it will file. It thus has great influence over policy, inasmuch as it exercises control over the pace of racial desegregation in education, housing, and employment.

Another consideration, which is not necessarily last in the order of reasons why a President needs a strong and loyal Attorney General, is the FBI. J. Edgar Hoover was named director of the FBI in 1924 when Calvin Coolidge was in the White House and the Bureau was small, inept, and politically controlled. Four decades and seven Presidents later, Hoover still was director, even though he was not entitled by the Constitution to lifetime tenure and his appointment had not been subject to Senate confirmation. His truly remarkable staying power was due largely to his administrative and public relations abilities and to the total dedication of this wifeless, childless man to the FBI. Under Hoover's direction, and his alone, the Bureau grew by the late 1960s into an efficient, nonuniformed national police with a work force of 20,000 which operates the nation's largest computerized crime information network and maintains the nation's most complete police files on hundreds of thousands of individuals. Hoover's control of this highly effective and largely secretive police apparatus became in turn an element of his staying power, and the unique kind of independence he acquired rested also on his close association with the most senior and powerful conservatives in the Senate and House.

Hoover's independence thus was a problem to Johnson as it had been to other Presidents. No President, presumably, wanted to take personal control of the FBI, but neither could he risk that this massive police apparatus would be run out of his control entirely. Consequently, there often were unfruitful tensions between the Bureau director and the Attorney General, and especially between Hoover and Robert Kennedy.[1]

For these various reasons, the role of Attorney General has become very important to presidential policies and politics, displacing the position in the cabinet once held by the Postmaster General, when the Post Office Department offered more patronage jobs than any other department. In earlier Administrations the President's campaign manager frequently chose to become Postmaster General. But Robert Kennedy, who had been his brother's campaign manager, became Attorney General and a few years later Richard Nixon's campaign manager, John Mitchell, similarly chose the same post.

When Robert Kennedy in September, 1964, handed in his resignation, President Johnson wanted Abe Fortas to become his Attorney General. Inasmuch as the election was two months off, and Johnson had no desire unnecessarily to offend liberal voters who esteemed the Kennedy name, Fortas's appointment presumably would not have been made public until after the election. But Fortas declined the position and therefore Johnson on the day after Kennedy's departure promoted a Kennedy man. He was Nicholas Katzenbach, a member of the original Kennedy team. Katzenbach was a product of Phillips Exeter Academy, Princeton University, and Yale Law School and he had served Robert Kennedy well, at Oxford, Mississippi, and elsewhere.

61

In November Johnson soundly defeated Republican candidate Barry Goldwater. Robert Kennedy won his bid for a seat in the Senate. A few days after Johnson was sworn in on a freezing January 20, 1965, the President elevated to sit at Katzenbach's right hand, as Deputy Attorney General, a Texan named Ramsey Clark, a tall, skinny thirty-seven-year-old lawyer whom Johnson had known since Ramsey was a boy.

The rise of Ramsey Clark is an unusual Washington story in various respects, the most significant being that in time he and Dean Rusk and a small number of other men were the very few who successfully bridged the Administrations of John Kennedy and Lyndon Johnson. Clark served both of these dissimilar Democratic Presidents, but as a Texan he did not really belong to Kennedy and as a young, consummate liberal he did not really belong to Johnson. Clark's link to Johnson was familial and his kinship with the Kennedys was intellectual and emotional. The latter proved the stronger.

Johnson had known young Ramsey Clark as the son of Tom Clark, a tall Texas lawyer who, like Johnson, had come to Washington in the 1930s during the Roosevelt Administration. Tom Clark and Johnson both had been close to Representative Sam Rayburn of Texas who in the 1940s became the powerful and famous Speaker of the House. In 1937, the year Johnson was first elected to the House, Tom Clark went to work at the Justice Department. Clark's professional accomplishments and political associations with Rayburn, Johnson, and other Democratic Party leaders led to successively higher positions in the Department and finally to his appointment by President Truman as Attorney General. In 1949 Truman nominated Thomas Campbell Clark, then only forty-nine years old, to be a member of the Supreme Court. The nomination initially aroused considerable liberal opposition in the Senate, where it was thought that Clark was anti-labor and anti-Negro.* But, with the support of then Senator Lyndon Johnson, Clark was confirmed and in time (still preferring to be known simply as Tom Clark, and still wearing bow ties) he became a member of the

*The initial opposition of Senate liberals to Clark's confirmation apparently stemmed more from his Texas background than from his actions as Attorney General. However, as Truman's Attorney General, Clark aroused liberal suspicions because of his defense of government loyalty programs and other anti-Communist activities. His nomination to the Supreme Court was confirmed in the Senate by a vote of 73 to 8.

Warren Court's liberal majority, except on certain issues including government loyalty and internal security programs.

So Ramsey, although born in Dallas, grew up mainly in Washington and mostly in the Justice Department. He went back home to the University of Texas for a bachelor's degree, but then strayed. He went to the University of Chicago, where in 1950 he received a master's degree in American history and a law degree. He might have gone into teaching and done some writing, but he instead went back to Dallas and practiced law until John Kennedy won the Presidency. In 1961, Ramsey Clark at the age of thirty-four came back to Washington as one of Robert Kennedy's half-dozen assistant attorneys general. But he was in charge of the Justice Department's Lands Division, a job far removed from the important functions of the Department. Clark did a respectable job in the Lands Division and became a liberal admirer of the Kennedy style, but he did not belong to the Kennedys' inner circle and was unknown to the general public. He was not rescued from the obscurity of the Lands Division until Johnson named him Deputy to Katzenbach.

Nicholas Katzenbach's stay as Attorney General was not to be for long. On October 3, 1966, President Johnson moved Katzenbach out of the Cabinet and into the State Department as Under Secretary.* On the same day Johnson named Ramsey Clark acting Attorney General. As Washington puzzled over Katzenbach's promotion, it began after a time to wonder also why President Johnson for weeks and then months kept Ramsey Clark in the "acting" capacity at the Justice Department.

The President told no one, not even Ramsey Clark. But finally, on the last day of February, 1967, Johnson informed the White House press corps of his intention to nominate Clark to be Attorney General. The Senate confirmed Clark forthwith, and on March 10 Lyndon and Lady Bird Johnson, Justice and Mrs. Clark, Chief Justice Warren, Director Hoover, and well-wishers in large numbers from the Administration and Congress gathered in the Great Hall at the Justice Department for the occasion of Clark's swearing in. The President was paying a special compliment to the Clarks, father and son, by coming to the Justice Department instead of having them come to the

*Katzenbach remained as Under Secretary of State through the end of the Johnson Administration in January, 1969.

White House. There in the Great Hall, a high-ceilinged mausoleum of marbled walls and silvered statuary whose architecture seemed the inspiration of the WPA, Texas accents were as numerous as at a barbecue on the LBJ Ranch. Almost everyone on the dais was embracing almost everyone else. When "Hail to the Chief" finally stopped echoing from the marble walls, the President rose and addressed the assembled crowd with words which must have embarrassed the new Attorney General.

"I remember him when he was serving his apprenticeship in the Department as a boy in knee pants," Johnson declared benignly. "His father [Attorney General Tom Clark] was soliciting suggestions on morale and how to improve the efficiency of the Department to bring all of the different bureaus up to the high standards of efficiency to which Mr. Hoover had brought the FBI. Even then, Ramsey made his contribution. When they opened the box and looked at the suggestions, one of them was a rather unusual suggestion. Tom Clark asked Hoover to find out who made the suggestion that the Attorney General quit wearing those bright bow ties. Hoover replied, 'It was your son.' "

The story, true or not, was a more fitting introduction to the Attorney Generalship of Ramsey Clark than Lyndon Johnson may have realized. If J. Edgar Hoover pried unwelcomingly into the affairs of Ramsey Clark as a boy, the FBI director got on even less well with Ramsey Clark as a man. As Attorney General, Clark had a number of run-ins with Director Hoover. After Clark left office he wrote a book in which he accused Hoover of being self-centered and Hoover replied by calling Clark a "jellyfish."* J. Edgar Hoover, Lyndon Johnson, and Tom Clark were of the same political generation and they understood one another well enough to tolerate one another. Ramsey Clark, as it turned out, was of another generation. But on this, Clark's swearing-in day, even the Director smiled.

Having moved Nicholas Katzenbach out and Ramsey Clark up, President Johnson went on to the next logical move in his political game.

*In *Crime in America* (New York: Simon and Schuster, 1970), Clark made only a brief reference to Hoover, p. 82, but it was that reference which in large part made the book newsworthy. Hoover replied by granting a rare interview with a reporter, Ken W. Clawson of the Washington *Post* (November 17, 1970, pages A1, A7).

When Johnson on February 28, 1967, first told the White House press corps of his intention to nominate Ramsey Clark as full-fledged Attorney General, reporters had asked whether the appointment would "present any problem" for Justice Tom Clark. Johnson's reply was, "It is a problem for his father. I haven't discussed it with his father or with his son."

If the President did not discuss his intention of nominating Ramsey with Tom Clark, it was because men such as Lyndon Johnson and Tom Clark had known one another for so long that each can make his move sure of the response of the other. Johnson conceded to the White House reporters that the Ramsey Clark nomination would present "a problem" for the Justice, and certainly the President knew specifically that Tom Clark could not remain on the Supreme Court. Because the Justice Department frequently is a party to cases before the Court, and the Attorney General personally may argue a few of the most important of such cases, Justice Clark could not remain without appearing or risking the appearance of deciding cases in favor of the position argued by his son. Alternatively, the elder Clark theoretically could have declined to participate in any cases to which the Justice Department was a party, but that course would have unduly burdened the other members of the Court. The only course was for Justice Clark to retire, as he and the President well knew.

Indeed, Tom Clark was quite prepared to retire. On February 28, the very day Johnson made his announcement at the White House, Justice Clark issued a statement at the Supreme Court announcing his intention to retire. Now sixty-seven years old and on the Court for seventeen years, Tom Clark was perfectly willing to leave so that his son might become Attorney General. He said in his statement, "Mrs. Clark and I are filled with both pride and joy over Ramsey's nomination by the President. We deeply appreciate the high confidence that the President has placed in him." The statement disclosed that back on October 3, 1966, the day Nicholas Katzenbach moved out and Ramsey became Acting Attorney General, Justice Clark had notified Chief Justice Warren privately that "in the event Ramsey becomes the Attorney General it is my intention to retire from the Court."*

Justice Clark's retirement became effective on June 12, 1967, follow-

*The statement was released February 28, 1967, by Justice Clark through the Supreme Court's press officer.

ing the close of the Court's term, and Johnson thus acquired his second opportunity to nominate a member of the Court. The second vacancy, like the first, was not delivered to the White House by unassisted fate. Whether Johnson in his private mind intended a Texas double play, gaining the opportunity to name Ramsey Clark as Attorney General and also to name another Texas friend to the Supreme Court, is not known. Certainly Johnson in moving Katzenbach to the State Department was motivated at least in part by the desire to nominate as Attorney General the son of his friend of long standing, Tom Clark. Ramsey Clark, to Johnson still that "boy in knee pants," was as much a son as Lyndon and Lady Bird Johnson ever had. It seems not unlikely that the President similarly had private plans to nominate a Texas crony to fill the new vacancy on the Court. Informed speculation in Washington was that Johnson probably would nominate either Homer Thornberry, a personal and political friend of many years from Austin, Texas, or Leon Jaworski, a Houston lawyer whom Johnson had known for many years and who, like Abe Fortas, had risen to high position in the legal profession.*

But events and Ramsey Clark persuaded the President to defer his wishes to name a second personal choice to the Supreme Court. In the spring of 1967 America was in turmoil and President Johnson faced mounting difficulties, domestically and in Vietnam. The willingness of the great majority of Southern blacks to move forward nonviolently seemed to be wearing thin. Racial violence had erupted with growing intensity in each of the past three summers. In the summer of 1964 the incidents of white and black violence were confined largely to cities in the South. Thereafter they spread to the North and West in a perplexing new pattern. Young blacks, the children and grandchildren of Negroes who had migrated from the South, rioted in the inner city ghettos and public housing projects where they lived. Such young blacks, more militant than Negroes who had remained in the South, in the summer of 1965 led massive riots in the Watts section of Los Angeles. The Watts violence left thirty-five persons dead, 883

*Although speculation in the press concerning Justice Clark's successor centered on Jaworski, Thornberry, and a few other white lawyers, it also was mentioned that Johnson had an interest in naming the first Negro as well as the first woman to the Supreme Court. See, for instance, the New York *Times,* March 1, 1967, page 1, article headed "Ramsey Clark Nominated To Be Attorney General" and "Father To Quit High Court."

injured and more than 3,500 under arrest. In the summer of 1966, racial violence flared in the Hough section of Cleveland, in Chicago, and in more than forty additional cities. There were some deaths and scores of injuries and arrests, but more bloodshed was avoided because governments, state and federal, were learning to quickly deploy thousands of troops against such black uprisings. Still, there seemed no logical pattern to the violence. It was unplanned, almost always erupting in overheated, crowded streets after a run-in between local police and young blacks.[2]

In the spring of 1967, Martin Luther King, Jr., warned at a press conference in New York that at least ten cities could "explode in racial violence"; in the days and weeks that followed blacks rioted in Nashville, Louisville, Cleveland, and a number of other cities, and in Montgomery, Alabama, a bomb exploded near the home of a U.S. district court judge who was a member of a three-judge panel which had ordered the desegregation of Alabama's public schools by the next fall. Also in that spring of 1967, black protest appeared from Washington to be taking another new and dangerous turn. Johnson, deeply troubled by campus disorders and rising white opposition to his escalation of the war in Vietnam, saw Dr. King threatening to bring together the civil rights and antiwar movements. King in April had urged American youths, white or black, to boycott the war by declaring themselves conscientious objectors. He had drawn parallels between the sending of American youths to Vietnam and the German concentration camps of World War II and he had alleged that "twice as many Negroes as whites are in combat" in Vietnam. Later in April King led an antiwar demonstration in New York in which more than 100,000 persons marched from Central Park to the United Nations headquarters.

It was those events and the "strong recommendation" of Attorney General Ramsey Clark that led President Johnson to nominate as Tom Clark's replacement the first black member of the Supreme Court in American history. On June 13, the day following Justice Clark's retirement, Johnson nominated Thurgood Marshall. With Marshall at his side in the White House rose garden, the President said that Marshall "is best qualified by training and by very valuable service to the country" to sit on the Supreme Court. "I believe it is the right thing to do, the right time to do it, the right man and the right place," Johnson added.

It was the right thing to do, even though the time was late. Whether Thurgood Marshall was the right man is a question that will be debated in history. The rise in Negro militancy bought the first black seat in history on the Supreme Court, as the reawakening of blacks to all of their civil rights a century after the Civil War bought for them the Civil Rights Acts of the new era. The selection of Thurgood Marshall to fill that seat was, for white liberals in Washington, an appropriate and acceptable symbolic act. The selection was not equally appropriate and acceptable to blacks in the spring of 1967.

Thurgood Marshall, fifty-eight years old when Johnson nominated him to the Supreme Court, had been born in Baltimore and received his law degree from Howard University, a predominantly black school in Washington. He was a member of the Class of 1933 at Howard, and in the years following he played a large and important role in the beginnings of black reawakening. After graduation, like the relatively few other educated young Negroes of his generation, Marshall joined the National Association for the Advancement of Colored People without even thinking of direct confrontation. He did legal work for the NAACP branch in Baltimore and then moved to New York where in 1938 he became chief legal officer of the NAACP and helped to found the Legal Defense and Education Fund as a separate litigation arm of the association. For nearly a quarter of a century he initiated and argued civil rights cases, thirty-two of them in the Supreme Court. He argued against the "separate but equal" doctrine before the Supreme Court in *Brown* v. *Board of Education* and the other school desegregation cases the Warren Court decided in 1954 and 1955. There, and in a number of other voting, school, and public accommodations cases, he was a participant in arguments that led to the Warren Court's momentous civil rights decisions.

But it was not until a new generation of civil rights leaders emerged in the South that Thurgood Marshall was elevated from advocate to judge. As Dr. King of the new generation led black people into the streets and went to jail, Marshall rose ever higher in the councils of government. In 1961, the year that a newer black organization, the Congress of Racial Equality, began to sponsor freedom rides across the South, President Kennedy named Marshall to the U.S. Second Circuit Court of Appeals in New York. In 1965, the year of the bloody riots in the Watts section of Los Angeles, President Johnson brought Marshall back to Washington to become Solicitor General, the third-ranking position in the Department of Justice. And in June, 1967, as the racial violence Dr. King predicted was erupting in American cities, Johnson nominated Marshall to be a member of the Supreme Court.

Thurgood Marshall's very substantial contributions to civil rights progress, as an advocate prior to 1961, are not to be discounted. Nor is the good faith of Lyndon Johnson and Ramsey Clark, in urging his appointment to the Supreme Court, to be impugned. Yet, their good faith illustrated the difficulty that even well-meaning, white liberals encounter in attempting to see America as blacks see her and, as a result, there was deep, deep irony in the nomination and confirmation of Thurgood Marshall to be the first black member of the Supreme Court. He was nominated and confirmed because he had accumulated what Richard Nixon might have called an acceptable "track record." At a time when racial violence was sweeping the nation, Marshall was picked to fill the first black seat on the Court precisely because he was a symbol of gradualism and nonviolence. "No black man can lay just claim to the title 'black leader' until he has gone through the proper ritual and been appointed by white folk."[3] Marshall in 1967 was not a black leader among the masses of young blacks. To whites and blacks, he stood for order and for law and, to the extent that "law and order" was becoming a code word for rising white opposition to rising black militancy and violence, his nomination and confirmation carried a brooding implication, intended or not by his white supporters.

There had been overt white racial opposition in 1961 when Marshall first was nominated for federal office. President Kennedy nominated a total of five blacks to judgeships, including Marshall's nomination to the U.S. Second Circuit Court of Appeals in New York. The Senate took no action, so Kennedy gave Marshall a recess appointment and resubmitted the nomination as Congress reconvened on January 15, 1962. The Senate Judiciary Committee, under the leadership of senior Southern Democrats, did not begin hearings until May 1 and it did not vote out the nomination until September 7, when the threat of a discharge petition became serious. The committee recommended confirmation by a vote of 11 to 4, and on September 11 the Senate confirmed Marshall by a vote of 44 to 16. In 1965, when President Johnson nominated Marshall to be Solicitor General, he was confirmed without delay or difficulty.

Clearly, whatever fears the Senate initially harbored that Marshall, once in high federal office, would be a civil rights zealot were satisfac-torily answered by 1967. Marshall had accumulated his track record.

When the Senate Judiciary Committee in July took up his nomina-tion to succeed Tom Clark on the Supreme Court, Marshall's race was not an overt issue.⁴ No organized black support appeared for him and no organized white opposition appeared against him. The National Association for the Advancement of Colored People did not testify in favor of the nomination, for instance, and no White Citizens Council testified against it. The only senator who raised questions concerning racial matters was Strom Thurmond, Republican of South Carolina. Thurmond posed a seemingly endless series of questions, intended to show that the Warren Court was not interpreting the Thirteenth, Fourteenth, and Fifteenth Amendments as their framers intended.

He asked Marshall, for example, "What constitutional difficulties did Representative John Bingham of Ohio see, or what difficulties do you see, in congressional enforcement of the privileges and immunities clause of article IV, section 2, through the necessary and proper clause of article I, section 8?"⁵

To this, and most of Thurmond's other questions, Marshall replied: "I don't understand the question," and inasmuch as no one else in the hearing room understood either, the senator from South Carolina scored no points against the nominee.

But, more significantly, Southern Democrats on the Judiciary Committee questioned Marshall for five days about the criticisms of the Warren Court that had been raised in 1958 by the thirty-six state chief justices and about the Warren Court's decisions concerning the rights of the criminally accused and the powers of police. Marshall proved himself a skillful witness by refusing to tell the Southerners how he would vote, as a member of the Supreme Court, in future cases concerning criminal rights. But, in these times of black rioting and violence which had brought Thurgood Marshall before the Judiciary Committee, the Southerners succeeded in sowing the implication that black militancy was somehow connected with the Warren Court's decisions upholding the constitutional rights of alleged criminals.

The committee approved the nomination 11 to 5 and the Senate on August 30 confirmed Marshall by a vote of 69 to 11, after six hours of uneventful floor debate. Marshall took his seat when the Court opened its new term on Monday, October 2, 1967, as President John-son quietly sat in the Court's chamber to watch the swearing in.

Marshall's nomination and confirmation were evidence, then, that in 1967 political opposition to the Warren Court was rising but the White House and a majority of the members of the Senate remained willing, under pressure of rising black militancy, to advance further the cause of racial equality. The number of votes cast against confirmation was fewer than those recorded in 1959 against confirmation of Potter Stewart, the last Supreme Court nominee whose confirmation was decided by roll-call vote. The eleven votes against Thurgood Marshall were those of ten Southern Democrats and the eleventh was a renegade conservative Northern Democrat, Robert C. Byrd of West Virginia. Four Southern Republicans voted for confirmation of Marshall. They were Senators John Sherman Cooper and Thruston B. Morton of Kentucky, Howard H. Baker, Jr., of Tennessee, and John G. Tower of Texas. The total membership of the Senate at the time consisted of ninety-nine white members and one black, Edward W. Brooke, Republican of Massachusetts, who was elected in 1966, the first black to serve in the United States Senate since the Reconstruction era.

Marshall's nomination and confirmation came at a time when Congress still was debating new civil rights legislation. The policy of the White House still was to explain and deal with black race riots not in terms of criminal behavior but rather in terms of the social causes of Negro unrest.[6] And, so far as the Supreme Court was concerned, the arrival of Marshall was neither intended nor expected to alter Warren Court doctrines.

Yet, the arrival of this first black man to sit on the Court marked the beginning of the end of white and black willingness to move forward, in the Court, Congress, and the White House, toward racial equality through nonviolent, constitutional means. Marshall was not a cause of the end of racial accommodation under law; he was a symbol.

For many whites the symbolism was acceptable and indeed necessary. Marshall was not a representative of the increasingly insistent and strident brand of nonviolence preached by Martin Luther King, Jr. Marshall was a legalist, King a moralist. After he took his seat on the Court, Marshall on various occasions affirmed the faith that whites had had in his track record. He traveled to Phillips Exeter Academy, in Exeter, New Hampshire, to discuss black militancy and the Court with students there, and declared, "Negroes are nonviolent

71

people and they always have been and always will be." Asked by a curious student about his thoughts concerning younger black leadership in general and Eldridge Cleaver in particular, Marshall asserted: "Cleaver is a refugee from justice. I think his idea of a government is taking a carbine and joining others and shooting at police. That's not the way to protest." While many blacks in the civil rights movement and young whites in the antiwar movement were marching in protest against Lyndon Johnson, to Marshall the President was "the greatest man I've ever known in my life."[7]

For many blacks the symbolism was unacceptable and perhaps offensive. In July, as Marshall sat before the Judiciary Committee talking not about civil rights but about law and order, racial riots still more violent than in previous years broke out. In Detroit thousands of blacks rioted, burned, and looted. Police, National Guardsmen, and Army paratroopers moved in against them and by the time the violence ended forty-three persons, thirty-three black and ten white, were dead. Riots in Newark, New Jersey, in the same month left twenty-three dead, twenty-one of them black and two of them white.

When the next springtime came, and Mr. Justice Marshall was completing his first term on the Court, Martin Luther King, Jr., was assassinated. Blacks rioted in Washington and throughout the nation, and Congress enacted its last major civil rights act and for the first time made it a federal crime to incite riot. And also for the first time, the demand for "law and order" was heard above the cry for racial equality.

CHAPTER 6

# The Perils of Cronyism

A month after the President had sat in the Supreme Court chamber, witnessing the swearing in of Thurgood Marshall with hope that this historic appointment would help to calm black turmoil in the nation, Johnson met at the White House with some of his political friends and advisers to talk for the first time about strategy in the 1968 election campaign.[1]

There was no intended relationship between the two events. Yet there was a connection between the President's hopes that lay behind the Marshall appointment and his upcoming campaign for reelection. The nomination had had no perceptible effect on black militants, and Martin Luther King, Jr., at the tenth annual convention of the Southern Christian Leadership Conference in Atlanta, had called for a continuation of racial protest through the mounting of a campaign of civil disobedience in Northern cities. King at the same recent convention had urged a repudiation of the war through the election of a peace candidate in the 1968 presidential election.

Nothing was firmly decided at the initial strategy meeting held in November, 1967, and subsequent White House staff discussions in the weeks that followed produced no definite campaign plans. Johnson seemed indecisive, exhausted, and dispirited.

Liberal opposition to his Vietnam policy was growing more vehement in Congress with each escalation of the war. Antiwar militancy was growing on college campuses. In October some 35,000 demonstrators, most of them young whites, had marched on the Pentagon and clashed with troops and police. Now King was planning to join whites and blacks in a united political front against the President.

Apparent also was the growing opposition on Johnson's right. The President and his young Attorney General sensed the rising reaction of older, more affluent white citizens and conservative members of Congress against the black militants, the campus radicals, and the tenor of the times that seemed to have spawned a plague of street crimes and lawlessness throughout the country. But Johnson's and Clark's response to the fear and anger of more conservative, middle-class, and suburban Americans often appeared to be confused and contradictory. Johnson, for instance, early in 1967 proposed to Congress a crime control bill, under which the federal government among other things would make available hundreds of millions of dollars to strengthen state and local law enforcement. Congress enacted the legislation as the Omnibus Crime Control and Safe Streets Act of 1968, but Clark refused to use the new authority Congress provided to utilize wiretaps and electronic devices, under court warrants, as crime-fighting tools. "Nothing so mocks privacy as the wiretap and electronic surveillance," Clark declared. "They are incompatible with a free society."[2] His position was applauded by liberals and condemned by conservatives.

Johnson thus was caught in a hailstorm of criticism that came from all sides. The popularity poll results he carried around in his pocket showed sharp declines. A Louis Harris poll in November reported that, if the election were held then, he would be defeated by any one of six Republican presidential possibilities. As winter came on, the abuse became more personal. Johnson was the target of threats and obscenities. Crude caricatures of him were drawn in books, and in a play that opened in New York he was portrayed as an inarticulate country clod who had risen to power not by legislative skill but by wheeling and dealing and worse.

Johnson's sinking popularity and his apparent confusion and indecisiveness made the 1968 presidential election ever more attractive to all sorts of presidential possibiliites, Republican and Democratic. Senator Eugene McCarthy announced at a press conference in Washington on the last day of November that he intended to oppose Johnson for the Democratic nomination. McCarthy made the announcement after he was assured that Robert Kennedy would not run against Johnson.[3] McCarthy's liberal young followers promptly began to prepare for the primary election in New Hampshire, the earliest of the state primaries which have become so important to all presidential

74

aspirants as gauges of popular appeal. Early in February Richard Nixon flew into New Hampshire to open his campaign for the Republican nomination for President. The results of the primary showed that Johnson was in deep trouble indeed.

On March 12 Nixon as expected won the Republican popularity race in New Hampshire, and among the Democrats McCarthy did vastly better against President Johnson than had been expected. Johnson, at the White House in Washington, was informed that he had received only 230 votes more than the hitherto almost unknown senator from Minnesota. So impressive was Gene McCarthy's antiwar vote that, four days after the New Hampshire primary, Senator Robert Kennedy changed his mind and decided that he would enter the race against Johnson for the Democratic presidential nomination.

Kennedy's abrupt seizure of opportunity embittered Johnson perhaps even more than McCarthy. The President since that initial campaign strategy meeting in November had been immersed in the dispatch of more American troops to Vietnam to meet the Tet offensive which the North Vietnamese opened in late January. In the ensuing days combat in South Vietnam extended even into the United States Embassy there, and liberal opinion in this country grew ever more hostile to the war. In early March Johnson was faced not only with the results of the New Hampshire primary but also with a request from General William Westmoreland, his commander in Vietnam, for 206,000 additional troops.

In Washington the rapid buildup of the political campaigns of 1968 was being watched with intense interest not only at the White House and the Capitol but also at the Supreme Court.

One observer was Mr. Justice Fortas. More than that, however, Fortas was a participant, if not in the political discussions at the White House concerning Johnson's reelection chances, then in the conferences concerning Vietnam policy, which patently would be one of the two dominant political issues in the 1968 election. Notwithstanding the separation of powers doctrine, Fortas, after he became a member of the Supreme Court in 1965, continued to maintain a personal, confidential relationship with Johnson. On March 26, 1968, Fortas participated in a meeting at the White House of the nation's highest military and diplomatic leaders that was of crucial importance to the future of the war and to Johnson's political future.[4] His participation in such conferences was kept secret at the time, but Fortas later conceded there were "stages in the fantastically difficult decisions about the war in Vietnam where I participated in meetings."⁵ He admitted also to having played a role in the decision Johnson made in the summer of 1967 to send troops to quell racial rioting in Detroit.⁶ After having known Johnson for "many years, many, many years," Fortas explained, the President "did me the honor of having some trust in my discretion, some belief in my patriotism, and some respect for my ability to analyze a problem."⁷

Another at the Supreme Court who observed with interest the unfolding political campaigns was Chief Justice Earl Warren. Warren and Fortas had become close friends as brothers on the Court. The Chief Justice saw the President rather often, but his relationship with Johnson was totally unlike the personal friendship of Fortas and Johnson.

The Chief Justice and the President frequently were drawn together by official occasions. Warren had been present, for example, when Johnson in February had addressed the Washington chapter of the National Conference of Christians and Jews. The following month, in the East Room of the White House, Warren administered the oath of office when Clark Clifford became Johnson's new Secretary of Defense. In April, at a White House dinner for the Shah of Iran, the President had been unusually gracious in addressing his toast to "Your Imperial Majesty, our beloved Chief Justice, distinguished guests . . ." But on these and all other occasions Warren very carefully kept Johnson at arm's length, not apparently because of a personal dislike of the President but because of his strong belief in the independence of the Court. Still, Warren knew the President well enough to know the man's mind.

After the crucial meeting attended by Fortas on Tuesday, March 26, the tenor and pace of activity at the White House quickened. Political and military decisions facing Johnson could not be further delayed.

Johnson requested time on the national television networks for nine o'clock in the evening of Sunday, March 31, for a major policy statement on Vietnam. McCarthy, learning of the President's request, demanded equal time. Nixon, who had scheduled a Vietnam statement of his own for release on Saturday, changed his plans to see first what Johnson was going to say.

On Sunday night Johnson spoke to the nation from his office in the White House. He made a lengthy defense of his Vietnam policy and renewed his offer to stop the bombardment of North Vietnam if the Communists would begin peace talks. He also outlined steps he was taking to limit the war "in the hope that this action will lead to early talks." And then, in conclusion, Johnson said:

> For thirty-seven years, in the service of our nation, first as a Congressman, as a Senator, and as Vice President, and now as your President, I have put the unity of the people first, I have put it ahead of any divisive partisanship. There is division in the American house now. What we won when all of our people united just must not now be lost in suspicion and distrust and selfishness and politics. And believing this, I have concluded that I should not permit the Presidency to become involved in the partisan divisions that are developing in this political year.
>
> Accordingly, I shall not seek and I will not accept the nomination of my party for another term as your President.

Johnson was a beleaguered President but he also was an obstinate and vain man and therefore his withdrawal was a stunning surprise. He was exhausted and apparently believed he could not win reelection. But if he unselfishly hoped his withdrawal would heal the nation's divisions, that hope was not fulfilled.

In the primary election battles that continued, Robert Kennedy in May won the Democratic primaries in Indiana and Nebraska and Gene McCarthy won in Oregon. Then the candidates began campaigning for the primary in California. Richard Nixon was running unopposed in some of the primaries and initially was worrying more about the independent conservative third-party candidacy of George Wallace of Alabama than about late arriving opponents for the Republican nomination. But Nixon's appeal to white conservatives appeared to be proving so successful that he was challenged from his right by Governor Ronald Reagan of California, who made plans to seek the Republican nomination at the convention in Miami Beach.

Nixon at his campaign headquarters in New York in May released a long position paper addressed to those whom time and again he called "the great majority of Americans, the forgotten Americans— the non-shouters, the non-demonstrators." The paper, titled "Toward Freedom from Fear," was skillfully drawn to respond to the demand for law and order without taking a position on race relations or the war. In it Nixon talked of crime and the cities which, he said, are "neither safe nor secure for innocent men and women." He blamed the Supreme Court's decisions for "seriously hamstringing the peace forces in our society and strengthening the criminal forces." He blamed Attorney General Ramsey Clark for being an "unwitting" handmaiden of crime and of the Court. Nixon thus drew the Supreme Court squarely into the political campaign and he repeated these themes throughout his race for the presidency.[8]

Then on June 5 came the big California primary. In the Democratic vote tally, Robert Kennedy defeated Gene McCarthy, and that evening, at a victory celebration at the Hotel Ambassador in Los Angeles, Kennedy, forty-two years old, was assassinated. Among all those who might have become President, he was the candidate who could have best united the young, blacks, browns, and other minorities in a common political front that might have pressed civil rights forward at the ballet box rather than in the streets. But now both Kennedy and Martin Luther King, Jr., were dead.

The assassination of Robert Kennedy, less than five years after the slaying of his brother, was yet another national disgrace that raised one notch more the level of confrontation between violence and reaction. Politically, the death of Senator Kennedy was a disaster for many liberals who saw the war as only one of several major campaign issues and therefore were not prepared to support McCarthy. It threw the Democratic presidential race into chaos, so much so that there were indications Johnson was seriously considering changing his mind and running again. It was an unexpected advantage for the Republicans and their front-runner Richard Nixon, and it lent new urgency to Nixon's law and order campaign.

The assassination of Robert Kennedy and its political ramifications were particularly poignant for Earl Warren. Warren had served at Johnson's request as chairman of the official commission that had investigated the assassination of President Kennedy. Presidents Kennedy and Johnson had upheld the Warren Court, in their appointments to it and in their enforcement of its school desegregation doctrines. Warren also had sensed the rising tide of reaction against the Court. The year before he had read the roll-call vote in the Senate on the nomination of Thurgood Marshall. He also had made a speech in which he declared, "This is no time for cavil or recrimination." Crime and violence, he suggested in the speech, were not caused by the people's exercise of their civil liberties but by "deep-seated cancerous conditions" in our society.* Now, more than ever before, the Court was becoming a political issue because Nixon was attacking it rather than the cancerous conditions in the black ghettos and elsewhere.

At that moment, however, the Warren Court was secure. Hugo Lafayette Black, eighty-two, was having some trouble with his eyes and in his judicial outlook was wavering a bit on some issues, including criminal rights matters. But by and large Black had remained a liberal, good and true. William Orville Douglas, sixty-nine, never wavered in his liberalism. Black and Douglas were the only Roosevelt appointees remaining on the Court. William J. Brennan, Jr., an Eisenhower appointee, was a certain fourth member of the liberal bloc. Johnson's two appointees, Abe Fortas and Thurgood Marshall, were the fifth and sixth members. Potter Stewart, Eisenhower's appointee, was a conservative on some issues, but he consistently voted with Warren on important racial discrimination issues. Indeed, Stewart had just written the majority opinion holding that under the 1866 Civil Rights Act a black man can sue to buy a home in the white suburbs.⁹ Byron R. White, John Kennedy's remaining appointee on the Court, had turned out to be surprisingly conservative on many issues, although not on all. Finally, in order of philosophic adherence to libertarianism, there was a new John Marshall Harlan, grandson of the great Mr. Justice Harlan whose dissent to the separate but equal doctrine in 1896 had been made the law of the land by the Warren Court in 1954. The first and the second John Marshall Harlan took their middle name from the great Chief Justice John Marshall. Paradoxically the new Justice Harlan did not espouse the doctrine of federal supremacy, as had John Marshall or the first John Marshall Harlan. Justice Harlan, appointed to the Court by Eisenhower in 1955, was the Court's most conservative member and the most consistent opponent of Warren's liberal activism. But he also was an intellectually honest man who respected judicial precedent.

So the Warren Court stood, as strong as, if not stronger than, at any time since Chief Justice Warren had arrived in 1953, and with political controversy swirling furiously outside it.

*Speech was delivered before the National Conference on Crime Control, Washington, March 29, 1967.

A little more than a week before Johnson had announced his withdrawal from the presidential race, Warren had celebrated his seventy-seventh birthday with his family. He remained in good health and looked fine. Despite the aloofness he intentionally maintained from the President, politicians generally, and the press, he still wore the warm, broad smile that had stood him in good stead when he had been a practicing politician himself. As spring passed, the Court handed down, as usual, the most important decisions of the term. June arrived, and the end of the term was approaching once more. And as the days came and went after Robert Kennedy's assassination, it became clear that Johnson was not going to change his mind and run again.

If Warren retired now, allowing Johnson while still in office to name the next Chief Justice, anyone who knew the President's mind could know what Johnson would do. HIs habit of installing old friends in high offices now was so firmly established that Washington was full of Johnson cronies. In addition to Abe Fortas and Ramsey Clark, Johnson's personal friends held office at such diverse places as the United States Information Agency, the Interstate Commerce Commission, and the U.S. Embassies in Australia and Sweden. Johnson had named his old friend Homer Thornberry to a federal judge-ship in Texas, and Thornberry the year before had been rumored to be the President's choice to fill the Clark vacancy on the Court. Just recently Johnson's friend Clark Clifford had become Secretary of Defense.

If he retired now, Warren could not be sure which friend Johnson would nominate as the next Chief Justice. Conceivably he might name Thornberry. Arthur Goldberg still enjoyed a rather surprisingly large following, particularly in the Eastern liberal press, which felt that Johnson had an obligation to return Goldberg to the Court. But Goldberg was no crony of Johnson's, and the President almost certainly would not pick him to be Chief Justice. Within a month after Johnson had announced his withdrawal, Goldberg had resigned as U.S. Representative to the United Nations and disappeared from government service into a private law firm in New York. Among all the names Johnson might consider to succeed Warren, one was as sure a guess as anyone possibly could make: Abe Fortas, the President's oldest and most trusted friend.

But it really did not make that much difference which of the names Johnson would settle on. The next Chief Justice, whomever Johnson selected, would be a liberal. He would sit for years to come and, no matter what political party occupied the White House, he would cast a libertarian vote, certainly in civil rights cases, and the Court would remain secure. This much of Johnson's response could be predicted with certainty. Warren's health was good now, but at his age he could not be certain it would remain so. If he did not retire now, he might be forced to leave the Court later, and later Richard Nixon might be in the White House. With Nixon campaigning now against the Warren Court, there was no question at all of what he would try to do to the Warren Court, if he won the White House and the chance to name Earl Warren's successor.

On June 13, 1968, eight days following the assassination of Robert Kennedy, after drawing up the appropriate papers in consultation with the White House, Warren notified Johnson that he would retire. The Court closed its term on June 17 and the White House on June 26 announced the Chief Justice's intention to retire.

Conservative Republicans, alarmed at what was afoot, raised loud objections without waiting to find out whom Johnson would nominate to succeed Warren. Governor Reagan told a press conference that Chief Justice Warren displayed a "lack of faith in this system of ours" by retiring so that President Johnson could choose a successor before leaving the White House. Warren had no right "to choose which President he thinks should dominate for the next twenty years the Supreme Court," Reagan claimed.[10]

There was, however, historic precedent for Warren's action. Admittedly, the precedent was somewhat remote in time. It was provided by Chief Justice Oliver Ellsworth, who resigned from the Court in the year 1800. But it also came at a time in American history when the future of the Court and the nation were deeply entwined in political controversy.*

The controversy then, as later, was between those who adovcated states' rights and others who argued for federal supremacy. It divided

*For a discussion of the resignation of Chief Justice Ellsworth, see Charles Warren, *The Supreme Court in United States History* (Boston: Little, Brown and Co., 1928), vol. I, pp. 172–88. The circumstances of Ellsworth's unusual departure are examined also in Albert J. Beveridge, *The Life of John Marshall* (Boston and New York: Houghton-Mifflin Co., 1916), vol. II, p. 547. The animosity between Jefferson and Marshall is described by Charles D. Harris, in "The Impeachment Trial of Samuel Chase," *American Bar Association Journal,* vol. 57 (January 1971), pp. 53–57.

patriots, including Washington, Jefferson, Hamilton, Madison, Marshall, Ellsworth, and the several Adams, who not many years before had been together in the Revolution and the establishment of the nation. President Washington, a strong Federalist, named Ellsworth Chief Justice in 1796. Ellsworth, a Connecticut Yankee, believed as Washington did in nationalism and federalism. When Washington declined a third term, John Adams ran against Thomas Jefferson and Adams in 1797 became the second President. Adams, from Massachusetts, also belonged to the Federalist party. Jefferson, from Virginia, believed strongly in the rights of states and was opposed to a strong central government. Four years later Jefferson, as the candidate of the new Republican party, defeated Adams and ended twelve years of Federalist administration. But Jefferson did not take office until March 4, 1801.

Chief Justice Ellsworth, citing poor health, although only fifty-five years of age, on December 15, 1800, gave President Adams his resignation. The "lame duck" President quickly nominated John Marshall, a Federalist. The Senate confirmed Marshall and he became Chief Justice on February 4, 1801, one month before Jefferson was inaugurated as President. There can be no doubt that Ellsworth resigned in order to allow Adams to name the new Chief Justice and to avoid the possibility that Jefferson would have that privilege. Ellsworth apparently did not know specifically that Adams would name Marshall. But Adams's choice was a logical one, from the Federalist view. Jefferson and Marshall had been at odds for some years. When Adams nominated Marshall, Jefferson called the appointment "an outrage on decency" and argued, unsuccessfully, that such appointments to the federal judiciary were void unless made with the consent of the President-elect. A Republican newspaper accused Adams of naming Marshall "because President Jefferson will not be able to turn him out of office." Marshall in turn penned a letter to a friend in which he called Jefferson an "absolute terrorist."

After Jefferson became President, he did turn many Federalists out of office. Marshall of course remained Chief Justice for thirty-four years and was historically successful in maintaining and strengthening the doctrine of federal supremacy. Unfortunately, the happy precedent created by Oliver Ellsworth and John Adams for Chief Justice Warren and President Johnson did not yield similar results.

On June 26, 1968, when Johnson at a White House press conference disclosed Warren's intention to retire, the President simultaneously announced that he had selected Abe Fortas to be the next Chief Justice. True to form, Johnson also announced that, to fill the Associate Justiceship vacancy that would result, he was nominating Homer Thornberry. Thornberry was a former mayor of Austin, Johnson's base of operations in Texas, and for fourteen years had occupied the House seat that once belonged to Lyndon Johnson. After becoming President, Johnson had named Thornberry a federal district court judge and then had elevated him to the U.S. Fifth Circuit Court of Appeals.

Earl Warren's knowledge of Lyndon Johnson was thus confirmed. "An entirely splendid appointment," the Chief Justice said at the unusual press conference he held on July 5 in the East Conference Room at the Supreme Court. "I feel Justice Fortas will be a great Chief Justice. I don't know Judge Thornberry as well as I do Justice Fortas, but I believe he will be an excellent Justice."

The Chief Justice and the President in concert did the best they could to assure that the Warren Court's philosophic and judicial activism would be preserved, through Johnson's selection of Warren's successor. Warren's retirement letter to Johnson did not fix a retirement date; they provided that Warren would leave when his successor was confirmed. The Chief Justice wrote, "I hereby advise you of my intention to retire as Chief Justice of the United States effective at your pleasure." Warren in another letter explained that he was not leaving "because of reasons of health or on account of any personal or associational problems," but because every man "eventually must bow" to age. The President's letter, which completed the transaction with Warren, said, "In deference to your wishes, I will seek a replacement to fill the vacancy in the office of Chief Justice that will be occasioned when you depart. With your agreement I will accept your decision to retire at such time as a successor is qualified."

Little wonder then that, when the Senate Judiciary Committee convened July 11 to open hearings on the nominations, there was much disputation over whether Warren in fact had retired and there was indeed a vacancy for Johnson to fill. Republicans and Southern Democrats on the committee pressed the question and Ramsey Clark, the Attorney General, was the chief spokesman for Johnson and Fortas, insisting that, "From the earliest years of the Union, Presidents have nominated and the Senate has confirmed persons to high office when no vacancy existed at the time."[11]

But the disputation obviously was a game. All knew that, when the

Senate confirmed Fortas, Warren would leave. The real question that intrigued the conservative senators was, would Warren leave if Fortas was not confirmed? At this stage, however, the conservative opposition was not well organized and the general assumption in Washington was that the Senate would confirm Johnson's nominations. For one thing, the opposition leadership was assumed by Robert P. Griffin, a forty-four-year-old Republican lawyer from Michigan who had been in the Senate only two years, rather than by a member of the Republican leadership in the Senate. In fact, the Senate Republican leader, Everett McKinley Dirksen, supported the Fortas and Thornberry nominations. Richard Nixon, who happened to be campaigning in Griffin's home state of Michigan, delivered a carefully worded statement saying, "We need a Court which looks upon its function as interpretation rather than breaking through into new areas," but not mentioning Warren or Fortas by name. Griffin, who was accusing Johnson of "cronyism," was himself accused of trying to save the nomination for Nixon.

Still, the initial consensus in Washington was that Johnson certainly would win. The President's party controlled Congress and the Senate previously had confirmed Fortas to be an Associate Justice and Thornberry to be a circuit court judge. Moreover, Johnson had paved the way for his nominees by talking privately with the leaders of the Senate, including his old friend Dirksen. Further, the Senate only once in this century had failed to confirm a Supreme Court nominee. That single instance had occurred back in 1930, when President Hoover nominated John J. Parker to the Court.

Fortas's first and foremost mistake was to appear in person before the Judiciary Committee. No nominee to the position of Chief Justice before in history had appeared in person before the Senate. When nominated, each of the fourteen men who served as Chief Justice, through Earl Warren, had allowed his record to speak for him, and the Senate had not demeaned the office by insisting that the nominees submit to interrogation. The committee asked Fortas to appear. He could have refused. But he came, saying, "I am very happy to be here."[12] Quite apparently, he did so in the belief that his personal appearance would hasten his confirmation. Senator Griffin doggedly had raised questions about the relationship between Johnson and Fortas, since Fortas had gone on the Court in 1965, and succeeded in suggesting that their relationship somehow compromised the independence of the Court. Griffin's questions also succeeded in publicizing the "cronyism" issue. Fortas felt he could respond satisfactorily to the senator's questions. He was mistaken. By breaking with precedent, Fortas committed the tactical error of exposing himself to increasingly hostile interrogation. The questions probably would have gone unanswered had he not appeared. He committed the strategic error of exposing himself to questioning about his Superme Court opinions. If the Court is to maintain its independence, no Justice can allow himself to be questioned by members of Congress about his written opinions; Fortas tried to resist but his resistance was unsatisfactory. Justices' opinions standing alone, of course, may be discussed by members of Congress or anyone else, but the law itself is questioned when a Justice exposes himself to hostile congressional interrogation and is drawn into a combative defense of his opinions.

Such questioning by Congress of a Justice's official opinions has the inevitable appearance of, and often the purpose of, influencing the future decisions of the Court. When the Court's decisions even appear to have been influenced, by Congress or the President, the constitutional separation of powers doctrine is violated, the independence of the Court is compromised, and the integrity of the Court is damaged.

Fortas, accompanied as he had been in 1965 by liberal Senator Gore of Tennessee, sat before the Judiciary Committee for four long days, as some of the most conservative members of the United States Senate alternately grilled him. Strom Thurmond of South Carolina read for nearly two hours from selected documents that were critical of the Warren Court. Sam Ervin of North Carolina held the floor for longer to inform Fortas and the nation why he believed the Court had erred in deciding that the poll tax was unconstitutional, that the 1866 Civil Rights Act had real meaning, and so forth. James Eastland of Mississippi pressed on Fortas his views of the meanings of the Constitution. Roman Hruska of Nebraska questioned Fortas concerning a labor case the Court had decided, which led the senator to the assumption that, inasmuch as Fortas played the violin, "You have a card" in the musicians union. "I do not," Fortas replied. John McClellan of Arkansas was less vicious and more blunt. McClellan reserved the right to disagree "wholly and completely with some of the philosophy you have expounded."

Fortas tried not to respond when he was asked about decisions of the Court, but he was less than successful. Senator Eastland asked, for example, "To what extent and under what circumstances do you believe that the Court should attempt to bring about social, economic, or political changes?" Fortas, drawn into response, gave a curious answer: "Zero. Absolutely zero."[13]

But the senators returned again and again to the "cronyism" charge and to questions concerning Justice Fortas's relationship with President Johnson, and Fortas supplied his interrogators with the answers they so eagerly sought. He responded with an earnestness that at times was emotional, as if compelled by sincere conviction that no man in the service of President Johnson could do wrong. He seemed almost oblivious to the fact that the more answers he gave, the more partisan his nomination became. Senator Griffin, never pausing in his pursuit of Fortas, declared: "Never before has there been such obvious political maneuvering to create a vacancy so that a 'lame duck' President can fill it and thereby deny the opportunity to a new President about to be elected by the people. And never before in history has any President been so bold as to subject himself to the charge of 'cronyism' with respect to two such nominations at the same time."[14]

The senators drew from Fortas admissions that he had been at the White House when the President decided to send Federal troops to quell the race riot in Detroit in 1966, and that in 1967 he had telephoned to complain to a former business associate about the businessman's criticism of Johnson's Vietnam war budget. Fortas's testimony left the impression that his old relationship with Johnson had not changed much at all in the years he had been an Associate Justice. Fortas was not entirely convincing when he insisted time and again that his continuing association with the President had no effect on his decisions and other judicial work at the Court. The committee still had not finished when Congress recessed for the Republican and Democratic National Conventions in August.

On the eighth day of August in Miami Beach, Florida, Richard Nixon won the Republican nomination on the first ballot and in an acceptance speech addressed to the American majority that was neither young nor black he spoke of violence and crime and fear. "Let us always respect, as I do, our courts and those who serve on them," he declared. "But let us also recognize that some of our courts in their decisions have gone too far in weakening the peace forces as against the criminal forces in this country and we must act to restore that balance." Also in his acceptance speech, Nixon went further than he

86

THE PERILS OF CRONYISM

had before in attacking Ramsey Clark as a symbol of libertarian permissiveness that allegedly caused crime and violence. "I pledge to you a new Attorney General," Nixon told the cheering Republicans in Miami Beach.

Two weeks later the divided and disorganized Democrats met in convention at Chicago. Amidst violent street demonstrations met by an ugly counterforce of police and soldiers, the party faithful on the first ballot nominated Hubert Humphrey over Eugene McCarthy as the Democratic presidential candidate. In his acceptance speech, Humphrey made no real effort to defend the courts or Ramsey Clark. He said, to Democrats on his left, that violence will not be quelled by attacks on "our courts, our laws or our Attorney General." But he also declared, to those on his right, "Rioting, burning, sniping, mugging, traffic in narcotics, and disregard for law are the advance guard of anarchy, and they must and they will be stopped."

On September 13 the Judiciary Committee resumed its hearings on the Fortas and Thornberry nominations and the Republicans further strengthened their case against Fortas. Fortas declined to reappear before the committee. So the committee, without Fortas's participation, called as a witness B. J. Tennery, dean of the American University Law School in Washington, who testified that Fortas had been paid $15,000 to conduct a series of seminars at the school during the summer of 1968. Dean Tennery said that the money came from a fund of $30,000 which was raised by Paul Porter through contributions from five men: Gustav L. Levy, John Loeb, and Paul D. Smith, all of New York; Troy Post of Dallas and Maurice Lazarus of New York. Each was a wealthy businessman or lawyer; some were friends or clients of Fortas before he went to the Supreme Court. Paul Porter, of course, was one of Abe Fortas' former law partners at the old firm of Arnold, Porter & Fortas. Tennery's testimony apparently was intended by Fortas's enemies in the Senate to be further evidence of the Justice's alleged insensivity to the independence of the Court and its members. The conservatives on the Judiciary Committee also discussed at length, and without the benefit of Fortas's presence, the Warren Court's decisions concerning the First Amendment rights of book publishers and movie makers, and left or attempted to leave the distinct impression that the Supreme Court and Justice Fortas were responsible also for glutting America with pornography.

The committee on September 17 voted 11 to 6 to recommend confirmation of the nomination of Fortas to be Chief Justice. Eight Democrats and three Republicans voted for confirmation; the three included Senator Dirksen. Three Democrats and three Republicans voted no.

The nomination moved to the Senate floor and on September 25 a conservative coalition of Republicans and Southern Democrats began a filibuster, the first in the Senate's history to prevent a vote on the confirmation of a nominee to the Supreme Court. All the criticisms of Fortas heard in the committee were voiced again on the floor. But the political objection to the nomination was predominant. Hiram Fong, Republican of Hawaii, said, "Particularly at this juncture in the history of our nation, this crucially important appointment should be left to the new President soon to be elected by the people." Howard H. Baker, Jr., Republican of Tennessee, added, "The Supreme Court has fallen to a low estate and it must be reconstructed . . ."

Southern Democrats helped the Republicans along. Senator Ervin declared, "The tragic truth is that in recent years the Supreme Court has repeatedly usurped and exercised the power of the Congress and the states."

At one o'clock in the afternoon of October 1, a roll-call vote began on a motion to stop the filibuster and take up consideration of Johnson's nomination of Fortas. To pass, a motion to invoke cloture needed fifty-nine votes, or two-thirds of the senators present and voting. The tally showed forty-five votes in favor of halting the filibuster, far short of the fifty-nine required. The Republicans and Southern Democrats had won, not on the merits but on the question of their right to filibuster indefinitely. Ten Republicans and thirty-five Democrats had voted for cloture, but the balance of power was held by the forty-three votes, twenty-four of them Republican and nineteen Democratic, cast against cloture.

The following day Johnson, at Fortas's request, withdrew the nomination.

"I hope," Fortas said in his letter to the President, "that my withdrawal will help put in motion a process by which there will be an end to destructive and extreme assaults upon the Court."

Johnson in reply declared that the Senate action was "tragic." For Johnson, it was doubly tragic; with no promotion for Fortas, Warren would stay and with Warren staying there was no vacancy for Thornberry to fill.

And thus was joined the battle for control of the Supreme Court of the United States.

In the joining, the well-laid plans of Warren, Johnson, and Fortas were destroyed, laid waste by Johnson's peculiar view of presidential power applied without limit to the manipulation of men for the rewarding of personal friends with public offices. True, the conservative opposition to the Warren Court was rising, Johnson was a "lame duck" President without popular strength, and the Republicans were determined to save the Chief Justiceship for Richard Nixon. Still, Johnson was President and his party controlled Congress. Johnson almost certainly could have won confirmation of a new Chief Justice who would have preserved the essential concern for human justice and equality, the independence and the integrity of Earl Warren. Had Johnson only nominated the right man.

Johnson probably could have won confirmation even of Abe Fortas to be the next Chief Justice. If the Republicans and Southern Democrats in the Senate had been confident of their case against Fortas, they would not have had to resort to filibuster. Fortas committed an indiscretion in accepting the $15,000, but he was proved guilty of nothing worse. Fortas's continuing relationship with the President after he became an Associate Justice was offensive to the independence of the Court, but probably was no worse than similar relationships in history of certain other Justices with their Presidents. More to the point, Johnson in six months would have left the presidency. But the nomination of Fortas could not carry the weight of a second Johnson crony. All Presidents need friends, but the Fortas nomination thus weighted down broke under the charge of cronyism. Johnson gave the Warren Court's enemies the leverage they needed, and in the final analysis he offended the dignity of the Supreme Court.

It was said by some liberals, after the Fortas debacle, that Johnson should have nominated another liberal to succeed Earl Warren. There were discussions at the Justice Department and the White House that centered on the idea of nominating Senator Hart of Michigan as the next Chief Justice. Johnson was willing, but not enthusiastic. Ramsey Clark, true to the end in his miscast role, argued against the idea on the ground that the nomination would further politicize the Supreme Court. Clark prevailed, for the moment.

CHAPTER 7

# Into Nixon's Lap

Anyone who might have escaped Washington on the final day of the Supreme Court's term in June, 1968, and gone fishing all summer where there was no newspaper, television, or radio could have returned when the Court reopened in October and assumed he had missed absolutely nothing. At ten o'clock on the morning of Monday, October 7, the same red velvet curtains parted and the same nine black-robed Justices stepped through to their high-backed leather chairs behind the long mahogany bench. Chief Justice Warren announced the opening of the Court's new term. Associate Justice Fortas was in his place. Justices Black, Douglas, Harlan, Brennan, Stewart, White, and Marshall were in their accustomed seats. To all appearances, the Warren Court remained intact. Intact, but not in the way Warren in the spring had intended that his Court should be preserved. Spring, summer, now fall, then winter.

The return of Earl Warren was anticlimactic. Not Warren but events outside this quiet place would determine whether the Supreme Court would continue to assert a doctrine of constitutional supremacy or would be forced once more into a role subordinate to the majoritarian branches of government. Some of the events outside seemed absurd. The Gallup Poll, for example, recently had surveyed public opinion concerning the Court, the same way the pollsters sampled the political popularity of presidential candidates. "In general," they asked a nationwide sample of 1,534 adults, "what kind of rating would you give the Supreme Court—excellent, good, fair or poor?"* If the Supreme Court were to be judged on the basis of its

*New York *Times*, July 10, 1968, p. 22. The poll reported that unfavorable

90

political popularity, there would be no need for a Court and perhaps no reason for a Bill of Rights in the majoritarian scheme.

Yet, there was a peculiar and unhappy relevance to the popularity poll in the fall of 1968. Justice Holmes had said in 1913, "We are very quiet, but it is the quiet of a storm centre."[1] In October, 1968, the Supreme Court faced a crisis more serious than any time since 1835 when Chief Justice Marshall died in office. The Warren Court's decisions against states' rights had carried the federal supremacy doctrine far beyond the place it had been in 1956, when one hundred members of Congress pledged in the Southern Manifesto to "bring about a reversal" of the decisions requiring racial desegregation of schools in twenty-one states. Earl Warren's plan to retire so that a President who supported the Court could name the next Chief Justice had backfired. The successful filibuster of Republicans and Southern Democrats against Johnson's nomination of Fortas, while Nixon campaigned against the Warren Court, intensified the political storm. Now, with the presidential election less than a month away, both Warren and Fortas were back and the Court was opening for business again. It could not be business as usual because the Court now was under intense political assault. Its independence, and the future of America's blacks and her other minorities, were at stake.

During the final weeks of the political campaign, Richard Nixon said the Supreme Court should not "become a political issue" and then proceeded to make it even more so. He had made "law and order" the major theme of his campaign, insisting that crime and violence were larger problems than the Vietnam War. He declared that slums, hunger, and unemployment were not the major causes of crime and violence and asserted, "The war on poverty is not a substitute for a war on crime." Racial violence and street crime, which Nixon seemed to believe were a single problem, were to be blamed on the Supreme Court and Attorney General Ramsey Clark. Nixon promised not only to get rid of Clark but also to enlist in his war on crime the wiretaps and electronic surveillance devices Clark refused to use. As late as three days before the election, Nixon still was promising what he would do concerning the Supreme Court. He

attitudes toward the Court outweighed favorable sentiment by a 3 to 2 ratio. The Gallup Poll, which had been checking public attitudes toward the Court for thirty years, added that an individual's opinion of the Court is closely related to his political identification.

would appoint to the Court "strict constructionists who saw their duty as interpreting law and not making law. They would see themselves as caretakers of the Constitution, not super-legislators with a free hand to impose their social and political viewpoints upon the American people."[2]

Presidential election campaigns in America are nationally televised popularity contests in which soap opera pitchmen in the employ of the candidates attempt to reduce the issues to subliminal slogans and simplistic rhetoric. Nixon as a lawyer knew that the term "strict constructionist" meant whatever one wants it to mean, depending on one's politics or philosophy as the case may be. He was using it to communicate to political conservatives, and particularly those in the South, his opposition to the Court's racial and criminal rights decisions.

On November 5 Nixon was elected by the smallest percentage of the popular vote for a successful presidential candidate since Woodrow Wilson's election in 1912. But the narrowness of his victory did not mean that he had been mistaken in pitching his campaign to that part of the American mind which did not identify with the blacks, the young, or the Warren Court. Nixon won only about 43.4 per cent of the popular vote, but George Wallace who had spoken even more venomously against school desegregation and the Warren Court received 13.5 per cent of the total national popular vote and Wallace had carried the states of Alabama, Arkansas, Georgia, Louisiana, and Mississippi. There were various issues in the 1968 campaign, but the combined 57 per cent of the popular vote won by Nixon and Wallace must be accepted as valid evidence of the white majoritarian backlash against dissenting blacks and young people and against the civil rights decisions of the Warren Court.

With the election over, one of the first questions to which Washington pundits turned their typewriters was the question of Earl Warren. Had Warren tendered his retirement only to President Johnson and, Johnson's choice of a successor having been defeated by filibuster, was it now Warren's intention to remain as Chief Justice? There really was no question, however. Warren's refusal to retire would be a concession that he had tried to give Johnson the right to name his successor. The attacks by Republicans and Southern Democrats on Warren and the Court surely would grow more furious day by day if he now refused to retire. He had no choice.

Before the month of November had passed, Warren let it be known through the press that he would retire and that Nixon could nominate his successor.[3] The Chief Justice would prefer to remain until the end of the Court's term, which would be in June, 1969, but he left the date of his leaving to Nixon. In December the Chief Justice and the President-elect came to an understanding. Warren would remain until the end of the term and on that day he would retire.

After the election there also was uncertainty as to whether the Chief Justice in January would perform his traditional role of swearing in the new President.[4] But Earl Warren in November also let it be known through the press that, if asked, he would swear in Richard Nixon. On January 20, 1969, the air of conciliation that fortunately prevails for at least the moment of presidential inaugurations was much in evidence at the Capitol Plaza as Nixon took office as the thirty-seventh President. Before a crowd of 65,000 Chief Justice Warren swore him in, and the new President in his inaugural address promised Democrats he would "build on what has gone before." He pledged to blacks that he would try "to give life to what is in the law: To insure at last that as all are born equal in dignity before God, all are born equal in dignity to man." And of young people he said he was "proud that they are better educated, more committed, more passionately driven by conscience than any generation that has gone before." But the loudest and longest applause came when, after talking about his desire for peace, Nixon added: "But to all who would be tempted by weakness, let us leave no doubt that we will be as strong as we need to be for as long as we need to be."

One of Nixon's first acts as President was to be rid of Ramsey Clark as Attorney General; the act can be noted even though the Republican candidate's promise to replace the Democratic Attorney General was a fine example of campaign rhetoric. President Nixon installed as his Attorney General John N. Mitchell, his dour-faced political campaign manager. One of Nixon's second acts as President was to settle down to a two-hour luncheon with Attorney General Mitchell two days after the inauguration. Nixon and Mitchell shared the instinctive personal conservatism of many wealthy lawyers whose success is self-made instead of handed down. Despite the hurrah of the campaign, neither was or ever could be completely a public man who genuinely enjoyed the crowds, as, say, Franklin Roosevelt did, and who in turn was genuinely embraced in popular esteem. There still was a certain reserve, a stiffness, in Nixon's and Mitchell's public appearances. There also was the inherent discomfort and distrust that lawyers often seem to feel in the presence of the press.

Privately and politically, the President was closer to his Attorney General than to anyone else in the Cabinet, and at their long luncheon on their second day in office they talked of many things. They talked of law and order. They talked of crime in Washington which, with 70 per cent of its population black, had given Nixon 18 per cent of its popular vote. (Among large cities, Washington had the largest ratio of Negroes and it had given the President the smallest share of its popular vote.) And they talked of Earl Warren.[5]

In this Warren's last and final term as Chief Justice, the Supreme Court surrendered neither its independence nor its integrity to the executive and legislative branches. Indeed, one of the final acts of the Warren Court was to assert its constitutional prerogative by ruling that the House of Representatives acted unconstitutionally in excluding Adam Clayton Powell, the flamboyant black Democratic congressman from New York, from the seat in the Congress to which Harlem voters had elected him.[6] Chief Justice Warren delivered the Court's opinion. In its final weeks and days the Warren Court asserted its constitutional authority also in a number of other important decisions. Holding that states and cities cannot impose "special" burdens on legislative actions to assist racial minorities, the Court voided an Akron, Ohio, city charter provision requiring that city council-enacted fair housing laws be submitted to a referendum vote.[7] The Court threw out a North Carolina literacy test for voting, on the grounds that previously segregated and inferior Negro schools had so restricted educational opportunity that use of the test now to disqualify blacks was illegal.[8] And the Court held unconstitutional, under the First Amendment, state laws making a crime of the mere possession in a private home of obscene books and magazines.[9]

And then, as the end of the Court's term drew near and Earl Warren prepared to take his leave and President Nixon readied his announcement of the election of the new Chief Justice, fate once more came to play a role which was not foreseen in the nomination and confirmation of Earl Warren's successor.

President Nixon had said that he would appoint to the Supreme Court "caretakers." Patently the Constitution needs more than caretakers. But Nixon's purposes demanded a caretaker, a Chief Justice who would lead the Supreme Court back to its place, passively behind and unobtrusively out of the way of the executive and legislative branches. Now was the time, as Nixon time and again had said during the campaign, to strengthen "the peace forces, as against the criminal forces, in this country." It was the time for law and order, for new strength to local and state police and the Federal Bureau of Investigation. It was the time for "benign neglect" of civil rights and criminal rights and constitutional rights generally as against the police powers of the state. Inasmuch as President Nixon sought to upset the Warren Court whereas President Johnson had sought to preserve it, the former's search for a new Chief Justice led him in directions different from those Johnson had followed. But every President who has had the opportunity to name a Chief Justice almost certainly has thought of his best friends; one's best friends mirror in the mind one's best self.

So Richard Nixon thought initially about his friends and considered first of all John Mitchell, his Attorney General, the manager of his successful 1968 political campaign and former law partner. Mitchell "is superbly qualified," the President later said. "He is my closest adviser, on all legal matters and on many other matters as well."

The President next considered Herbert Brownell, a wealthy New York lawyer and close friend who had been Attorney General in the Eisenhower Administration when Nixon was Vice President. "He was the man, next to Attorney General Mitchell, who was my closest adviser in selecting the Cabinet," the President later commented. "I think he would have made a superb Chief Justice."

There was Thomas E. Dewey, former governor of New York, twice the unsuccessful Republican candidate for President and still an important figure in the Republican Party. Nixon also considered Potter Stewart, the incumbent member of the Supreme Court who thought most like the President. And he jotted down the name of Charles Rhyne, a man prominent in legal circles who had been a Nixon classmate at Duke University Law School and who had helped Nixon in the 1968 political campaign. Rhyne was "perhaps my closest friend among all of those considered," Nixon said.

But Nixon scratched off his list of candidates for the Chief Justiceship the names of all those men with whom he had a personal relationship. For Lyndon Johnson personal and political friendship had been the overriding consideration. But few Presidents have taken friendship as far as did Lyndon Johnson, and, because Johnson had gone too far, the personal friendship of Richard Nixon could not be an asset but would be a political liability for a candidate for nomination to the Supreme Court.

There were other reasons why Nixon eliminated each of those names from his list. John Mitchell professed personal reasons for not wanting to be Chief Justice and, whatever they were, his reasons apparently were held as sincerely as those which once upon a time had led Abe Fortas to resist, unsuccessfully, Johnson's insistence on making him an Associate Justice. Brownell when he had been Attorney General had made enemies in the Senate who now might try to block his confirmation. Anyway, Brownell might be too liberal; he had wanted John Lindsay, mayor of New York, as Nixon's running mate in the 1968 campaign.[10] Tom Dewey would be risky. He had too much stature in his own right and might turn out to be too independent-minded as Chief Justice. Anyway, Dewey and Warren had been running mates once. Potter Stewart had requested that his name be scratched from the list. Charles Rhyne, for Nixon's purposes in 1969, was not well enough known outside the legal community.

So there were reasons for scratching each name. But a perhaps larger reason why Nixon scratched all of them was that the Senate remained after the 1968 election in control of the Democrats, and Richard Nixon almost certainly was going to have trouble getting the Senate to confirm his nominee to succeed Earl Warren. Johnson's nomination of the liberal Mr. Fortas had after all not been defeated on its merits by a majority of the Senate, but by a filibuster. Had the Fortas nomination been put to a vote, requiring only a simple majority, Fortas might well have been confirmed by a slim margin. And now a slim majority of liberals might defeat Nixon's nominee or filibuster it to death.

Nixon in pondering his choice took only one other man into his confidence, John Mitchell. They weighed all the considerations and decided together that all of the President's personal and political friends must be scratched. With all of the potential trouble ahead, Nixon could not add to his difficulty by exposing his nomination to the charge of cronyism. With the Fortas rejection so fresh and Senate liberals so anxious now to take revenge, this was no time to repeat Johnson's cardinal error.

So Nixon looked elsewhere and found his caretaker. And then all of the potential trouble with the Senate suddenly evaporated. Even one of Nixon's cronies probably could have been confirmed. For the evaporation of the liberal opposition in the Senate had almost nothing to do with the President or his nominee. The opposition was reduced to a weak vapor by another untimely and unexpected liberal debacle. It was an historic accident, through which Abe Fortas walked off the Court and Warren Earl Burger walked on.

The annual dinner of the White House Correspondents Association was to be held on Saturday evening, May 3, 1969, in the cavernous ballroom of the Washington Hilton Hotel. The association, despite its name, is made up not exclusively of news media people assigned to cover the White House, but newspaper, wire service, television, and other reporters who cover anything and everything in Washington. The association's sole reason for being appears to be to sponsor an annual dinner at which members and their guests may honor the President. Presidents in recent years sometimes have attended and at other times have sent the Vice President instead; the President's decision seems to depend not so much on the state of world affairs as on his disposition of the moment to demonstrate either a friendliness or a hostility toward the Washington press corps. But the press does not know beforehand whether the President will appear, so invariably the black tie dinner is a large, noisy affair peopled with reporters of all stripes and their guests, many of whom are officials high and low of the political party which happens to be in control of the White House that year.

As the ballroom filled with chattering, drinking, smoking people the evening of May 3, some of the officials of Attorney General Mitchell's Justice Department went from one table to another and from one reporter to the next familiar face they could see, wearing on their own faces the special kind of controlled anticipation that bureaucrats portray when they have a state secret which now they want to tell. The message they were carrying from table to table was that *Life* magazine, in its new issue which would be available in Washington the next day, would have a very important story concerning the Supreme Court. By the time dinner was served, *Life*'s promised revelation was a larger topic of speculation in the ballroom than whether President Nixon was going to appear. (He did.)

On Friday, the day before the dinner, the Justice Department had dispatched a United States marshal to New York to pick up proof copies of the *Life* article. The marshal flew back to Washington with the proofs and, prior to the time the dinner began on Saturday evening, the article already had been read by top officials at the Justice Department and the White House. Clearly the Nixon Administration had prior knowledge of the article. It was not known how long the Administration had been aware or how much the Administration knew, but the article had been in preparation since late in 1969.[11]

On Sunday morning, the stacks of *Life* magazines which had arrived in Washington contained an exclusive story in which William Lambert, an associate editor of *Life,* reported that Abe Fortas, after he became a member of the Supreme Court, was paid $20,000 by a charitable foundation set up by financier Louis Wolfson and his brothers.[12]

Wolfson's name was well known in Washington and Wall Street. Only a week before, the *Wall Street Journal* had carried an interview with Wolfson on the occasion of his impending surrender in Miami Beach to begin serving a one-year Federal prison sentence imposed for selling corporate stock that had not been registered with the Securities and Exchange Commission.[13] In the interview Wolfson had said that he could have been spared the jail sentence by accepting a pardon which he said was available, allegedly through political connections, in the preceding December from President Johnson. The interview also recalled that Wolfson, now fifty-seven years old and graying, a decade earlier had been an industrial giant commanding a $400 million conglomerate of shipbuilding yards, paint factories, chemical plants, and moneylending operations.

The *Life* article recounted details of Wolfson's more glorious past and noted the disclosure, before the Senate Judiciary Committee almost a year earlier, of Fortas's acceptance of $15,000 for lecturing at American University. Then the article said that on January 3, 1966, three months after Fortas became an Associate Justice, a check for $20,000 drawn on the bank account of the Wolfson Family Foundation was paid to Fortas. It said that in March, 1966, the Securities and Exchange Commission recommended to the Justice Department that criminal proceedings be brought against Wolfson and an associate for allegedly failing to register with the SEC a public offering of stock of Continental Enterprises, Incorporated. In June, the article continued, Fortas paid a one-day visit to Harbor View Farm, Wolfson's home near Ocala, Florida. The article said that in July Wolfson wrote to Manuel Cohen, a Democrat who then was chairman of the SEC, asking that the criminal proceedings recommendation sent to the Justice Department be withdrawn and that Wolfson be given an opportunity to appear before the commission. In September, the *Life* article continued, a federal grand jury in New York, to which the Justice Department had presented the Continental Enterprises case, indicted Wolfson and his associate. In December Fortas returned the $20,000 to the Wolfson Family Foundation, the article said.

Subsequently, Wolfson was convicted, the Supreme Court refused to review the case, and in the late spring of 1969 Wolfson began to serve his one-year prison sentence. The *Life* article concluded by noting that Wolfson in the *Wall Street Journal* interview had asserted that he could have gone free, had he been willing to accept a pardon from President Johnson in December, 1968.

The article quoted Justice Fortas as saying there was "no impropriety" in his conduct, and added that Fortas "ostensibly" was paid the $20,000 "to advise the foundation on ways to use its funds for charitable, educational and civil rights projects." The article further stated that *Life* had not "uncovered evidence making possible a charge that Wolfson hired Fortas to fix his case."

On Sunday, the same day the stacks of *Life* magazines were available in Washington, Justice Fortas, without making himself available to the press, issued a statement through the Supreme Court's press officer. The statement began: "I have not accepted any fee or emolument from Mr. Wolfson or the Wolfson Family Foundation." It said that in 1965, before Fortas went on the Court, his law firm represented a Wolfson company, and "in this connection I met Mr. Wolfson and discussed with him the significant and commendable work of Mr. Wolfson and his family foundation in the field of harmonious racial and religious relations." In 1966, the statement continued, the foundation "tendered a fee to me, in the hope that I would find time and could undertake, consistently with my Court obligations, research functions, studies and writings connected with the work of the foundation." Fortas said he returned the fee when he concluded "I could not undertake the assignment." Fortas said he never believed the fee was tendered with "any hope or expectation that it would induce me to intervene or make representations on Mr. Wolfson's behalf." Fortas added: "At no time have I spoken or communicated with any official about Mr. Wolfson, whether with respect to a pardon or his criminal cases or his SEC matters. At no time have I given Mr.

Wolfson or any of his family, associates, foundations or interests any legal advice or services, since becoming a member of the Court."

On Monday morning, the Court's marshal chanted his familiar "Oyez! Oyez!! Oyez!!!" and Fortas took his accustomed place as if nothing had happened. Privately, he discussed his problem and what he should do about it with his friends among the "brethren" of the Court. He decided he would ride out the storm for the few weeks remaining in the term and, he hoped, by the time the Court opened its new term in October the storm would have passed.

Instead, the storm Fortas had seeded grew worse. His Sunday statement did him more harm than good. It seemed less than frank in saying no fee was accepted and then conceding a fee was tendered and returned. It did not mention the figure of $20,000 nor did it explain why the fee had been kept for eleven months. Fortas's lack of candor inevitably was seen against a background that flashed with the old charges of cronyism and wheeling and dealing. Some of the more exuberantly conservative members of Congress prepared impeachment proceedings to remove him from the Court and none of the more prominent liberals in Congress spoke out in his defense. But most of the members of Congress, including its senior conservatives, and many prominent legal scholars in universities were publicly silent, so great was their shock and so strong was their expectation that Fortas must out of conscience resign. Instead, Fortas kept speaking engagements in Boston, Massachusetts, and in Richmond, Virginia, still seeming to ignore the storm.

The Nixon Administration seemed outwardly to be ignoring it also. In fact, the wheels inside the White House and the Justice Department had been spinning at least since the proofs of the *Life* magazine article had been studied late on Friday, May 2. The stakes for Richard Nixon were almost as high as for Abe Fortas. If Fortas resigned, Nixon would have the opportunity, rare in any President's first year in office, to name two conservatives to the Supreme Court. If, on the other hand, Fortas refused to resign and Congress began impeachment proceedings against him, not only might the President's legislative program be sidetracked but the result could be acrimony permanently poisoning the new Republican Administration's relations with the Democrats in Congress.

Far from ignoring the Fortas affair, Attorney General Mitchell decided that Wolfson should be interrogated concerning his foundation's relationship with Fortas. FBI agents, armed with a grand jury subpoena, questioned Wolfson. Then Mitchell called Earl Warren to ask whether he could see the Chief Justice privately. On Wednesday, May 7, the Attorney General paid his secret call. He laid before the Chief Justice additional information on Fortas.

No one but the two of them knows precisely what was said, but clearly it was Mitchell's purpose to enlist Warren's help in obtaining Fortas's resignation. Persons who are extremely close to both Warren and Fortas say there are conflicting stories about whether Warren advised Fortas to resign or to stay and fight it out. But the fact is that Mitchell went back to the Justice Department and waited while the rest of the week passed. Fortas did not resign.

On Sunday Mitchell's secret began to leak. *Newsweek* magazine reported that the Attorney General had gone to the Supreme Court Building to tell the Chief Justice that, unless Fortas resigned, more damaging information about the relationship between Fortas and Wolfson would become public knowledge. The following day Mitchell and Warren confirmed the fact of their meeting. That was Monday. Tuesday passed and still Fortas did not resign. On Wednesday, May 14, the more damaging information began to leak out and finally, that afternoon, Fortas caved under the mounting pressure and sent to President Nixon a short letter of resignation and to Chief Justice Warren a long letter of attempted explanation. The resignation letter reached the White House at 5:30 P.M. on Wednesday, just before the President was to speak on national television about the Vietnam war. The White House, not wanting to bury the President's war message under headlines about Fortas's resignation or vice versa, withheld public announcement of the resignation. At 8:45 A.M. on Thursday, when the White House still had not disclosed the resignation, Fortas released it himself through the Supreme Court's press office. What Fortas released was, until that moment, his and John Mitchell's secret: that Justice Fortas had agreed to accept from the Wolfson Family Foundation not just $20,000 but an annual payment of $20,-000 for so long as he lived and thereafter to Mrs. Fortas, if she survived him.

Fortas spelled out the arrangement in his long letter to the Chief Justice. He said he came to know Wolfson in 1965, before Lyndon Johnson nominated him as an Associate Justice, when Wolfson retained Fortas's old law firm of Arnold, Fortas & Porter to represent two Wolfson companies, one of which was even then involved in certain securities problems with the SEC. At that time, according to the Fortas letter to Warren, Wolfson invited Fortas's attention to the charitable works of the Wolfson Family Foundation. Shortly after Fortas joined the Court in October, 1965, Wolfson came to Washington again and talked with Mr. Justice Fortas about the foundation. Fortas agreed to a "long-term" association with the foundation and the annual stipend of $20,000 also was agreed upon. The $20,000 check which *Life* magazine discovered to have been paid in January, 1966, was merely the first payment.

Fortas in his letter recalled the night spent in June, 1966, at the Wolfson farm in Ocala, Florida. Later that month, the letter to the Chief Justice continued, Fortas decided to terminate his relationship with the Wolfson foundation. There were two reasons, he told Warren. First, Fortas's work at the Court was too heavy and, second, "I learned that the SEC had referred Mr. Wolfson's file to the Department of Justice for consideration as to criminal prosecution."

Fortas said he canceled his agreement with the foundation on June 21, 1966. Wolfson was indicted on two charges in September and October, 1966. Fortas said he returned the initial $20,000 in December, 1966. The letter did not explain why the $20,000 was not returned more promptly.

Fortas concluded his letter to Warren with the assertion that he had not "interceded or taken part in any matter" affecting Wolfson and "there has been no wrongdoing on my part." He was resigning, he said, "in order that the Court may not continue to be subjected to extraneous stress."

And thus did Lyndon Johnson's best friend fall into Richard Nixon's lap.

CHAPTER 8

# Nixon Runs with the Ball

One day, after the Nixon Administration had been in office only six months, a small group of Negroes from several Southern states walked into the Justice Department building on Pennsylvania Avenue and went up to the fifth floor, where they staged a quiet sit-in in the outer office of Attorney General Mitchell to protest the Administration's civil rights policies. A summer later, after the Nixon-Mitchell policies on law and order and civil rights had been developed more fully and dissenters were making real and imaginary threats to bomb a number of Washington buildings, the Department of Justice became a guarded fortress, barring entry to persons without proper identification. But in the summer of 1969, the huge, steel doors remained open and the blacks simply walked in. After they had sat for a time in the Attorney General's office, they were told that if they would move out quietly, Mitchell would talk with them in the Great Hall downstairs. The Great Hall of course was the large room used for the swearing-in of Ramsey Clark as Attorney General and for similar ceremonial occasions. The blacks moved out and it was in the Great Hall that Attorney General Mitchell delivered, inadvertently, his famous line: "Instead of listening to what we say, watch what we do."[1]

It may be that the American people, black and white, are accustomed enough to political rhetoric that, to paraphrase Abraham Lincoln, they do not believe all politicians all the time. But politicians rarely concede publicly that they are trying to fool the people, and, as Nixon's and Mitchell's struggle with Senate liberals over control of the Supreme Court grew into a classic confrontation of governmental power, differences arose time and again between what each set of combatants said and what they did.

Mitchell's Justice Department said certain things and did certain things, relative to Abe Fortas and Louis Wolfson, which were or which became public knowledge. It also engaged in conversations and actions, the detailed contents of which remain secret. What then was the Nixon Administration's total role in the fall of Abe Fortas? Did Mitchell merely push Fortas when Mitchell went to the Supreme Court to tell Chief Justice Warren of the more damaging information against Fortas? Or did Mitchell, perhaps with threats or promises, shove with all the muscle at the command of the Justice Department and the FBI?

Whatever the full contents of Mitchell's briefcase and his mind, and however they were revealed to Warren, the Attorney General's secret visit with the Chief Justice was unusual in the extreme, from constitutional and political points of view. The Department, of course, had prosecuted Louis Wolfson, and it had access to the Securities and Exchange Commission's investigative files. It is not known what the Department knew prior to receipt of the proofs of the *Life* magazine article about Wolfson's relationship with Fortas. But it is unlikely that the Department, with the FBI's vast investigative resources available to it, knew nothing of the relationship. Certain of Richard Nixon's close Republican friends knew as early as the fall of 1968, at the height of Nixon's presidential campaign, that there was some sort of potentially explosive tie between Justice Fortas and Louis Wolfson.[2]

After the *Life* magazine article appeared, the Justice Department attempted to maintain the fiction that it was not investigating Justice Fortas; rather, after FBI agents were sent to question Wolfson, the Department said its investigation was to determine whether there was any "obstruction of justice" in connection with Wolfson's attempt to combat the federal charges of selling unregistered stock. Ironically, it was in the end the Justice Department that officially closed the book on the Fortas affair, by failing to bring any legal action against him. Some weeks after Fortas resigned from the Supreme Court the Department spread the word that the FBI investigation had uncovered no reason for bringing action against Fortas and therefore the case was closed.

Inasmuch as the Justice Department brought no action against Fortas after he resigned, it must be concluded that, whatever the reasons he was tendered $20,000 annually for life, there was no evidence that his relationship with Wolfson violated any federal laws. If that were the case, Fortas could have tried to ride out the storm, bracing for the possibility of impeachment proceedings. Had he had that kind of fortitude, it is doubtful that Congress would have removed him from the Court. A vote of impeachment by the House of Representatives was not imminent when Fortas resigned, but if the House had impeached Fortas it is very doubtful the Senate would have convicted and removed him. Had there been a trial before the Senate, the charges against Fortas would have become inextricably interwoven with political opposition to the Warren Court, as the impeachment of Justice Samuel Chase, 164 years earlier, had become bound up with the opposition to the Marshall Court of that day.[3] The Senate refused then to place constitutional government in jeopardy by trying the Supreme Court and almost certainly it would not do so now. Principle and rhetoric do not become that confused in the Senate. It acquitted Samuel Chase, and the House has never impeached any other member of the Supreme Court.

But Fortas, unlike Chase, was unwilling or unable to ride out the storm. Instead, he made history by becoming the first Justice in the history of the Supreme Court to resign under fire for his personal conduct. His resignation was a personal tragedy. Not even his enemies denied that he was a brilliant lawyer. What then was the flaw in this brilliant, quiet, 58-year-old man? One can only guess but, at the time Fortas was sitting before the Senate Judiciary Committee as nominee to be the next Chief Justice, he said that the Court "was not part of my life plan."

In an emotional rejoinder to conservative senators, who were attempting to demonstrate that his relationship to Johnson made him unfit to be the new Chief Justice, Fortas quietly and haltingly told his detractors:

"I did not seek the post of Justice of the Supreme Court of the United States. That was not part of my life plan. I wrote the President by hand a letter, of which I have no copy, but I wrote it to him in longhand, after he first suggested that I accept the position. I wrote it to him in longhand, Senator, because I was not writing it for the record. I dislike being in the position of rejecting a call by the President of the United States to public service. He nevertheless, as is well known, insisted that I do this—that it was my duty to do it."[4]

Perhaps Fortas knew that the boldness and skill which had made him a highly successful advocate were not the qualities that contributed to greatness or to personal satisfaction on the Court. Perhaps Fortas knew that the $39,500 annual salary of an Associate Justice (it was raised to $60,000 in 1969) was not adequate to support the Rolls-Royce, the Georgetown mansion, the summer house in Westport, and the other material elements of the lifestyle to which he was accustomed.

Whatever the reasons, Fortas resigned from the Court and went back to the practice of law, although not to the Victorian mansion on Nineteenth Street occupied by Arnold & Porter, as the firm was known after Fortas went to the Court in 1965. Some of the newer partners in the old firm reportedly threatened to leave if Fortas came back, not so much because of the notoriety as because Fortas might take back some of the clients he had distributed among the junior members of the firm in 1965. Instead, Fortas organized a new firm, Fortas & Koven, that opened for business in a modernistic, glass-walled building in the Georgetown section of Washington.

Elsewhere in Washington, the resignation of Abe Fortas left behind waves of self-righteous indignation and of anger. There was much talk in the Judiciary and in Congress of ethics and conflicts of interest, as there always is after a Washington scandal, in whatever branch.[3] The Judicial branch hastily prepared to require all federal judges to disclose their sources of private income and senators were saying that, if the Judiciary did not act, Congress would force complete disclosure by judges—though not necessarily by members of Congress. In addition, some conservative Republicans in Congress wanted a congressional investigation to further probe the extra-judicial activities of Fortas and other members of the Judiciary. On the other hand, some liberal Democrats in Congress wanted a congressional investigation to determine whether the Nixon Administration, in pursuing its role in the Fortas affair and particularly by taking the case against Fortas to Chief Justice Warren, had violated the constitutional separation of powers doctrine.

In the end there were no congressional investigations. The liberal Democrats were too dejected and unnerved by Fortas's resignation to press for an investigation of the Nixon Administration's role. The conservative Republicans were willing to let Mitchell's Justice Department handle any further investigation of Mr. Fortas. Moreover, a number of leading Republicans and Democrats in Congress hesitated to pursue investigations which might ultimately damage the integrity of the Supreme Court. For its part, the Judiciary adopted rules under which the extra-judicial activities of judges would be screened, but the rules were not applied to Justices of the Supreme Court.

At the White House the resignation of Abe Fortas was not a matter for righteous indignation or anger. The President had no time for retrospection.

After the news of the resignation had broken on Thursday morning, May 15, the papers that afternoon and on Friday morning told the story of Fortas's fall in big, black headlines. The President read the papers, cleared his desk of other matters, and left the White House to spend the weekend at Camp David, the presidential retreat in the Catoctin Mountains in Maryland, north of Washington. He took with him his lists and Mitchell's files concerning the selection of the new Chief Justice and, over the weekend in quiet privacy, he went through the materials a last time and confirmed his decision. Satisfied that his choice was right, he telephoned John Mitchell. After they had again discussed their man and talked about the Senate and the Court, the President gave orders to move. Nixon told Mitchell to get in touch with J. Edgar Hoover and have the FBI run a quiet check on the nominee. The Bureau similarly investigates all men the President wants to name to high office, checking with his neighbors and employers, looking into his bank account, to make sure there is nothing hidden in the man's background that would embarrass the President. The FBI does not always find everything, but it tries.

On Monday morning Nixon again talked with Mitchell. By Wednesday morning the FBI check was completed and all was in order. At the President's direction, Attorney General Mitchell asked the nominee to come over to the Justice Department and at 12:30 that afternoon Mitchell informed him that the President had selected him to be the next Chief Justice. Until then no one except the three of them (Hoover probably did not know the position the man would occupy) knew of the selection. Nixon and Mitchell made their choice without confiding even in the top White House staff people. By Wednesday afternoon activity was underway all through the White House. Prime evening time on the national television networks was requested for the President. Nixon himself telephoned Herbert Brownell to tell his old friend of what was going to take place. The President told Mitchell to phone Chief Justice Warren, as a matter of courtesy. Tom Dewey was informed, by Mitchell or Brownell, or perhaps both. Mitchell also informed Vice President Agnew.

At 7 P.M. on Wednesday, May 21, 1969, one week almost to the hour after Abe Fortas's resignation was delivered to the White House, President Nixon went on national television and into the nation's living rooms to introduce Warren Earl Burger, the man he had chosen to succeed Earl Warren as Chief Justice. The President told the television audience that Burger was "superbly qualified" to be the next Chief Justice and, in reference to the headlines of a week earlier, added that Burger was above all a man of "unquestioned integrity." The sixty-one-year-old man who appeared beside the President on TV screens throughout the country looked rather like Earl Warren. Burger's hair was flowing white, his smile was pleasant, and his appearance was distinguished. The similarities ended there.

Nixon's nomination of Burger was no snap judgment, notwithstanding the President's quick movement after Fortas fell. In fact, Nixon had known Burger for twenty-one years, since 1948. And, rather ironically, Fortas also knew Burger.

Earl Warren and Richard Nixon were Republicans and Californians and they never had gotten on well together. Warren, twenty-two years Nixon's senior, already held high office in the state and the party in 1946 when Nixon entered politics as a candidate for the U.S. House of Representatives. Warren had been district attorney of Alameda County, attorney general of California, and in 1943 was elected governor of the state. In 1944 he was keynote speaker at the Republican National Convention. As governor, it was Warren's custom not to endorse Republican candidates and he refused his endorsement when Nixon ran for the House in 1946 and for the Senate in 1950.

In 1948, the fifty-seven-year-old governor of California was a Republican presidential hopeful and the thirty-five-year-old congressman from California was establishing his reputation as an alert fighter against alleged subversives in government. The political paths Nixon and Warren were pursuing, not harmoniously, were crossed by Warren Earl Burger, a forty-one-year-old lawyer from St. Paul, Minnesota. Burger was a leader in the St. Paul Junior Chamber of Commerce and an active member of the Republican Party in the state.

The three were brought together in 1948 by the Republican National Convention in Philadelphia. One of the contenders for the Republican nomination for President that year was Harold Stassen, who had first been elected governor of Minnesota in 1938. Burger was Stassen's floor manager at the 1948 convention. Nixon, by his own recollection, went to the convention as one of the "great Stassen men." But the convention nominated Thomas Dewey and Earl Warren. Herbert Brownell managed the GOP election campaign, which lost to Truman and Barkley.

In 1952 Nixon, Warren, and Burger came together again and the results were different. Nixon by 1952 was a member of the United States Senate from Calfornia, Earl Warren still was governor of Califorina, and Warren Burger still was out in Minnesota supporting Stassen. At the Republican National Convention held in Chicago, the leading contenders for the presidential nomination were Senator Robert A. Taft of Ohio, General Dwight D. Eisenhower, and Governor Warren. The Minnesota delegation came again supporting Stassen, and, again according to Nixon's recollection, Burger "helped to bring the Stassen delegation over to Eisenhower." When his bandwagon broke down in Chicago, Warren also supported Eisenhower. Eisenhower won the Republican nomination and Nixon, who, although pledged to Warren, apparently left the governor's bandwagon early, became the Vice-Presidential candidate.*

After Eisenhower was inaugurated in 1953, Earl Warren became Chief Justice and Warren Earl Burger was given a job in the Justice Department, as assistant attorney general in charge of the Department's Civil Division. Herbert Brownell was Eisenhower's Attorney General. Burger did a competent enough job in the Civil Division, but his star did not begin to ascend until one day when Attorney General Brownell needed help and Burger stepped out of ranks to offer his assistance. The Attorney General's problem grew out of a case that also interested the Vice President. Nixon had, and still has, a particular interest in government loyalty programs and internal security matters.

The case was that of John F. Peters. When it reached the Supreme Court, Warren Earl Burger was on one side and Abe Fortas was on the opposite side. Peters was a professor of medicine at Yale and a part-time consultant to the U.S. Public Health Service. He was paid by the government only for the ten or so days a year he was required to be in Washington and his work was not of a confidential nature that involved access to classified material. But in January, 1949, a govern-

---

*Nixon's role at the 1952 convention, relative to Earl Warren's candidacy, is discussed in John D. Weaver, *Warren: The Man, the Court, the Era* (Boston and Toronto: Little, Brown and Co., 1967) pp. 180–84.

ment Board of Inquiry on Employee Loyalty informed Peters that derogatory information concerning his loyalty had been received. Peters responded in writing and the Board of Inquiry informed him of its conclusion that there was no reasonable grounds for doubting his loyalty to the United States.

But in May, 1951, the Inquiry Board reopened the case, notifying Peters that sixteen charges were specified against him, alleging among other things membership in the U.S. Communist Party. The board in 1952 held a hearing and Peters again denied, under oath, the charges against him. Then the board, still without identifying Peters' accusers or the sources of its information against him, notified Peters that he was barred from federal service for three years. Peters sued the government, claiming that the board's action was arbitrary and unlawful and that the board had acted unconstitutionally by denying him the right to confront his accusers.

Attorney General Brownell's problem, when the case reached the Supreme Court, was that Solicitor General Simon E. Soberoff refused to sign the government's brief or argue the case before the Court. The Solicitor General and his staff normally argue the government's cases before the Supreme Court, except the few which the Attorney General decides to argue personally. But the loyalty program was controversial within the government, even then, and Soberoff apparently felt he could not support the government's position in the Peters case. Soberoff's refusal was potentially of great embarrassment to the Eisenhower Administration because the constitutional issues raised by Peters were substantial and the case was drawing wide attention.

The Administration was saved from embarrassment, however, by Warren E. Burger, who volunteered to sign the brief and argue the case. It is unclear whether Burger was motivated by sincere belief in the loyalty program or political ambition, or both. Abe Fortas' law firm undertook the defense of Peters, as it did Owen Lattimore and others who, during the McCarthy era, were accused of disloyalty. Fortas, among others, signed the briefs that were filed in the Supreme Court in defense of Peters. Fortas's law partners, Thurman Arnold and Paul Porter, conducted the oral argument before the Court.

The Supreme Court decided the case in 1955 without reaching the constitutional issues. The Court's opinion, written by Chief Justice Warren, held that the Board of Inquiry had exceeded its lawful authority in barring Peters from federal employment, and on that basis its order against Peters was unlawful. The Court also ordered the board's findings against Peters expunged from government records.[6]

If Burger did not win the case for the government, he at least did not lose it. Had the Court decided the case on constitutional grounds, the decision could have had serious effects on the entire federal security program. The following year, a vacancy occurred on the U.S. Circuit Court of Appeals for the District of Columbia and the Eisenhower Administration showed its gratitude to Warren Burger by naming him to the position. In the fourteen years Burger sat on the Court of Appeals in Washington, Nixon saw him "off and on," as President Nixon recalled after nominating Burger as Chief Justice. They also corresponded. "In fact, I wrote him when I thought he made a good speech a couple of years ago," President Nixon said.

In his fourteen years on the bench, Burger acquired a reputation as a conservative judge who frequently dissented from the majority decisions of the District of Columbia Circuit Court, which was dominated by liberal judges. He placed a high priority on an orderly society and was impatient with what he felt was excessive judicial concern with the rights of individuals accused of crimes. He felt that courts should leave the country's major social and educational problems to the legislative and executive branches of government, but he did not hesitate to be critical of "big government" and to uphold the right of individuals to have their say before federal regulatory agencies.

Off the bench, Burger took an active part in American Bar Association activities and particularly in the association's programs dealing with reform of court procedures. He also made an increasing number of speeches which in time marked him as one of the judiciary's most outspoken critics of the Warren Court. Burger, as a judge, did not speak as caustically of the Warren Court as did Nixon. Yet Burger and Nixon often seemed to be saying much the same things about the Supreme Court and both were aroused mainly by its criminal rights decisions.

For example, in September, 1968, at a time when the Supreme Court was deeply involved in political controversy because of President Johnson's nomination of Fortas to be Chief Justice, Burger delivered a blistering speech that attracted the attention of Nixon, then the GOP candidate for President. "Over these past dozen years," Judge Burger declared, "the Supreme Court has been revising the code of criminal procedure and evidence 'piecemeal' on a case-by-case basis, on inadequate records and incomplete factual data. I suggest that a large measure of responsibility for some of the bitterness in American life today over the administration of criminal justice can fairly be laid to the Supreme Court. To put this in simple terms, the Supreme Court helped make the problems we now have." Burger spoke of the Warren Court's "almost undignified haste to clothe detailed rules of evidence and police station procedure in the garb of constitutional doctrine." He also commented in the speech that "too many law professors for a long time gave uncritical applause to anything they could identify as an expansion of individual 'rights,' even when that expansion was at the expense of the rights of innocent citizens."[7]

In a circuit court opinion more recent than the speech, Judge Burger declared: "The seeming anxiety of judges to protect every accused person from every consequence of his voluntary utterances (in a police station) is giving rise to myriad rules. We are approaching the predicament of the centipede on the flypaper—each time one leg is placed to give support for relief of the leg already 'stuck,' another becomes captive and soon all are securely immobilized."[8] The very basic contrast between the philosophies of Earl Warren and Warren Burger, concerning the role of the Supreme Court in the federal system, was vividly demonstrated in connection with the lawsuit in which Adam Clayton Powell challenged the constitutionality of his exclusion from the House of Representatives. A federal district court dismissed the suit. The Court of Appeals for the District of Columbia affirmed the dismissal. The appellate court's opinion, written by Judge Burger, held that courts should not decide such "political" questions. A ruling in Powell's favor, Burger wrote, "would inevitably bring about a direct confrontation with a co-equal branch and if that did not indicate a lack of respect due to that branch, it would be a gesture hardly comporting with our view of separate branches of the federal establishment." Anyway, Burger added, "That each branch may occasionally make errors for which there may be no effective remedy is one of the prices we pay for independence.[9] When the Supreme Court reversed the decision authored by Burger, Chief Justice Warren, without fear of the consequences of confronting another branch, held that "the Constitution does not vest in the Congress a discretionary power to deny membership by a majority vote."[10]

Burger was the kind of man President Nixon was looking for to be the next Chief Justice. When Nixon and Mitchell, soon after they took office in January, 1969, decided that Nixon could not nominate a close personal friend, Burger became a leading candidate on their list. They reread his opinions and speeches and took a closer look by inviting Burger to come to the White House for an apparently routine swearing in of a group of lower-level Administration officials. That was in February. Two months later they looked closer by inviting Judge and Mrs. Burger back to the White House to attend a dinner which also was attended by such old friends as Herbert Brownell and Thomas Dewey.[11]

Burger passed all the tests. He probably was not the man Nixon most would have liked to name Chief Justice, had Nixon felt entirely free to exercise his personal or political choice. He was a compromise in the sense that he was the man whose conservative philosophy was most like that of President Nixon and at the same time he was least vulnerable to attacks of Senate liberals. Burger could not be accused of not wanting the job, or of being a crony of the President, as Fortas had been a crony of Johnson. His Republican background, his conservative judicial philosophy, and his attacks on the Warren Court were matters of public record. But philosophy and speeches are not easily attacked in a Senate confirmation hearing; the headlines and popular support that opponents of a nominee must generate are much better made of dramatic instances of bad conduct or poor judgment. Burger might be vulnerable if liberals could mine useful specifics out of the opinions he had written as a circuit court judge. But while the liberals might find some nuggets of potential usefulness, they probably could not locate a rich vein, because the District of Columbia circuit court on which Burger sat gets relatively few civil rights, labor, or other such cases involving issues that stir liberal passions. So Burger could not be accused by the liberals of being anti-Negro or anti-union. He could be accused of being against the Warren Court, but that issue belonged not to the liberals but to Nixon.

President Nixon and Attorney General Mitchell had all but decided privately that Burger was their man to be Chief Justice when the Fortas affair burst. Even so, the President either had not recognized how totally the Fortas matter had decimated the liberals, or he decided out of extreme caution to take no chances. Whichever the reason, the Administration made elaborate efforts to smooth the way for Burger's confirmation. After introducing the nominee on national television, the President took an additional extraordinary step to generate popular and press support for Burger. On May 22, 1969, the day after the television appearance, Nixon called reporters into his office and, in a lengthy, on-the-record briefing, offered what for any President was a unique explanation of how and why the nominee was selected.[12]

"We have never done this before," the President began. "Some of you, I am sure, will find that this does not have immediate news impact. It is more color and background."

Nixon reminded the reporters that, "before the Inauguration, I knew that I would have this decision to make. Let me begin by trying to spell out the processes that I went through in making the decision."

Nixon explained the nature of the Chief Justiceship and his understanding of it. "Because of the Fortas matter," he said, "I determined that the appointee should not be a personal friend." He sought a man who would be confirmed "without violent controversy, but a strong vote of approval." During the campaign, he recalled, "I set forth my philosophy. I think I used the term strict constructionist. I happen to believe that the Constitution should be strictly interpreted." Using the late Justice Frankfurter as exemplar of the qualities he sought, Nixon said he wanted a Chief Justice who would feel that "it was his responsibility to interpret the Constitution, and it was the right of the Congress to write the laws and have great leeway to write those laws, and he should be very conservative in overthrowing a law passed by the elected representatives at the state or federal level."

Nixon explained that he had passed over Brownell, Mitchell, Dewey, and others who were his personal or political friends. And he said that he had selected Burger on the basis of "my study of his opinions and my knowledge of his views" which, Nixon frankly said, "indicate that we happen to share many views."

The President did not mention Burger's role in the Peters case or other elements of their earlier careers.

In addition to his meeting with the press, Nixon made plans to marshal the organized bar on behalf of the Burger nomination. Dozens of current and past presidents of the American Bar Association, the Federal Bar Association, and other bar associations inundated the Senate Judiciary Committee with letters and telegrams in support of the nominee.

Meanwhile on Capitol Hill, during the week that elapsed between the resignation of Fortas and the nomination of Burger, many members of the United States Senate, mindful of how close Fortas had come to being the Chief Justice, were saying publicly that henceforth the Senate must give long and careful consideration to anyone any President nominated to sit on the Supreme Court. But the consideration they gave to the nomination of Warren Burger was not long or careful.

The Judiciary Committee took up the Burger nomination on June 3.[13] It convened at 10:35 A.M. and was finished at 12:20 P.M. The conservative and the liberal members of the committee were fully aware of Burger's speeches and writings. Burger was there to answer the senators' questions, but there were almost none. The conservatives made reference to his speeches and writings for the purpose of expressing their approval. Senator Strom Thurmond of South Carolina, for instance, said in his soft Southern drawl, "I congratulate you and President Nixon upon your selection as Chief Justice." Senator Sam Ervin of North Carolina expressed his belief that "we are very fortunate in having one who has manifested his devotion to the Constitution and to the law." Among the liberals, Senator Edward Kennedy of Massachusetts had "no questions;" Senator Birch Bayh of Indiana asked no questions; Senator Joseph Tydings of Maryland engaged the nominee in a brief bit of pleasant conversation about court administration. Then the committee unanimously voted to recommend confirmation of Burger.

The nomination was called up on the Senate floor on June 9 and the nomination was confirmed by a vote of 74 to 3. The three dissenting senators were Eugene McCarthy of Minnesota, Stephen Young of Ohio, and Gaylord Nelson of Wisconsin—independent-minded Democratic liberals in the extreme.

The speed and near unanimity with which the Senate confirmed Burger were astonishing. The Senate had considered Earl Warren's nomination for five months before confirming him. It had considered Abe Fortas's nomination to be Chief Justice for longer than three months before rejecting him. It confirmed the Burger nomination in eighteen days.

In view of what went before and what came after the nomination of Warren Earl Burger, the story of his confirmation was an aberration in the larger story of the struggle for control of the Supreme Court. The speed with which the Senate moved and the very lopsided vote by which it confirmed the new Chief Justice can be attributed only to the Fortas affair and the state of voicelessness and impotence in which it left the liberals. The decline and fall of Abe Fortas, particularly at this time and place in the Supreme Court's history, was, then, much more than a personal tragedy.

# CHAPTER 9

# Nixon Scores in Court

Politics is a slippery, treacherous business. The President one day is hailed by almost all as a hero and the next he is pummeled with criticism by some and with revolutionary obscenities by others. He reads the newspapers or watches television, he ponders the latest findings of his favorite public opinion poll, and he listens to his chosen advisers. But the view from the White House is distant. The moods of the country are as many, as complex, and as changeable as the colors in a child's kaleidoscope. The voters seem fickle and those who sit in Congress constantly turn in hot pursuit of the voters. Sometimes, by the time the President sees beyond the iron fences and guardhouses that surround the White House, it is too late. It was too late for Lyndon Johnson. Richard Nixon of all people should have known the uncertain nature of the business, inasmuch as his political career had been a slippery roller coaster ride, up to the Vice Presidency in 1952, down to defeat when he ran for the Presidency in 1960, down deeper when the voters of California refused even to elect him governor in 1962, and then way back up into the White House in 1968. But President Nixon in his hero days either forgot or chose not to remember.

Because Nixon in his 1968 campaign had made the Warren Court one of the issues that carried him into the White House, the speed and decisiveness with which he won Senate confirmation of his choice of Earl Warren's successor was taken inside the White House and outside also as a major victory for the new President, gained after less than five months in office. The hero decided he would take full advantage of his triumph.

Earl Warren had agreed with Nixon the previous winter that he would retire as Chief Justice when the Court finished the work of its current term. After the Senate confirmed Warren Burger on June 9, Chief Justice Warren and his seven remaining brothers of the Court sat another Monday morning to hand down decisions on the remaining cases they had heard and they fixed June 23, 1969, as the final day of the term. A few minutes before ten o'clock on that Monday morning, Chief Justice Warren left his office and for the last time walked the few steps to the oak-paneled room to the rear of the marble courtroom where the Justices put on their robes before they step through the velvet curtains. At almost the same minute Richard Nixon left his oval office at the White House, stepped into a black limousine, and was driven along the route to the Supreme Court that his Attorney General, on another mission to the Chief Justice, had taken but seven weeks earlier.

The route between the White House and Capitol Hill, where both Congress and the Supreme Court sit, is a symbolic pavement. It has been travelled by innumerable presidential inaugural parades, military processions, and other trimphant marches, and, in more recent years, by massive protest demonstrations. Nixon was not the first President to ride from the White House to the Supreme Court and, as when other Presidents had made this particular journey, there were no crowds and there was no fanfare. Nevertheless, President Nixon's triumphal ride was a historic occasion.

There are strict constructionists who believe that democracy is best served when there is no social or political intercourse among the executive, legislative and judicial branches, and no personal communication between individual members of the three branches, that would create the opportunity for undue influence or the appearance of control by one branch of another. Throughout the turmoil over Earl Warren's successor, lip service was paid to the separation of powers doctrine as written by the Founding Fathers. For instance, there were the conservative senators who, in filibustering to death President Johnson's nomination of Abe Fortas in 1968, had argued that Fortas should not be Chief Justice because his closeness to Johnson might allow the executive branch to influence the judiciary. Then, only a few weeks before there were the liberal senators who wanted a Senate investigation to determine whether Attorney General Mitchell's mission to Chief Justice Warren, to lay before him additional information concerning Fortas and Wolfson, constituted a violation of the separation of powers doctrine. For his part, President Nixon also seemed in complete agreement with the Founding Fathers. The President, in the course of his extraordinary meeting with the press after he had announced the Burger nomination, said to reporters of Warren Burger: "While . . . we happen to share many views, I think it is vitally important that the Chief Justice and all Judges of the Supreme Court know that they are absolutely independent of the executive and legislative" branches.[1]

There have been times in history, most notably during the eras of the Warren and the Marshall Courts, when the strict constructionist view prevailed. The President and members of the Supreme Court came together at presidential inaugurations and thereafter intercourse was limited largely to state funerals and dinners. But, the Founding Fathers notwithstanding, the separation of powers doctrine, like all the other great principles set forth in the Constitution, takes its contemporary meaning from what men say and do.

There have been throughout history and, despite the Fortas debacle, there will be in the future instances of continuing private communication between a President and an individual member of the Supreme Court. Chief Justice Ellsworth in 1800 gave his resignation to his friend President Adams. President Lincoln in 1862 named to the Court David Davis, a personal and political crony who did not become a great Justice and who retained a close personal relationship with the Lincoln family. William Howard Taft, after he had served as President, was named Chief Justice by President Harding in 1921, and Taft thereafter maintained an active relationship with the White House. President Franklin Roosevelt and Felix Frankfurter, whom Roosevelt appointed to the Court in 1939, maintained a remarkably personal correspondence, which seems to have been inspired more by the Justice's almost fawning admiration of the President than by Roosevelt's initiative.[2]

At various times of national crisis or acute persidential need, Presidents also have called upon individual members of the Court to perform public services that have no relationship with the constitutional role of the Court but, paradoxically, have much to do with the public image of the Court as an independent and honorable institution. Franklin Roosevelt summoned Chief Justice Harlan Fiske Stone to assess responsibility for the unpreparedness of American military forces when the Japanese attacked Pearl Harbor in 1941. After World War II, President Truman designated Associate Justice Robert H. Jackson as chief prosecutor at the Nuremberg trials of Nazi war criminals. And after John Kennedy was assassinated in Dallas in 1963, President Johnson prevailed upon Chief Justice Warren to chair the commission which was to investigate the murder and still the rumors and fears that were sweeping the nation.

Various students of the law have criticized each of the various known instances in history of private and public intercourse between Presidents and individual members of the Supreme Court, and certainly some of the members of the Court have engaged in such political entanglements with great reluctance.* Whether such relationships with the President in fact have a compromising effect on the Court would seem to depend on the men and the circumstances. The public can never know the whole truth, but clearly all such relationships are not wholly innocent. Disclosures made after his death revealed that Chief Justice Taft maintained active relationships with certain members of Congress as well as with President Harding and that Taft obtained not only legislation affecting the judiciary but also the nominations of several new Justices he wanted on the Court. Taft's political involvement therefore had some effects on the institutional independence of the Court. Since no other member in recent history has brought to the Court the political experience that Taft carried with him, presumably none has had similar opportunity for involvement with the executive and legislative branches. In any event, each of the affairs has been a unique, personal relationship between a President and a Justice, and, so far as the Supreme Court as an institution is concerned, no President yet has been able to pack the Court with his cronies. Moveover, the relationships by their nature are passing affairs, because Presidents go and the Justices they appointed remain.

There is also, of course, the kind of intercourse between the President and the Supreme Court that takes place in public and involves the Court as a whole. But hard-line strict constructionists take offense, nonetheless. At one end of the spectrum of such encounters are state dinners and funerals. At the other are overt, widely publicized presi-

*Warren reportedly refused to preside over an investigation of the Kennedy assassination, when first asked. He agreed after Johnson personally insisted that it was Warren's patriotic duty to undertake the investigation. Weaver, *Warren*, p. 302.

dential attacks on the Court. Fortunately, Presidents have not often found it expedient or necessary, as Franklin Roosevelt and Richard Nixon did, to influence the Court to the extent of mustering popular opinion against it. But, as those two proved, a President can be highly effective when he addresses the Court from the stump, the lectern, or the television tube.

Strict constructionism notwithstanding, in rather recent years the President and the Court have come together in public settings that fall somewhere between the extremes of state dinners and funerals, on one hand, and publicized harangues, on the other. For example, all the members of the Supreme Court, dressed in their black robes, have become dependable, front-row attendants in the House chamber of the Capitol when the President delivers his annual State of the Union address to Congress and to a prime-time evening television audience.* In modern times, Presidents have come to the Supreme Court to see one or more of their nominees sworn in. President Truman started the practice, and it was followed by Presidents Eisenhower, Kennedy, and Johnson. Since there is no television in the Court's chamber, each President came quietly, sat amidst the other spectators, and quietly left, but each felt the trip worthwhile.

When Richard Nixon stepped out of his limousine at the Supreme Court building and made his way into the chamber, he made the trip more worthwhile still by becoming the first President in American history to stand before the long mahogany bench and address the Supreme Court.

It was a historic day. Until Richard Nixon, no President since Franklin Roosevelt had entered the White House to face a Supreme Court which he regarded as hostile. Roosevelt, after he entered the White House in 1933, had had to wait four years until the first Court vacancy occurred for him to fill, and in those years his only recourse was to bear down on the Court's majority with all the influence that fireside chats and court packing proposals could contain.³ Roosevelt had had to wait eight years to name a Chief Justice. Nixon not only

*Radio and television have helped to bring the three branches of the government together, it would seem. For a century before the Administration of Franklin D. Roosevelt, most Presidents did not appear before Congress but instead sent their messages to be read for them. Roosevelt began the modern practice of appearing before both houses of Congress in joint session to deliver his messages, which were broadcast.

had the opportunity to name a new Chief Justice awaiting him when he first entered the White House, but after a mere five months in office he had a second vacancy awaiting his pleasure.

Nixon sat quietly for seventeen minutes as the Warren Court announced its final decisions, and then Chief Justice Warren recognized the President. Nixon rose and stepped to the lectern from which all lawyers address the Court. It stands facing the mahogany bench, immediately in front of the center chair occupied by the Chief Justice.

"Mr. Chief Justice, may it please the Court," the President began.

In addressing Earl Warren, the seven Associate Justices, and the empty ninth seat, President Nixon did not crow triumphantly. Now he had no need to bear down on a hostile majority. To the contrary, he acknowledged the separation of powers doctrine and paid homage to appearances by stating that he was addressing the Court not as President of the United States but as a lawyer who some years before had been admitted, like thousands of others, to practice before the Supreme Court and indeed, on two occasions in 1966, had stood at this very lectern to argue cases before the Court. Nixon with calm and dignity then delivered a six-minute oration in honor of the departing Chief Justice, Earl Warren.

"Looking back" on those two occasions in 1966, at a time when Nixon was a lawyer in private practice in New York, "I can say, Mr. Chief Justice, that there is only one ordeal which is more challenging than a presidential press conference and that is to appear before the Supreme Court of the United States." He had come, Nixon said, to extend to Earl Warren "the best wishes of the Bar and the Nation for the time ahead."

Warren had held positions in local, state, and national government for fifty-two years and "the Nation is grateful for that service." Throughout those years, Nixon declared, Earl Warren embraced "humanity," in "the dedication to his family, his personal family, to the great American family, to the family of man. The Nation is grateful for that example of humanity which the Chief Justice has given to us and to the world.

"These sixteen years," in which Earl Warren sat as Chief Justice, "without doubt, will be described by historians as years of greater change in America than any in our history." But with change there also must be continuity, the President said. "To the Chief Justice of the United States, all of us are grateful today that his example, the example of dignity, the example of integrity, the example of fairness, as the chief law official of this country, has helped to keep America on the path of continuity and change, which is so essential for our progress."

Nixon had neither lauded strict constructionism nor damned judicial activism. He had mentioned none of the things he had told the press in explaining his selection of Warren Burger to succeed Earl Warren. There was no rancor and only the slightest reminder that there had been a partisan political fight the year before over Warren's successor. There was in the Court, as Nixon spoke, the same air of momentary conciliation that pervades presidential inaugurations.

But in Chief Justice Warren's reply to the President, who remained standing a dozen feet away as Warren sat, there was a reminder to Nixon and to the nation of the role of the Court in a constitutional government. Calmly but pointedly, Warren defended the Warren Court:

> Mr. President, your words are most generous and are greatly appreciated, I assure you. I accept your personal, kind words, but in doing so I must confess that I sense in your presence here and in the words you have spoken your great appreciation of the value of this Court in the life of our Nation and the fact that it is one of the three co-ordinate branches of the government and that it is a continuing body.
>
> I might point out to you, because you might not have looked into the matter, that it is a continuing body to the extent that if any American at any time in the history of the Court—one hundred eighty years —had come to this Court he would have found one of seven men on the Court, the last of whom, of course, is our Senior Justice, Mr. Justice Black. Because at any time an American might come here he would find one of seven men on the bench in itself shows how continuing this body is and how it is that the Court develops consistently the eternal principles of our Constitution in solving the problems of the day.
>
> We, of course, venerate the past, but our focus is on the problems of the day and of the future as far as we can foresee it.
>
> I cannot escape the feeling that in one sense, at least, this Court is similar to your own great office and that is that so many times it speaks the last word in great governmental affairs. The responsibility of speaking the last word for not only two hundred million people, but for those to follow us is a very awesome responsibility.

It is a responsibility that is made more difficult in this Court because we have no constituency. We serve no majority. We serve no minority. We serve only the public interest as we see it, guided only by the Constitution and our own consciences. And conscience sometimes is a very severe taskmaster.

But the Court through all the years has pursued a more or less steady course, and in my opinion has progressed and has applied the principles set forth in those five thousand general words of the Constitution in a manner that is consistent with the public interest and consistent with our future so far as it can be discerned.

We do not always agree. I hope the Court will never agree on all things. If it ever agrees on all things, I am sure that its virility will have been sapped because it is composed of nine independent men who have no one to be responsible to except their own consciences.

It is not likely ever, with human nature as it is, for nine men to agree always on the most important and controversial things of life. If it ever comes to such a pass, I would say that the Court will have lost its strength and will no longer be a real force in the affairs of our country. But so long as it is manned by men like those who have preceded us and by others like those who sit today, I have no fear of that ever happening.

I am happy today to leave the service of my country with a feeling of deep friendship for all these men whom I have served with for sixteen years, in spite of the fact that we have disagreed on many occasions. In the last analysis, the fact we have often disagreed is not of great importance. The important thing is that every man will have given his best thought and consideration to the great problems that have confronted us.

Warren, looking straight into Nixon's eyes, thus tried to warn the President, "because you might not have looked into the matter," of the grave danger which can confront the nation when the Supreme Court is shorn of its constitutional independence, its continuity, and its essential conscience. Warren's words, spoken without a show of emotion toward the man whom he had known for so long and who still was not a friend, will be quoted years hence as a classic defense of the independence of the Supreme Court.

Perhaps such words invariably are not heard by the ears for which they are intended. But the truth of Warren's statement was so fundamental, and the conflict between majoritarian rule and individual rights was so basically a part of the American fabric, that Chief Justice Marshall one hundred forty-five years earlier answered his critics with an opinion that serves equally well as an answer to Richard Nixon and like purveyors of presidential power.

The Constitution, Marshall wrote, "contains an enumeration of powers expressly granted by the people to their government. It has been said that these powers ought to be construed strictly. But why? Is there one sentence in the Constitution which gives countenance to this rule?"

There is not "one sentence in the Constitution that prescribes this rule," Marshall answered. "What do gentlemen mean, by a strict construction? If they contend for that narrow construction which would deny to government those powers which the words of the grant import, which would cripple the government and render it unequal to the objects for which it is declared to be instituted, then we cannot perceive the propriety of this strict construction.

"As men, whose intentions require no concealment, generally employ the words which most directly and aptly express the ideas they intend to convey, the enlightened patriots who framed our Constitution must be understood to have employed words in their natural sense, and to have intended what they have said."[4]

After President Nixon had addressed the Court and Chief Justice Warren had responded to him, Warren administered the oath to his successor, Warren E. Burger. And thus did Earl Warren retire on June 23, 1969.

After that day Warren thought he might go home to retire, leaving behind the recent turmoil in Washington. He did return to California, and there were reports in Washington that he and Mrs. Warren were looking for a house in Sacramento. But he decided to come back to Washington, where he and Mrs. Warren stayed, living where they had lived for sixteen years, in an apartment suite at the rambling old Sheraton-Park Hotel just off Connecticut Avenue. As the weeks and months passed, the former Chief Justice took on more speaking engagements and his speeches were not in a happy vein. He refused to comment directly on the President or the Court he had left, but he said, "We have just gone through a great national campaign in which the major issue announced was 'law and order.' The entire campaign was one of harsh rhetoric and a search for scapegoats."[5] On another occasion he said, "Still 102 years after the Fourteenth Amendment was adopted, we find that hundreds of thousands of black children are denied equal opportunities of education; like numbers of adults are denied the privilege of voting; litigants, witnesses and jurors are deliberately humiliated in courtrooms; people are denied the right to live wherever they choose; and a myriad of other indignities are imposed on millions merely because of their color."⁶ And on a third occasion he said, "There has been a great upsurge of demand for liberty everywhere. But the very demand of those who have suffered oppression through the ages has also triggered activities of repression."⁷

It could not be doubted that Earl Warren's retirement day of rapprochement with Richard Nixon had quickly passed, and in time it was said among Warren's friends that the former Chief Justice's feelings had turned to bitterness.

President Nixon on that day returned in his limousine to the White House and did nothing for nearly two months about the vacancy Fortas had left on the Court. There was no reason to hurry, and there were no elaborate preparations to be made this time. The Court was adjourned until the first Monday in October, and the President had until then to run through the motions of nomination and confirmation of his man to fill the ninth seat. Nixon and Mitchell had fixed their standards for selecting Court nominees when they had selected Chief Justice Burger; the selection process had been unnecessarily laborious but highly successful and certainly need not be repeated now. As the President had explained to the press in May, by his standards no cronies would be appointed to the Court; his nominees would be picked from among sitting federal judges "who have proved themselves on the line of battle, on the firing line, to be capable, able Judges who have a track record"; they would go through no "political clearance process"; and they would be selected for their "competence . . . representing all segments of the country" and not because they are representatives of any "racial, religious or geographical" segment of the nation.⁸

But as Nixon and Mitchell approached the vacant ninth seat, they did insist on a nominee who was a representative of a particular geographic and racial segment of the nation—the white South—and in so doing they utilized a particular kind of political clearance process. As it unfolded, their effort to fill the seat was marked with an especial irony. For their success in replacing Earl Warren, flowing in large part from the Fortas debacle, made Nixon and Mitchell bold. Unwilling to give Fortas his due, however, the bolder they became the more they fumbled.

The President waited until August 18 to send to the Senate a nomination to fill the Fortas vacancy, even though Nixon and Mitchell apparently had decided on their choice in May, before the Fortas seat had cooled.[9] Completely in contrast with the elaborate security measures Nixon and Mitchell took in connection with the Burger nomination, the identity of their new nominee became common knowledge around Washington, so much so that opposition began to sprout weeks before it was announced. But neither the prior public knowledge nor the budding opposition bothered the President as, on August 18, 1969, he casually announced from his vacation home in San Clemente, California, the nomination of Clement F. Haynsworth, Jr., to be Associate Justice of the Supreme Court.

CHAPTER 10

# Nixon Fumbles

The senior senator from South Carolina, Strom Thurmond, a Republican, introduced Clement Haynsworth to the Senate Judiciary Committee with the oratorical assurance that "he is a gentleman . . . a scholar." The junior senator from South Carolina, Ernest F. Hollings, a Democrat but no less enthusiastic for all that, declared in his introduction that Haynsworth would be "a brilliant addition to the Court."

Clement F. Haynsworth, Jr., age fifty-seven, was a gentleman of the Old South who smilingly looked at the members of the Judiciary Committee from behind rimless spectacles and spoke softly and courteously even to the most disagreeably liberal of the senators. He was an erect, old-family pillar of the white social and business establishment of the city of Greenville, South Carolina (pop. 58,161), a textile manufacturing center in the newly industrializing South. Greenville was the city where he had been born, where he lived, and where surely he would be buried. Four generations of Haynsworths, lawyers and South Carolinians all, had preceded him. He had gone to school in Georgia, come home to attend Furman University in Greenville, and then went north to Cambridge to get a law degree from Harvard University. After Harvard he followed his father and his grandfather into the Greenville law firm of Haynsworth, Perry, Bryant, Marion and Johnstone, which was said to be the largest law firm in South Carolina. He was wealthy and he once had been a Democrat, like his forefathers, but he supported Dwight Eisenhower for the presidency in 1952 and 1956, and in 1957 President Eisenhower appointed him to the U. S. Fourth Circuit Court of Appeals. The Fourth Circuit is based at Richmond, Virginia, and it covers the states of Maryland, North Carolina, South Carolina, Virginia, and West Virginia.

(In the small world of national politics, it happened that President Eisenhower also had promoted to the Fourth Circuit Simon E. Sobeloff, after Sobeloff as Solicitor General had refused, and Warren E. Burger had agreed, to sign the government's brief in the Peters case. So Haynsworth and Sobeloff for longer than a decade had sat together on the Fourth Circuit.)

The selection of Clement Haynsworth to replace Abe Fortas demonstrated the strength of President Nixon's determination to gain control of the Court and turn it rightward. Emboldened by the substantial majority by which the Senate had confirmed Burger, Nixon nominated Haynsworth with the dual purposes of bringing a strict constructionist to the Court and paying off a campaign debt to the South. But, as Nixon and Mitchell failed to realize, when they nominated Burger, how completely the Fortas affair had devastated the liberals, now they failed to recognize that the Fortas matter was past and the liberals were again prepared to fight.

Nixon had known of Haynsworth, but the President did not know him nearly so well as Senators Thurmond and Hollings knew him. Strom Thurmond had played a significant Southern role in Nixon's 1968 presidential campaign.[1] Thurmond, who had been the States' Rights, or "Dixiecrat," candidate for the presidency in 1948 and had carried four Southern states, once had been a Democrat, but he switched to the Republican Party in 1964. Hollings was younger and still a Democrat. They both recommended Haynsworth to Nixon for the Fortas vacancy on the Supreme Court. Judge Haynsworth's record on the Fourth Circuit was one "which no fair and just and honorable man should oppose," said Thurmond. "Judge Haynsworth will give balance where balance is needed," said Hollings.

Nixon and Mitchell read Judge Haynsworth's record and they wholeheartedly agreed. Many school desegregation and other racial issues of course had come before the Fourth Circuit in the years after the Warren Court in 1954 held the "separate but equal" doctrine unconstitutional, and Haynsworth had a long track record that placed him far to the right of the Warren Court majority. He was no rednecked racist. He was a conservative, a strict constructionist, and a representative of the South who would give balance to the Supreme Court where, in the eyes of President Nixon and the white South, balance for so long had been so much needed.

By August 18, when the President announced the Haynsworth nomination, many others in Washington, liberals and conservatives, also had read Judge Haynsworth's opinions on the Fourth Circuit. The National Association for the Advancement of Colored People announced that it found his record "one of resistance to the movement for racial equality." Other liberal groups, including the American Jewish Committee, the American Federation of Labor-Congress of Industrial Organizations, and Americans for Democratic Action, also had found reason to object.

Nixon, vacationing in California, was not dissuaded from making the nomination, and among political experts who remained in hot, muggy Washington in mid-August of 1969, the nomination seemed reasonably certain to win Senate confirmation. But, unfortunately for Haynsworth's admirers, the start of confirmation hearings before the Senate Judiciary Committee was further delayed by the death of Senator Everett McKinley Dirksen, and liberals put the additional time to good use by digging deeper into the record of Judge Haynsworth.

When the Senate hearings finally got under way on September 16, only three weeks remained before Chief Justice Burger would open the Supreme Court's new term. Senator Eastland of Mississippi, chairman of the Judiciary Committee, gaveled the hearings to a start and, after the introductions by Senators Thurmond and Hollings, Eastland dispensed with further pleasantries and proceeded directly into a prepared defense of Judge Haynsworth.

The committee proceeded directly into combat because organized labor, Negro groups, and other liberal organizations already had begun to air their charges against Haynsworth in the press and on the Senate floor. In the Senate the leadership of the opposition fell to Birch Bayh, the junior Democratic senator from Indiana, largely because he was a liberal, he was friendly with labor leaders, and he was politically ambitious. He also was the most available senator among the liberal Democrats on the Senate Judiciary Committee. Among the other liberals on the committee, Senator Edward M. Kennedy of Massachusetts could not undertake the assignment because of personal problems; on the previous July 18, a car driven by Senator Kennedy had plunged off a bridge into a tidal pool on Chappaquiddick Island, Massachusetts, and the body of Mary Jo Kopechne was later found in the car. Senator Joseph D. Tydings of Maryland might have led the opposition, but he was busy with a reelection campaign. Senator Philip A. Hart of Michigan was liberal enough, but perhaps not sufficiently ambitious or tenacious to tangle with Nixon. So Senator Bayh, a handsome, ambitious, forty-one-year-old lawyer, was the logical choice to head up the opposition to Haynsworth.

Under questioning by Senator Bayh, it quickly became apparent that Judge Haynsworth was indeed a man of substantial wealth, an investor in common and preferred stocks in some forty large and small corporations, an owner of convertible debentures and tax-exempt bonds. Wealth alone, of course, does not disqualify any man for high public office, including the offices of federal judge and Supreme Court Justice, and the liberals had had to dig much deeper. What they had come up with did not concern any of Haynsworth's investments in large, national corporations but the relatively small sum of $3,000 he had invested in a one-seventh interest in Carolina Vend-A-Matic Company, a private corporation organized in 1950 by Haynsworth and a small group of Greenville friends to enter the business of operating automatic coffee vending machines in bus stations, textile mills, and the like.[2] The business grew quite rapidly as new mills and other industrial plants came to South Carolina, and Carolina Vend-A-Matic expanded with machines that dispensed many kinds of food products. In fact, Carolina Vend-A-Matic grew so rapidly that in 1964 when it was acquired by a larger company, Automatic Retailers of America, Incorporated, Haynsworth received for his one-seventh interest in Vend-A-Matic 14,173 shares in ARA which he sold for $437,000.[3] Some of those details of the judge's wise $3,000 investment were drawn from him by liberal members of the Judiciary Committee, but it was not simply the money on which liberals built their case.

Rather, the liberals were able to show that Haynsworth, after he became a judge in 1957, remained a vice president and director of Carolina Vend-A-Matic until 1963, and therefore to allege that maybe his interest in the company indirectly influenced certain decisions he made as a member of the Fourth Circuit Court of Appeals.

When Haynsworth went on the bench in 1957, he resigned as director of a number of corporations because, he told the Judiciary Committee, "somebody might attempt to influence what I did as a judge by trying to throw business or favors to a concern of which I was a director." But he didn't then resign from Carolina Vend-A-Matic because it was so "small." He related that he resigned in 1963 when

the Judicial Conference of the United States, a representative conference of federal judges, took official note of the fact that many judges
were on the boards of directors of banks and other enterprises and
recommended that no judge remain an officer or director of a profit-
making enterprise.[4]

The litigation on which liberals hung their allegation against
Haynsworth had begun in 1956. The Textile Workers Union that year
won an election to represent workers at Darlington Manufacturing
Company, which operated a textile mill at Darlington, South
Carolina. The company closed its plant, and the union filed an unfair
labor practice charge with the National Labor Relations Board. The
NLRB found that the Darlington company and Deering-Milliken,
Incorporated, a larger textile maker which owned 40 per cent of
Darlington's stock, had committed an unfair labor practice and or-
dered that Darlington's employes receive back pay or preference in
obtaining jobs at other Deering-Milliken plants. The Fourth Circuit
Court of Appeals, with Judge Haynsworth concurring, rejected the
NLRB decision and held that Darlington had unqualified right to
close down its only plant. The case then climbed to the Supreme
Court, which in 1965 vacated the Fourth Circuit's decision and remanded the case to the NLRB, holding that the Darlington closing
would be an unfair labor practice if Darlington were found to be "an
integral part of the Deering-Milliken enterprise."[5] The NLRB so
found, and in 1968, some twelve years after the litigation began, it
ended when the Fourth Circuit with Judge Haynsworth concurring
upheld the NLRB.

Senate liberals went to the trouble of reconstructing the Darlington
litigation for the purpose of alleging that Judge Haynsworth's decisions in the case may have been influenced because Carolina Vend-A-
Matic did business with Deering-Milliken. They drew from Haynsworth the information that Carolina Vend-A-Matic in 1963 was
providing full food vending service in forty-six industrial plants, three
of which belonged to Deering-Milliken.

"Did Deering-Milliken throw you any business at any time?"
Chairman Eastland asked the witness.

"No, sir," answered Judge Haynsworth.[6]

But the liberals pressed their Carolina Vend-A-Matic case against
Haynsworth anyway. With Birch Bayh heading the pack, they questioned Clement Haynsworth as tenaciously as the conservatives had

dogged Abe Fortas. The liberals proved little, but they made headlines with Carolina Vend-A-Matic. Then they moved on to another case and made more headlines. The liberals dug up a 1968 decision in which the Fourth Circuit, with Judge Haynsworth concurring, had decided that Brunswick Corporation was entitled to recover a small amount of money representing its investment in the equipment of a bankrupt bowling alley in South Carolina. Haynsworth owned 1,000 shares of the 18 million outstanding shares of Brunswick, a large, national manufacturer of bowling equipment. The liberals thus attempted to allege that Haynsworth's decision in the case may have been influenced by his stock ownership or that the Judge at the very least should have disqualified himself from participation in the Brunswick case, as well as the Darlington case.[7]

In response to these liberal allegations, the Judiciary Committee brought in as an expert witness John P. Frank, a lawyer from Phoenix, Arizona, who testified that Judge Haynsworth was under no obligation to disqualify himself and said no federal judge "has ever disqualified in circumstances in the remotest degree like those here."

The liberals countered by bringing George Meany to the witness chair. Meany, the president of the American Federation of Labor-Congress of Industrial Organizations, used the Darlington case as a springboard to reach the conclusions that Haynsworth not only had "demonstrated a lack of ethical standards" but also that "his decisions prove him to be anti-labor."

If these building blocks of the liberals' case against Haynsworth seemed insubstantial and inconclusive, they probably were no more so than those the conservatives piled on the nomination of Abe Fortas to be Chief Justice. Now as then, each specific allegation made headlines and the headlines blended together into a dark, murky suggestion of a conflict of interest between private wealth on the one hand and judicial ethics on the other.

Still, if the Senate liberals had no more evidence, Haynsworth might be confirmed, and the liberals in fact did not dig up much more in the way of headline-grabbing allegations that related to Judge Haynsworth's stocks and bonds and debentures. But as the Judiciary Committee hearings moved into the fifth and then the sixth long day, the more partisanly political and sensational charges against Haynsworth began to give way to the more fundamental and substantial elements of the liberal case against the nominee, and the essentially ideological bases of the contest began to take shape.

In such moments of high political and ideological tension in Washington, the most telling testimony often comes from unexpected sources who put into words the indignation felt by many who have been on the sidelines. Senator Griffin of Michigan played somewhat this role in the fight against Fortas's nomination to be Chief Justice. Representative William Fitts Ryan, a forty-seven-year-old liberal Democrat from New York City, and the son of a well-known judge, made a similarly unexpected contribution to the fight against Haynsworth. Ryan asked and received permission to testify before the Senate committee, and he addressed himself to what the Haynsworth nomination really was about.[8]

"The Supreme Court is a crucial and powerful institution in our society," he said. "In a period of deep controversy and division in our Nation about the direction and speed with which the fundamental American promise of equality and equal rights for all of our citizens is being fulfilled, this nomination is a litmus test of our resolve." The Nixon Administration, Ryan charged, "has slowed the already painfully slow process" of racial desegregation in America and "in this atmosphere, Judge Haynsworth is appointed. I am sad to say that a study of his record reveals that his votes on the bench may be the pivotal steps toward further retrenchment on the fundamental law of our land."[9]

Representative Ryan had researched Judge Haynsworth's opinions in civil rights cases as deeply as the Senate Democrats had dug into the judge's stock holdings. He found that, when a majority of the members of the Fourth Circuit Court of Appeals in 1962 held that the Charlottesville, Virginia, school board could not transfer students out of a school district where racial desegregation was in progress, Judge Haynsworth dissented on the ground that desegregation was a "searing experience." In the famous case of Prince Edward County, Virginia, where the public schools were closed for four years to avoid desegregation, Judge Haynsworth in 1963 voted with the majority to deny a Federal Court hearing to parents of black children, saying, "When there is a total cessation of [school] operation, there is no denial of equal protection of the laws, though the resort of the poor man to an adequate substitute may be more difficult and the result may be the absence of integrated classrooms in the locality." The

Warren Court soundly reversed Judge Haynsworth in the Prince Edward County case.[10] In 1965 the Warren Court again reversed a majority opinion of the Fourth Circuit, written by Judge Haynsworth, which delayed integration of the schools in Richmond, Virginia.[11] And the Warren Court in 1968 reversed still another majority opinion, written by Haynsworth, which sanctioned delay in school integration and approved "freedom of choice" plans to allow white children to elect to transfer out of integrated schools.[12]

Judge Haynsworth had participated in various other types of civil rights cases and his record was not one of total opposition to any expansion of the civil rights of blacks. He seemed more willing to accept the Supreme Court's interpretation of the Constitution in cases which did not require racial integration of black and white children. For instance, he wrote the Fourth Circuit court's decision which struck down a "white only" membership limitation of the North Carolina Dental Society.

But liberals charged that such decisions were exceptions. Judge Haynsworth's track record demonstrated that he spoke for the South as a judicial opponent of the Warren Court's commands that the civil rights of blacks be acknowledged and expanded, much as Judge Warren E. Burger's record demonstrated that he stood in judicial opposition to the Warren Court's expansion of the rights of the criminally accused. Indeed, Haynsworth, who sometimes was in the minority on his own court, was more representative of the reluctant, gradualist approach to civil rights than many federal judges in the South. It was then Haynsworth, as a symbol of Southern opposition to the Warren Court, who was scored not only by Representative Ryan but also by a parade of additional witnesses that appeared before the Judiciary Committee.

Representatives of the National Association for the Advancement of Colored People and of the Leadership Conference on Civil Rights testified that "the nomination of Judge Haynsworth is a deadly blow to the image of the U. S. Supreme Court."

Joseph L. Rauh, Jr., a white Washington lawyer and liberal gadfly, testified as counsel of the Leadership Conference that Haynsworth "is a sort of laundered segregationist . . . one who would try to have the least forward progress on integration, the most continuation of past segregation."

Five black members of the House of Representatives came in a group to testify, saying, "We submit that Judge Haynsworth has played a very prominent role in the fifteen years of frustration and delay which have followed" the Warren Court's historic 1954 decision which held school desegregation unconstitutional. "We urge you to reject the nomination."

When the Judiciary Committee hearings finally closed on September 26, the real issue then was clearly drawn: Would the Senate consent to President Nixon's effort to turn the Supreme Court away from the libertarianism which Earl Warren had symbolized?

Senator Philip A. Hart, Democrat of Michigan, summed up for the liberals:

> If I were a fifth-generation white South Carolinian lawyer, I would be amazed if I would have gone any further than Judge Haynsworth. I am sure that our able colleague from South Carolina, Senator Thurmond, would be in accord with Judge Haynsworth.
>
> The question is—is that the kind of system that at this moment in history we want to advise and consent to?
>
> There is great alienation and hostility in the country. It is not the young alone. It is not the black alone. It is not the poor alone. It has been my feeling that the direction of the Warren Court has strengthened the responsible leadership in this country which urges that inequities be corrected within the law. Slowing down the direction of the Warren Court assists only the irresponsible voices. That's my concern.[13]

And Senator Sam J. Ervin, Jr., Democrat of North Carolina, summed up for the conservatives:

"I think they ought to take the little school children of America away from the judicial activists and the bureaucrats and give them back to the parents to whom the Lord has given them."[14]

The same day that the Senate hearings ended, President Nixon held a press conference at the White House where he was asked if Judge Haynsworth "has become controversial enough to lead you to withdraw the nomination?"

"No," answered Nixon, "I do not intend to withdraw the nomination. I studied his record as it was submitted to me by the Attorney General before I sent the nomination to the Senate. I still have confidence in Judge Haynsworth's qualifications, in his integrity."

The President also was asked for "some insight into your thinking, sir, as to the difference between the situation that required Supreme Court Justice Fortas to resign and the recent disclosures concerning Judge Haynsworth?" Nixon said he would "simply stand on my statement that I was aware generally of Judge Haynsworth's background, of his financial status, before he was appointed."

If Nixon was unwilling to recognize any parallels between the Haynsworth and Fortas nominations, the similarities impressed others, Republicans as well as Democrats. Three Republican senators early in October publicly announced they could not support their President's nominee, and the opposition of these three placed a particular strain on Nixon's continuing statements about the "integrity" of his nominee. The first to openly break with Nixon was Senator Edward W. Brooke of Massachusetts, the only black member of the Senate. The second and third were Senators Griffin of Michigan and Margaret Chase Smith of Maine. Griffin, after he successfully led the opposition to President Johnson's nomination of Abe Fortas to be Chief Justice, had become Assistant Leader of Senate Republicans. He said that "legitimate and substantial doubt" had been raised concerning Haynsworth's sensitivity to judicial ethics. Mrs. Smith, a fearsomely independent Yankee, declared she could not, after having opposed the Fortas nomination, now apply a double standard and support Haynsworth.

On Monday, October 6, Chief Justice Burger opened the new term of the Supreme Court, and not only was the ninth seat vacant still but the Judiciary Committee had not even voted on the Haynsworth nomination. It voted three days later, and the vote was 10 to 7, to recommend that the Senate confirm Haynsworth. The ten were mostly Southern Democrats and five Republicans; the seven were mostly Northern Democrats and two Republicans, Senators Griffin of Michigan and Charles McC. Mathias, Jr., of Maryland. The majority found Haynsworth "extraordinarily well qualified" to sit on the Supreme Court and asserted, in answer to the attacks on him, that "nothing in his judicial conduct . . . would in any way justify recommending against his confirmation." The five Democrats who voted against Haynsworth recommended that Nixon withdraw the nomination.

Nixon stubbornly repeated almost daily that he had no intention of withdrawing the nomination. But by now the President and Attorney General Mitchell fully realized that the marvelous ease of their success in June with the Burger nomination would not be repeated. Their triumphal success had been won only four months before, but now even the Fortas mess was effectively being turned against them. Democratic liberals, blacks, and organized labor had ganged up and attacked Haynsworth so viciously that Nixon could not withdraw the nomination without conceding defeat to his enemies. Far more than Clement F. Haynsworth, Jr., was involved now. Politics and campaign promises were involved. Promises Nixon had made to American voters who were not black or young. Promises to reform the Supreme Court. Promises to the South that Richard Nixon for good reasons, past, present, and future, must redeem.

So Nixon and Mitchell belatedly abandoned their casual approach to the Fortas vacancy and went to work.

The President on October 20 called the press into his office for another informal chat, attempting to repeat the success he had had with reporters immediately after he had made the Burger nomination. "I want to give you my own thinking with regard to the nomination of Judge Haynsworth," Nixon told the press. The President said he still believed that Haynsworth, among all the appellate court judges in America, was "the best qualified to serve on the Supreme Court at this time." Haynsworth had become the target of "a vicious character assassination," Nixon said, and he reviewed the Carolina Vend-A-Matic case, the Brunswick case, and the other charges and opined that Haynsworth had not acted improperly in any of them. Some of the opposition, Nixon agreed, was directed at Haynsworth's philosophic conservativism, but the President argued that philosophy is not "a proper ground" for the Senate of the United States to consider. "I think he will be a great credit to the Supreme Court, and I am going to stand by him," Nixon declared with evident determination.

Clark R. Mollenhoff, once a reporter himself, who recently had joined Nixon's staff as White House deputy counsel, also went to work on the press. Mollenhoff's past credentials as an excellent investigative reporter stood him in supposedly good stead as he looked into the charges that had been made against Haynsworth, and, now, from his White House office, he dispatched statements to the press asserting, for instance, that there was no justifiable basis for comparing the activities of Haynsworth with those of former Associate Justice Fortas.

The organized bar began to line up behind Haynsworth, rather as it had supported the Burger nomination. Sixteen former presidents of the American Bar Association on October 24 sent a telegram to Senator Eastland urging Senate confirmation of Haynsworth. But the list did not include the current or immediate past presidents of the ABA.

Republican Party machinery in states all across the country was cranked up on behalf of Haynsworth. Pressures were applied mainly to Republican senators who had not committed themselves one way or the other on the nomination; though the pressures came from their home states, the senators attributed them to the White House. Senator Len B. Jordan, of Idaho, later said that pressure from Republican groups in Idaho had begun after he confidentially had told Attorney General Mitchell he would vote against Haynsworth. An aide to Senator William B. Saxbe of Ohio said the senator received "tens of hundreds of threatening letters from people in the state who have contributed to his campaign. It's as strong as anything we've seen." Almost the entire Illinois Republican delegation to the House of Representatives paid a visit to Senator Charles H. Percy of Illinois to ask him to vote for Haynsworth. Civil rights and labor groups at the same time, of course, were lobbying against the Haynsworth nomination. But the most crucial undecided votes belonged to Republican senators, and, if the outcome was to be decided by last-minute pressures, the White House obviously could twist Republican arms with a great deal more muscle than was available to black and labor lobbyists.

Senate debate on the Haynsworth nomination began November 13 and in the week that it lasted the cliquishness that normally dictates against harsh verbal assault by one senator on other members of the club was severely strained.

Senator Eastland of Mississippi declared on the floor of the Senate that Haynsworth had "withstood a trial-by-ordeal within the committee and a trial-by-rumor without the committee with no trace of bitterness, or anger, or outrage which others felt for him."

"The nomination in question is going to demonstrate how much power labor has in America," Republican Senator Robert Dole of Kansas added in defense of Haynsworth.

Conservative Robert C. Byrd, Democrat of West Virginia, asserted during the floor debate that "much of the opposition to this nomination comes from groups and blocs who are opposed to the philosophy of Judge Haynsworth, so that the matter of conflict of interest may be considered a smokescreen."

The liberals opposing Haynsworth in the debate were equally outspoken. Democratic Senator Lee Metcalf of Montana sharply attacked Nixon, saying: "In the light of Judge Haynsworth's record, it is plain that the highest qualification for a seat on the Supreme Court is complete ideological identification with the reactionary tenets of the Administration's southern strategy."

Jacob K. Javits, a liberal Republican from New York, told the Senate that Haynsworth was "so consistently insensitive to the centuries-old injustice which we as a nation have caused our black citizens to bear, that I could not support the introduction of Judge Haynsworth's philosophy into the nation's highest court."

"We cannot afford to fill the ninth seat with a man who enjoys anything less than the full faith and respect of those whom he serves," said the Senate's only black member, Edward Brooke. "We cannot afford to weaken the reverence on which the Court's power is ultimately founded."

The intense pressure that the Nixon Administration was putting on senators also became an issue in the debate, and the pressure to some extent backfired. Senator Jordan, for instance, told his colleagues: "During my more than seven years in the Senate, few issues have generated more pressure on my office than has the confirmation of Judge Haynsworth. Support of the President is urged as if it were a personal matter rather than an issue of grave constitutional importance."

The roll-call vote was scheduled to take place Friday afternoon, November 21. That morning a few senators, including Republicans John Sherman Cooper of Kentucky and Mark Hatfield of Oregon, still had not announced their positions. The result was sufficiently uncertain that at one o'clock in the afternoon, as the roll call began, Vice President Spiro T. Agnew was presiding over the Senate—a rarity for him—in the event his vote would be needed to break a tie. It was not. The roll call took ten minutes, and when the tally was handed to Agnew for him to announce, he glanced at the sheet of paper and then grimly told the crowded galleries, "There will be no outburst."

Haynsworth was defeated. The tally showed that forty-five senators voted to confirm Haynsworth and fifty-five voted against confirmation. The margin of defeat for Nixon and Mitchell was substantially larger than the White House had expected or the Senate liberals had hoped. It was unexpectedly large because the nomination was an affront to a relatively few senators whose votes were neither foreordained by politics or geography nor moved by pressure. The tally showed that, of the forty-five senators who voted for Haynsworth, twenty-six were Republicans and nineteen were Democrats, almost all of them southern Democrats. Of the fifty-five senators who voted against Haynsworth, seventeen were Republicans and thirty-eight were Democrats. Defections from the Republican Party, largely among senators who had not committed themselves until late, were more than enough to defeat the nomination. Among the seventeen Republicans who defected to vote against President Nixon and his nominee were not only Robert Griffin, Len Jordan, and Margaret Chase Smith, but also Hugh Scott of Pennsylvania, the Republican Leader in the Senate, Mark Hatfield of Oregon, John Sherman Cooper of Kentucky, Charles Percy of Illinois, John J. Williams of Delaware, and Jack Miller of Iowa.

The defeat of Clement F. Haynsworth, Jr., was the first major congressional setback suffered by President Richard M. Nixon. It was a stronger rebuke than the Senate had handed Lyndon Johnson, for Johnson's nomination of Abe Fortas to be Chief Justice was killed by filibuster, without reaching a vote, while Nixon's nomination of Haynsworth was finally and decisively defeated by vote of the United States Senate. It was, moreover, the first Supreme Court nomination to be defeated on a roll call vote since 1930, when President Hoover's nomination of John Parker was defeated.

Later in the afternoon of November 21 President Nixon issued from the White House a statement in which he insisted that Haynsworth "would have brought great credit to the Supreme Court."

It was an angry statement in which Nixon implicitly acknowledged that Haynsworth had been defeated because he represented the white South's continuing opposition to the Warren Court's declarations of equal justice under law for blacks. It was a defiant statement.

"I deeply regret this action. I believe a majority of the people in the nation regret it," Nixon's statement declared. "Especially I deplore the nature of the attacks that have been made upon this distinguished man. His integrity is unimpeachable. The Supreme Court needs men of his legal philosophy to restore the proper balance to that great institution."

Nixon promised that, when the Congress returned for its second session in January, he would send to the Senate a new nomination to fill the Fortas vacancy, and Nixon vowed, "The criteria I shall apply to this selection, as was the case with my nomination of Judge Haynsworth, will be consistent with my commitments to the American people before my election as President a year ago."

Nixon's recollection of political campaign promises notwithstanding, his attempt to place Judge Haynsworth on the Supreme Court was a rather dull episode in the struggle for control of the Court. It lacked the drama of Fortas's secret excursions to the White House to advise the President on mighty issues of war and peace and it had no supporting characters as interesting as Louis Wolfson. The reconstruction of the Judge's stock and bond holdings became tedious, even if members of the Senate who needed an excuse to vote against him found it in his strongbox. He was too straight a pillar of the Old South to be the subject of a really good fight. But when Nixon, as promised, tried again to fill the Fortas vacancy, he provided the Senate with a more lively strict constructionist.

# CHAPTER 11

# Nixon Fumbles Again

Of the opposition which defeated the nomination of Clement F. Haynsworth, Jr., Attorney General John Mitchell said: "If we'd put up one of the Twelve Apostles it would have been the same." The quality of the advocacy, relative to the nomination to fill the Supreme Court seat of Abe Fortas, vacant now for nearly eight months, declined from that level.

The Attorney General, manager of President Nixon's election and Supreme Court campaigns, tended to see all things and all people in their political light. Which is to say, in terms of the popular and electoral votes Richard Nixon would and would not receive in 1972. Attorneys general, according to the folklore of Washington, are not to be political persons because they are the nation's chief law enforcement officers and the laws must be enforced among Democrats and Republicans, rich and poor, black and white alike. Attorney General Mitchell knew his folklore, as had Robert Kennedy. After the 1968 campaign Mitchell in fact did not concern himself very much with the bothersome business of running the Republican National Committee, hearing the complaints or praises of state and local party officials or settling intra-party squabbles. Mitchell's gaze was higher and wider. North, South, East and West. There was no "Southern strategy," if that term, popularized by their enemies, meant the President and his Attorney General were interested only in the popular and electoral votes of the South. Mitchell was interested in votes for Nixon anywhere he could find them. But if by that term it was meant that Mitchell must pay particular attention to the winning of conservative, white, Southern votes, then of course it had validity; Mitchell, looking toward 1972, had to assume that in the South there again would be that narrow margin of votes which could mean for Richard Nixon victory or defeat.

Nixon and Mitchell, following the rejection of Haynsworth, went in search of a new nominee who would be equally "consistent with my commitments to the American people before my election as President a year ago." The new nominee also would be a sitting federal judge with a track record that demonstrated his conservative, or strict constructionist, credentials. He would be a Southerner, to give the Supreme Court the balance it needed. Being both a Southerner and a strict constructionist, his track record automatically would include decisions that again would prompt black people to oppose this nominee. But Mitchell could count very few black votes anyway. On the other hand, organized labor opposition this time should be avoided, insofar as that might be possible. Above all, the nominee must own no stocks or bonds or convertible debentures. It's difficult to find a poor judge, but he must not be rich as Haynsworth.

Nixon and Mitchell had no difficulty finding their nominee, and this time they wasted no time in dispatching the nomination to the Senate. The President announced the nomination on January 19, 1970, which was, as Nixon had promised, shortly after the new session of Congress began. Senator Eastland of Mississippi and the other conservative elders of the Senate Judiciary Committee this time also made haste. The confirmation hearings opened only a week after the nomination was made, despite liberals' complaints that they had not had time to study thoroughly the nominee's track record or much else about him.

The nominee was G. Harrold Carswell. The G. was for George but his friends at home in Tallahassee always called him Harrold. George Harrold Carswell was a judge on the U.S. Fifth Circuit Court of Appeals, which is based at New Orleans and is the federal appellate circuit for the states of Florida, Georgia, Alabama, Mississippi, Louisiana, and Texas. The Fifth Circuit had been involved as fully certainly in civil rights litigation as the Fourth Circuit on which Judge Haynsworth sat, but Judge Carswell did not have much of a track record as an appellate judge because President Nixon had named him to the Fifth Circuit but eight months earlier. Indeed, as coincidence would have it, Carswell was nominated to the Fifth Circuit in May, 1969, the same month Abe Fortas left the Supreme Court. For eleven years before that Carswell had been a U.S. district court judge for the northern district of Florida, and for five years prior to his appointment to the bench he had been U.S. Attorney for the northern district of Florida. President Eisenhower in 1953 had named him U.S. Attorney and in 1958 had elevated him to the federal district court, where he sat until the next Republican President, Richard Nixon, came along.

There were then impressive similarities between President Nixon's first and second choices to fill the ninth seat on the Supreme Court. Carswell and Haynsworth, in addition to being sitting federal appellate judges, were both from the Old South—northern Florida qualifying, sociologically and politically, for inclusion in the Old South even though the lower part of the state has been partially severed by the influx of retired persons and vacationers from the North. Carswell and Haynsworth also shared, along with Strom Thurmond, the distinction of having been Southern Democrats who had switched to the Republican Party back when Eisenhower was President and Nixon was Vice President. And, in the 1968 presidential election, Richard Nixon had carried Florida as well as South Carolina, outdistancing George Wallace in both of those Southern states.

There also were differences. Judge Haynsworth at fifty-seven was the archetype of the landed aristocracy of the South which was moving ahead, if at a conservative pace. He was not mean and he was not wholly lacking in compassion. After the Northern liberals in Washington abused and defeated him, he did not grow vengeful but instead went home to Greenville and commented that, while his defeat was "unhappy for me, for our country's sake, I hope the debate will prove to have been a cleansing agent which will smooth the way for the President's next and later nominees."[1] Judge Carswell was only seven years younger than Haynsworth, but his dark hair and boyish face reinforced the impression of an ambitious young man, a more direct and sharp and impatient person than Haynsworth. There were additional differences which ultimately proved, among other things, that there are degrees of strict constructionism. But the most important difference between Carswell and Haynsworth, for the purposes of the moment, was that Carswell was not a rich man. He also claimed no distinguished family lineage of five generations and he had not been to Harvard.

Carswell was born in the town of Irwinton, Georgia, on December 22, 1919. He went to Duke University, joined the Navy in World War

II and came out a lieutenant, and in 1946 enrolled at the Mercer University Law School in Macon, Georgia. While a student at Mercer, he obtained a franchise and borrowed $7,000 to start a telephone business in nearby Wilkinson County, Georgia. He received his law degree in 1948 and ran as a Democrat for the Georgia legislature and lost. Then he sold the telephone business and moved to Tallahassee, the capital of Florida. There he practiced law for about five years, first as an associate of the firm of which Leroy Collins, later governor of Florida, was a partner, and later he started his own firm. Carswell married a pretty Tallahassee girl of good family and he maintained a lively interest in politics, supporting Senator Richard Russell of Georgia for the Democratic presidential nomination in 1952. When the Democrats instead nominated Adlai Stevenson, Carswell switched to support the Republican ticket of Eisenhower and Nixon. Then, at the age of thirty-three and after only five years in Florida, Carswell in 1953 received from President Eisenhower appointment as U.S. Attorney and five years later he became the youngest federal district court judge in the nation. In May, 1969, President Nixon nominated and the Senate confirmed him to be a member of the Fifth Circuit Court of Appeals.

When the Senate Judiciary Committee on January 27, 1970, opened hearings on the nomination of Carswell to the Supreme Court, the point was quickly made that he was not a rich man. Roman L. Hruska, the senator with the mellifluous voice from Nebraska who appropriately had succeeded the late Everett McKinley Dirksen as the senior Republican on the committee and who would be Carswell's chief proponent in the Senate, made the point soon and often. "While he is not an impoverished man, he is far from well off," Hruska said. "He is far from affluent." Affluence, like strict constructionism, is variously defined. Under questioning by Hruska and other friendly Republican committee members, Carswell testified, "I have no stocks, I have no bonds whatsoever." He had "never received any fee for any outside activities of any nature." He and his wife shared an automobile, "a Pontiac," he volunteered. His house was mortgaged for $50,-347.20 and his monthly payments were $469.45. The house admittedly was handsomely spacious, located on a lake north of Tallahassee and worth maybe $90,000 on the current market. Carswell also owned by inheritance, with other members of his family, a three-sixteenths interest in 1,290 unimproved acres of undeveloped land in Wilkinson

County, Georgia. His wife owned by inheritance 78 shares of common stock of a crate and box manufacturing concern, worth perhaps $50,000. And that, Carswell told the Judiciary Committee, in a strong and almost proud tone, was all there was of his personal wealth.[2]

The liberal Democrats on the committee made an effort to dig into Judge Carswell's alleged poverty of stocks and bonds. Senator Bayh again led the attack, but this time Senator Kennedy, recovered a bit from the Chappaquiddick accident, took a more active role in the interrogation of the President's nominee.

Bayh and Kennedy tried the line of questioning that had proved fruitful in the Haynsworth hearings, by attempting to lay hands on cases which Carswell had decided but which perhaps he should have allowed some other judge to decide. Kennedy, for instance, tried to find out whether Carswell had ruled on cases involving parties who had been his clients during the five years he had been in private law practice. Bayh wanted to know whether Carswell had decided any cases involving customers of the crate and box company in which Mrs. Carswell owned stock. But the liberals dug only dry holes and Senator Hart of Michigan ended the search on a note of good humor.

"To ease the tension, if possible," Hart said to Carswell, "we are not to understand by reason of the fact that you own no stocks or bonds that you are opposed to the basic concept of a free competitive society?"

Everyone laughed, Carswell answered, "Certainly not," and the liberal and conservative senators on the committee concluded in silent unanimity that Nixon and Mitchell thus far had succeeded: this nomination would not fail, as the Fortas and Haynsworth nominations had, because of reasons allegedly related to the personal riches of the nominee.

Well, then, what of Judge Carswell's track record in labor cases? In fact, he did not have much of a record because relatively few labor cases had come before him, as an appellate or district court judge. There was, however, one case that was brought to the senators' attention by some woman liberationists and that interested the senators mildly. It was a case titled *Ida Phillips* v. *Martin Marietta,* which had been decided in 1969 by the Fifth Circuit. Martin Marietta Corporation had refused as a matter of policy to hire Ida Phillips and other women with children of preschool age, and the question was whether the policy constituted illegal sex discrimination under the 1964 Civil

Rights Act. The liberal senators were quite gentle in their questioning of Carswell concerning the case, but Representative Patsy T. Mink, of Hawaii, testified before the committee that she most adamantly opposed the Carswell nomination because of his part in the case. Worse, Betty Friedan, author of a book titled *The Feminine Mystique* and president of National Organization for Women (NOW), appeared in opposition to testify that Carswell was "a sexist judge."

But Committee Chairman Eastland of Mississippi said to each woman, as she seemed about to conclude and finally did conclude her testimony, "Thank you, ma'am," and Eastland said no more. Carswell's brush with women's liberation was not serious, and in fact it was rather unfair. A three-judge panel of the Fifth Circuit, which had not included Judge Carswell, had found that Martin Marietta's policy did not violate the 1964 Civil Rights Act. Mrs. Ida Phillips' lawyers then asked that the panel's decision be set for a hearing before all of the dozen Fifth Circuit judges and Carswell's only participation in the case was to vote with the majority to deny an *en banc* hearing. The case then followed the normal course of appeal to the Supreme Court.[3]

With the Carswell hearings barely three days old, the Judiciary Committee had rather well exhausted the more or less tangential issues of the kind which had proved useful to the liberals as handles for getting hold of Judge Haynsworth and to the conservatives for getting hold of Justice Fortas. So the senators had nothing more to talk about except the central issue, which was the merit of the nomination of Judge Carswell to fulfill President Nixon's stated purpose of giving new balance to the Supreme Court by placing on it a Southern strict constructionist.

But the members of the United States Senate, liberal and conservative, are generally not adept at deciding issues strictly on their merits when the stakes are very high and the pressures very great. Many senators are lawyers who are fully capable of exploring issues on their merits, but senators also are politicians who are subjected to many political pressures and who in the end must answer to their constituents, their party and, as the case may be, their President. If an issue can be disposed of solely or largely on some tangential basis, answering is relatively easy. The tangents almost always involve allegedly questionable personal ethics, so answering is easy because ethical questions lend themselves nicely to rhetoric, and anyway no senator is expected to be in favor of questionable ethics. If great issues cannot be so disposed of, answering is more difficult because the merits are complex and no amount of explaining will in any event satisfy all of those who pressured a senator to do the opposite of what he did.

All of which President Nixon and Attorney General Mitchell knew when they nominated Judge Carswell. It was an election year and they chose a nominee who was not vulnerable to the kinds of ethical allegations that had been raised against Haynsworth and Fortas. They chose wisely. The liberal Democrats in the Senate did not succeed in grabbing hold of Carswell. But Nixon and Mitchell did not choose wisely enough. Pressures, more professional than political, that were initiated outside the Senate forced the debate to the central issue, and in the end the Carswell nomination was decided more on the basis of merit than any of the other engagements in the struggle for control of the Supreme Court that began the day Adlai Stevenson fell dead in London. And the inevitable basis of the decision was the constitutional rights of black Americans, past and future.

During the brief period between the day Nixon nominated Carswell and the day the Senate hearings began, an enterprising journalist rediscovered a speech Carswell had made twenty-two years earlier. The speech was delivered before an American Legion audience in Georgia and the time was the period immediately following World War II. Carswell was running for a seat in the Georgia legislature.

In that context, Carswell, a twenty-nine-year-old war veteran, delivered a ringing "remember Pearl Harbor" speech in which he warned of Communists and of Northern liberals who, he declared, were invading states' rights by advocating federal action to force the South to grant equal employment and other rights to Negroes.

He then said:

> I am a Southerner by ancestry, birth, training, inclination, belief and practice. I believe that segregation of the races is proper and the only practical and correct way of life in our states. I have always so believed, and I shall always so act. I shall be the last to submit to any attempt on the part of anyone to break down and to weaken this firmly established policy of our people.
>
> I yield to no man as a fellow candidate, or as a fellow citizen, in the firm, vigorous belief in the principles of white supremacy, and I shall always be so governed.[4]

In the year 1970 the overt advocacy of white supremacy by any holder of public office was no longer acceptable in Washington, D. C. No member of Congress, even from the Deep South, would stand on the floor of the Senate or House and publicly call a black man a "nigger," or embrace segregation as a way of life, or advocate white supremacy. The most conservative members of Congress would advocate, as the President had, strict constructionism and law and order. But the leadership of the Warren Court, more than anything else, had carried the federal government forward by 1970 to a time when, for political if not moral reasons, no holder of public office, elective or appointive, could openly advocate in Washington a policy of apartheid for America.

Even before the Senate confirmation hearing opened, Carswell in the strongest terms repudiated his 1948 speech. In a CBS television interview, he said, "I denounce and reject the words themselves and the ideas they represent. They're obnoxious and abhorrent to my personal philosophy." On the first day of the hearing, as he sat before the Judiciary Committee toying with a yellow lead pencil and occasionally puffing on a filtered cigarette, he repeatedly and strongly reiterated "with all the conviction that I have, that these views are obnoxious and abhorrent to me."

If President Nixon and Attorney General Mitchell also recognized the rediscovery of the 1948 speech as a potential problem, they initially tried to meet it by insisting that the speech was of no relevance now. They said they had not known of the speech because the Federal Bureau of Investigation had failed to discover it when the Bureau checked into Carswell's background. The announcement sacrificed a bit of the FBI's vaunted reputation, but the choice was between allowing the FBI to look sloppy and making Nixon and Mitchell appear insensitive to Carswell's racist words. But the main point, Nixon said at a press conference three days after the Senate hearings had begun, was that Carswell's record of public service since 1953 was "without a taint of racism." As if to say that racism and strict constructionism are opposites, the President added that Carswell's record was one of "strict constructionism as far as interpretation of the Constitution" was concerned.

After some weeks passed and it became quite apparent that the Senate did not consider the 1948 speech to be irrelevant, Mitchell found it necessary to make a further statement concerning the Nixon

Administration's knowledge of the speech. The Justice Department issued a statement to the press which said: "Attorney General John N. Mitchell today described as 'categorically false' a report that an FBI investigation of Judge G. Harrold Carswell prior to his nomination to be an Associate Justice of the Supreme Court uncovered his 1948 speech."*

So the question, as it was posed for deliberation by the Senate Judiciary Committee, was one of Carswell's veracity. And thus the contradiction, acknowledged in the political world, between politics and principle—the difference between what is said and what is believed—itself became an issue in the struggle for control of the Court.

Carswell told the committee that he supposed he believed his words when he said them twenty-two years ago, but whatever he believed then, it was now 1970 and "I do not harbor any racial supremacy notions." His testimony seemed frank and unequivocal, and the senators seemed to be sympathetic to his plight. The speech was a long time ago, when a young Carswell was trying to talk American Legionnaires into voting him into the Georgia legislature.

A long line of witnesses appeared to testify to the worth of Carswell's character and ability. The president of the Florida Bar Association, Mark Hulsey, Jr., told the committee that Judge Carswell was a fine judge and no racist. Leroy Collins, now a former governor of the state, said he knew Carswell to be "a man of untarnished integrity." Both of Florida's senators, Democrat Spessard L. Holland and Republican Edward J. Gurney, testified in strong support of the nomination. The American Bar Association's Standing Committee on the Federal Judiciary said it had investigated Carswell and found him "qualified for this appointment." One of the many letters which came to the Judiciary Committee in support of Carswell was postmarked Austin, Texas, and it bore the endorsement of Homer Thornberry, a fellow judge on the Fifth Circuit, who hoped the members of the Senate would not think him "presumptuous" for writing.

But even if Carswell's veracity was accepted, a subtle note of ambiguity had crept into the confirmation hearing. If Carswell was no racist, it nonetheless remained that Nixon had by his own words selected this particular Southern strict constructionist for the purpose of balancing the Supreme Court against the libertarian philosophy of the Warren Court. If G. Harrold Carswell was no racist, what then

*The statement was issued on March 27, 1970.

was his position concerning civil rights? If the answer was not to be found in what Carswell had said, the liberals could examine what he had done.

During most of the first three days of the Senate hearing, as the liberals were conducting their fruitless search for ethical lapses and the conservatives were successfully establishing that Carswell was not a rich man, the 1948 speech and what Carswell had done since then came up intermittently a number of times. In most of the years since 1948, Carswell had been in Federal service, as a U. S. Attorney and a judge. But he had participated in few cases during his recent short stay on the Fifth Circuit Court of Appeals. During the eleven years he sat as a federal district court judge in northern Florida, he had decided many civil rights cases, involving racial segregation in schools, a barber shop, airport facilities, theaters, and so forth. But it was difficult or impossible to draw firm conclusions about Carswell's philosophy from readings of his decisions. Judge Carswell's opinions typically were short, direct, and lacking of the judicial reasoning and intellectual probing to be found in various other federal court opinions of the 1950's and 1960's which dealt with the many complex questions of fact and law that were left undecided by the Warren Court's initial civil rights decisions.

The liberal members of the Judiciary Committee made only feeble efforts to investigate Carswell's philosophy through his decisions. The liberals did make a somewhat more determined attempt to question the nominee about his membership in a Tallahassee golf club, suggesting that this bore on his racial views. But Carswell assured them it was only a "little wooden country club."

The conservative committee members, on the other hand, found merit in Carswell's record as a judge. They also did not dwell on his particular decisions but apparently relied on the President's judgment. Senator Thurmond told the committee that Carswell "has a reputation of having a conservative philosophy," adding that Nixon chose Carswell for his conservatism because "you cannot bring a balance to the Court unless that were done." Thurmond also said that Carswell was to be congratulated for his ability to "bring together the facts and applicable law, and succinctly state the conclusion with brevity and exactness. This style of writing judicial opinions is somewhat unique today, for the opinions of many of our judges are too long and superfluous," Thurmond said.[5]

Another Republican member of the Judiciary Committee, Senator Griffin of Michigan, on the same subject said to Carswell, "Frankly, I must register my disagreement with those who criticize your opinions by comparing them to a plumber's manual."[6] Inasmuch as the liberals at that point had not publicly compared Carswell's opinions with a plumber's manual, Griffin's remark seemed to raise a question as to whose side he was on this time.

Late on the third day of the hearings, the Judiciary Committee began to hear witnesses who had taken time to study Judge Carswell's opinions and who came to testify not on behalf of any bar association or other organization but as individuals.

One was William Van Alystyne, a professor at Duke University Law School, the school from which Richard Nixon had received a law degree in 1937, as it happened. Van Alystyne reviewed for the committee some of the particular cases Judge Carswell had decided.[7]

One was brought by several Tallahassee Negroes to enjoin the local sheriff from allegedly harassing blacks who were engaged in an effort to desegregate theaters; Carswell refused to hold a hearing and granted summary judgment for the sheriff. Under federal civil rights acts and Supreme Court decisions, Van Alystyne said, "a hearing should have been held," adding that Carswell was reversed by a court of appeals.

A second case was brought by four Negro children to desegregate the facilities of a juvenile institution to which they had been sent after being convicted of participating in a sit-in. Judge Carswell dismissed the suit and he again was reversed, the professor noted.

In a third case, Negro plaintiffs sued to enjoin alleged police harassment and Judge Carswell granted summary judgment against the Negroes without holding a hearing where the Negroes would have had an opportunity to establish that the police were in fact acting maliciously. He again was reversed by an appeals court which ordered Judge Carswell to hear the Negroes.

In a fourth case, suit was brought on behalf of black children to enjoin the assignment of school teachers on the basis of race. Van Alystyne said Carswell's opinion "manifested a severely restricted interpretation" of the Supreme Court's 1954 school desegregation decision. Carswell held that the Supreme Court decision applied only to segregation of children and that there was no basis for concluding that the Constitution similarly barred segregation of school faculties.

Professor Van Alystyne told the committee that, in his opinion, "it would be uniquely inappropriate" for the Senate to confirm Carswell's nomination to the Supreme Court unless the 1948 speech "can be significantly discounted by clear and reassuring events since that time. But an examination of his decisions and opinions as a district judge since that time provides no feeling for a basis of reassurance whatever."

Van Alystyne found it disturbing that in Carswell's opinions generally

> there is simply a lack of reasoning, care, or judicial sensitivity. There is, in candor, nothing in the quality of the nominee's work to warrant any expectation whatever that he could serve with distinction on the Supreme Court of the United States.
>
> If the Warren Court will be historically a monument, it will be because it gave that initial push to momentum of concern in the United States dating from 1954. There has been in my view a unique and admirable unanimity on this crucial question since that time.

"I can think of no more regrettable insult to the Warren Court" than confirmation of Carswell, unless the Senate finds in Carswell's record since 1948 reassurance that his speech then was "merely a forgivable incident," Van Alystyne concluded.[8]

The testimony was particularly damaging to Nixon and Carswell because Van Alystyne had been an assistant attorney general in charge of the Justice Department's Civil Rights Division during the Eisenhower Administration. Much more recently, he had appeared before this same Judiciary Committee to support the President's nomination of Judge Haynsworth. He had testified for Haynsworth because he had been familiar with that judge's decisions and felt that, although he did not always agree with Haynsworth's results, his opinions were arrived at with "reassuring care and reason." Having taken a position on Haynsworth, he now was here to express his "sharply different impressions" of Carswell.

Professor Van Alystyne's courage opened a floodgate through which poured a stream and then a river of opposition. It came from the academic community and the legal profession and its anger was directed more at Nixon and Mitchell as lawyers than as politicians. Some Republican sentors were swept up in it because, politics notwithstanding, as lawyers they seemed unable to take the Carswell nomination seriously anymore. Senator Griffin's remark about the plumber's manual was but the beginning.

Gary Orfield, an assistant professor of politics and public affairs at Princeton University, in testifying against Carswell applied the term "mediocre" to the nominee and it took hold, even in the mind of Senator Roman Hruska, who had defended Carswell so well against charges of affluence. When Hruska, as leader of the pro-Carswell forces in the Senate, was interviewed on television, he defended Carswell by saying, "even if he were mediocre, there are a lot of mediocre judges and people and lawyers. They are entitled to a little representation, aren't they? We can't have all Brandeises and Frankfurters and Cardozos."

Professor Orfield had testified also against the Haynsworth nomination, and as the Carswell hearing moved through its fourth and fifth days others who were against Haynsworth also appeared in opposition to Carswell. Clarence Mitchell, testifying for the Leadership Conference on Civil Rights, called Carswell "an advocate of racial segregation" and said, "We breathe a sigh of relief when Negroes go into the courts instead of into the streets, but we then confront them with judges who have decided to deny them relief even before they enter the courthouse door."[9] Thomas E. Harris, a lawyer who appeared for the AFL-CIO, testified against Carswell not because of his decisions in labor cases but because of the racial issue.

The stream of opposition to Carswell was turned into a river by lawyers and law professors who had remained silent on the Haynsworth nomination. John Lowenthal, a law professor at Rutgers University who had litigated civil rights cases before Judge Carswell in 1964, testified that the judge was "extremely hostile."[10] Ernest H. Rosenberger, who as a law student in 1964 had assisted in defending civil rights workers before Carswell, testified, "His reputation was bad. His reputation was one of obstruction in civil rights litigation."[11] Leroy D. Clark, associate professor at New York University Law School, testified on behalf of the National Conference of Black Lawyers: "It was not unusual for Judge Carswell to shout at a black lawyer who appeared before him while using a civil tone to opposing counsel," adding, "Black people do not want their destinies in the hands of G. Harrold Carswell."[12]

As the hearing neared its end, Louis H. Pollak, dean of the Yale Law School, took the witness chair.

Speaking out of "professional concern and citizen concern," Pollack said:

> When the President nominates and the Senate confirms an Associate Justice of the U.S. Supreme Court, it does an awesome thing. The President and the Senate in combination are entrusting a fair measure of the Nation's future to the man or woman, one can hope that in due course it may be a woman, who sits on that Court and participates in the shaping of our fundamental institutions.
>
> I in no way object to a President giving weight in the selection of a judicial nominee to geographic and indeed political considerations. [The appointment of a Republican and a Southerner add philosophic and geographic diversity] which strengthens the Court when rightly applied, that is to say when applied in appointing a man who at a minimum presents the highest professional qualifications. But when one adds to the criterion of Republicanism and southernism the criterion of lukewarmness on the greatest issue confronting our Nation, then it seems to me we have to take a second look.

Dean Pollack took a second look and he found Carswell a judge given to "a repeated use of dispositive techniques which avoided hearings." He found him a judge who "was failing to follow clear mandates of the court above him in failing to explore applications plainly alleging serious constitutional deprivations." He saw in Carswell no "signs of real professional distinction which would arise one iota out of the ordinary." And he found that "the nominee has not demonstrated the professional skills and the larger constitutional wisdom which fits a lawyer for elevation to our highest court."

> I am impelled to conclude [Dean Pollack said] that the nominee presents more slender credentials than any nominee for the Supreme Court put forth in this century; and this century began, I remind this committee, with the elevation to the Supreme Court of Oliver Wendell Holmes.

In conclusion, and even without questioning Carswell's good faith in repudiating his 1948 speech, Pollack asked:

> What symbolism would attach to Senate confirmation as Associate Justice of a lawyer whose later career offers so meager a basis for predicting that he possesses judicial capacity and constitutional insight

of the first rank? I say advisedly, if that speech had been an attack on Jews or on Catholics, his name would have been withdrawn within five minutes after the speech came to light.

Lukewarmness to the rights embodied in the Constitution, and most especially rights of black people, is not just Florida politics vintage 1948 but American politics vintage 1970, and on that reckoning it is not Judge Carswell who is accountable. What is called into account is the constitutional commitment of the American people today.[13]

President Nixon and Attorney General Mitchell could not have been attacked with greater eloquence nor could the merits of the nomination have been laid open more cleanly.

The hearing ended on February 3 but the professional indignation continued to build in telegrams sent to the committee, letters to the editors of newspapers, press releases, and speeches. Derek C. Bok, dean of the Harvard Law School, by letter fell in behind his counterpart at Yale. Francis T. P. Plimpton, president of the prestigious Association of the Bar of the City of New York, called a press conference to release a statement of opposition that was signed by more than 300 members of the bar from over the country. Some thirty-five members of the law faculty of the University of California at Los Angeles and nineteen law professors at the University of Virginia signed letters in opposition to Carswell. More than 500 lawyers employed by various federal agencies in Washington signed a petition against Carswell. Letters, telegrams, and petitions came in from law professors in more than two dozen universities. The entire faculty of the University of Iowa College of Law sent a letter of opposition to the President. More than 200 former law clerks to Supreme Court Justices, including Dean Acheson, who served as Secretary of State many years after he was a clerk to Justice Brandeis, signed a letter of opposition that was sent to every member of the Senate.

Professors ordinarily do not make good Washington lobbyists, but in this cause they excelled, and when they finished testifying and petitioning against Carswell, the professional politicians resumed their inquiry.

The liberal Democrats investigated Carswell's membership in the "little wooden country club" in Tallahassee and found circumstantial evidence that racial discrimination might have been involved.[14] The evidence was this. The City of Tallahassee since 1935 had operated a municipal golf course, apparently on a racially segregated basis. In 1956 the golf course with its little wooden clubhouse was acquired from the city by a private organization, the Capital City Country Club. The organizers were some of Tallahassee's leading white citizens, who planned to operate the property as a private club with necessary improvements including a new clubhouse, swimming pool, and the other refinements of private country clubs. The Senate liberals presented evidence indicating that the transaction also was motivated by the possibility that in 1956, two years following the Supreme Court's initial constitutional decision against state-enforced racial segregation in the South, federal courts would have ordered that the Tallahassee golf course be desegregated, had it remained under municipal operation. Harrold Carswell, then U.S. attorney, was one of the prominent citizens of Tallahassee who in 1956 paid an initial $100 to become an original subscribing member of the Capital City Country Club. He withdrew from membership in 1957 because he was not a golfer, rather than because of any reasons related to racial discrimination. Sometime later, when his sons were old enough to play golf, he joined again and in 1966 resigned his membership once more.

That was the evidence the liberal Democrats adduced from Carswell and other witnesses. It was tangential, more or less, but it was not unrelated to a determination of Carswell's veracity in renouncing his 1948 racist speech.

Contributions also were inadvertently made by conservative politicians in the Senate and the White House to the Carswell opposition. Senator Hruska's statement concerning Carswell's mediocrity was followed, for example, by Senator Russell Long, a Louisiana Democrat, who said on the Senate floor that it might be better for the Senate to accept "a B student or a C student who was able to think straight, compared to one of those A students who are capable of the kind of thinking that winds up getting us a 100 per cent increase in crime in this country." President Nixon publicly suggested it would be constitutionally improper for the Senate to refuse to confirm Carswell. Nixon, in the course of reaffirming his "total support" for Carswell, said that other Presidents had been accorded a "right of choice in naming Supreme Court Justices" and if the Senate "attempts to substitute its judgment as to who should be appointed the traditional constitutional balance is in jeopardy and the duty of the President under the Constitution impaired."[15] The statement was foolish because the very purpose of Senate confirmation is to check presidential power, and Nixon had not read his history. Fifteen Presidents, starting with George Washington, had seen twenty-four of their nominees to the Supreme Court fail to win Senate confirmation.

After several weeks of liberal pulling and conservative hauling within the Judiciary Committee, its members reported out the Carswell nomination on February 27, 1970. The majority found Carswell "thoroughly qualified" for the Supreme Court. The dissenting minority consisted of four Democratic liberals: Senators Bayh of Indiana, Hart of Michigan, Kennedy of Massachusetts, and Tydings of Maryland. Debate on the Senate floor began March 13 and for several more weeks the quality of the debate in Washington declined as the academic and professional criticism of the nomination continued to rise, and even in places as far south as the Florida State University and Washington and Lee University.

The Senate debate lasted for three and one-half weeks and, as one senator after another addressed himself to the issue, the most surprising observation to be made from outside was that the outpouring of professional opposition to Carswell had not been transformed into a flood of political opposition. A scorecard would have shown, as the debate progressed, that neither the Northern liberal Democrats who opposed Carswell nor the Southern Democrats and conservative Republicans who supported him had enough committed votes to assure victory. Nixon showed no intention, as lawyer or politician, of withdrawing the nomination. Again, the result would be decided by uncommitted senators, and most crucially by undecided Republicans.

Principle is most likely to be compromised with politics in an election year. This was an election year in which some of the uncommitted Republican senators would have to face their constituents and their President. So the liberals who were against Carswell offered a way out to the uncommitted senators who apparently felt they could not vote against the nominee on the merits. The liberals proposed that the Senate take a vote on a motion to recommit the nomination to the Judiciary Committee, thus killing it. But recommittal early in the debate was opposed by some liberal Republicans, as well as by Senate conservatives who supported Carswell.

Since the issue could not thus be evaded, the debate on the Senate floor continued. Senator Bayh declared that "if the advice and consent procedure means anything, this is a time when we have, in all respect, to say, 'Send us a man of bigger stature.'" Bayh and other liberals continued quoting Van Alystyne and other professors and kept reading into the *Congressional Record* excerpts from the anti-Carswell statements that still flowed into Washington from law schools across the country.

Bayh insisted that Carswell's professional credentials were "too threadbare" to justify confirmation of the nomination.

Harold E. Hughes, an Iowa Democrat, told the Senate that arguments being made in support of Carswell were "demeaning to the South, which has many better men to offer." Hughes added, "It is demeaning to the many federal and state judges throughout the nation who are conservatives in the traditional sense of that word, but are also great scholars of the law, while the present nominee is not."

Alan Cranston, Democrat of California, entered the floor debate emphasizing testimony before the Judiciary Committee concerning Carswell's conduct as a judge. "There is a consistent pattern in his behavior of bias and hostility toward anyone arguing a civil rights case, of emotionalism, intemperance and anger," Cranston said.

Senator Scott, the Republican leader, this time supported the President's nominee, but with less than total enthusiasm. Scott during the Senate debate said he was convinced Carswell was a "middle-of-the-roader."

Senator Hruska, the leader of the pro-Carswell forces, continued to make contributions of dubious worth to his cause. He declared that common sense and experience as a judge were more important than legal scholarship as qualifications for membership on the Supreme Court. Legal scholarship, Hruska said, "is too often the only qualification an outstanding legal scholar has."

On April 6, after the floor debate had gone on for just over three weeks and the liberals had renewed their attempt to have the issue decided by a vote on recommital of the nomination, the Senate voted on the motion. But the vote was 44 to 52 against killing the nomination by sending it back to the Judiciary Committee.

The result was taken as a victory for Nixon and Mitchell, but their satisfaction was misplaced and short-lived.

Two days later, on April 8, the Senate voted on the merits of the President's nomination of G. Harrold Carswell. Nixon and Mitchell still remained "confident" of final victory, it was said, but the fate of the nomination rested with perhaps a dozen uncommitted Republicans and a handful of Democrats. When the roll call was over, thirteen Republicans had voted against Carswell and he was defeated. The final tally was 45 to 51 against confirmation.

Perhaps the most dramatic vote against Carswell was cast by Marlow W. Cook, a Republican senator from Kentucky. Cook was a member of the Judiciary Committee. He had defended Carswell during the committee hearings and he had voted with the conservative majority in favor of the nomination. He had voted for Haynsworth. But he refused even at a late hour to commit his vote in the April 8 Senate floor action. President Nixon spoke privately with him just before the final Senate vote.

Therefore, when Cook cast his vote against Carswell, the packed Senate gallery gasped. The anti-Carswell spectators were elated not only at Cook's display of independence but also because his name came early in the roll call and his "no" was a strong indication that enough of the other uncommitted votes would be cast against Carswell to defeat him.

Cook never explained his vote fully. At the time, he told reporters in Washington that his vote was politically the most dangerous of his career and he added that, while he would like to see a Southern conservative on the Court, "Haynsworth satisfied my standard of excellence, Carswell did not." Cook's reaction to the Carswell nomination, after he had considered it for some time, may have been affected by the fact that he himself not only was a lawyer but also had served as a judge. Before Cook became a senator in 1968, he had sat for seven years as a judge of the court of Jefferson County, Kentucky.

Cook shed additional light on his thinking about the President, the Senate, and the Supreme Court in a speech he delivered before the Louisville Bar Association.* He did not comment specifically about the Carswell nomination, but talked about the role of the American Bar Association and the Justice Department in federal judicial nominations. He was critical of both the ABA and the department for their long-standing arrangement under which the department, as the President's representative, has been accorded the opportunity to pass on the qualifications of presidential nominations to Federal district courts and circuit courts of appeal. These selections, as well as those

*September 29, 1970.

of Supreme Court members, he insisted, should be the sole responsibility of the President and his Attorney General. The ABA, Cook charged, possesses "a certain unavoidable bias against a great class of outstanding lawyers who represent plantiffs in personal injury cases, criminal defendants and quite often practice alone or in small firms." The association is "large firm-oriented" and dominated by firms that do corporate work, Cook said.

In conclusion, and without being entirely clear about whom he was referring to, Cook quoted from Samuel Butler:

> Authority intoxicates,
> And makes mere sots of magistrates;
> The fumes of it invade the brain,
> And make men giddy, proud and vain.

Cook was one of three Republicans who had voted for Haynsworth and against Carswell. The other two were Senators Winston L. Prouty of Vermont and Hiram L. Fong of Hawaii. The Republicans who voted against Carswell and also against Haynsworth were Brooke of Massachusetts, Case of New Jersey, Goodell of New York, Hatfield of Oregon, Javits of New York, Mathias of Maryland, Schweiker of Pennsylvania, Packwood of Oregon, Percy of Illinois, and Mrs. Smith of Maine.

Four Southern Democrats also voted against Carswell. They were Fulbright of Arkansas, Spong of Virginia, Gore of Tennessee, and Yarborough of Texas.

After a major political fight is settled in Washington, one way or the other, the participants normally go on to the next order of business and forego personal recrimination, at least until the next election. But the nature of the Carswell nomination, the President's dedication to it and the bitterness that the defeat left behind all were such that normality did not prevail.

For example, Mrs. Smith on April 13 on the Senate floor charged that Bryce Harlow, a White House aide, "impugned the integrity and veracity of my office" in connection with the Carswell vote. "I am shocked at the repeated irresponsibility of Mr. Harlow both before and after the vote," Mrs. Smith said in her highly unusual attack.

Mrs. Smith did not make entirely clear how her integrity had been impugned but, shortly after her Senate speech, Harlow appeared on a television interview and he conceded that he had telephoned Senator

Cook just before the Senate floor vote to say that Mrs. Smith would vote for Carswell. Harlow said he had received the information from Mrs. Smith's office.

Mrs. Smith denied that she or her aides had made any such statement and asked Harlow for an apology. He made a qualified apology.

A second example of the recrimination and retribution that settled on the Carswell defeat was offered by some Senate conservatives. Senators whose hopes for the Supreme Court were most shattered by the Carswell defeat began to press their conclusion that the time had come to impeach Justice Douglas.

Still another example of conservatives' mood of angry retribution came from Senator Dole of Kansas. Dole declared, on the Senate floor, "It may be easier to change the Senate than the U.S. Supreme Court—in fact, it may be a prerequisite." Dole, a strong defender of both the Haynsworth and Carswell nominations, found that President Nixon agreed with his conclusion, and in 1971 Dole was named chairman of the Republican National Committee and thus given the opportunity to act on his political conclusion.

For his part, Nixon would not run again until 1972, but in the mid-term elections that were held in November, 1970, the President set out to do what he then could to change the Senate. He did not succeed, if his goal was Republican control of the Senate. But, among those thirteen Republicans and four Southern Democrats whose votes were crucial in the defeat of Carswell, five had to face re-election in 1970. Three of the five were defeated: Goodell of New York and Gore of Tennessee in the general election and Yarborough of Texas in a primary. Theirs ultimately were the most dramatic votes cast against G. Harrold Carswell.

But the Democrats and turncoat Republicans who were blaming the Attorney General for the Haynsworth and Carswell debacles did not know Nixon and Mitchell, these two partners in the law. The choices were theirs together, and they were right! Nixon and Mitchell stubbornly adhered to the belief that the Senate had no right, constitutional or other, to frustrate the President's fulfillment of his campaign promise to remove Earl Warren and his civil libertarianism from the Supreme Court. If the Senate would not consent to their nominations of Southerners such as Haynsworth and Carswell, then it was the Senate that must be changed.

Senator Dole, in arriving at that retributory conclusion following the defeat of Carswell, had suggested to President Nixon that he take the issue to the voters and postpone another nomination to fill the Fortas vacancy until after the mid-term election in November, seven months away. As Nixon and Mitchell talked on board the *Sequoia* and back at the White House they must have weighed the idea. There was some merit to it. Nixon and Mitchell already had examined the political situations in the states where thirty-five Senate seats would be up for election in November. They had helped Republican conservatives to move into running positions in certain states, North and South, for the elections in the fall. The Carswell and Haynsworth defeats would make effective issues in some of these states, but not all. So far as the Supreme Court itself was concerned, there was no longer much point in hurrying. The Court by now had heard argument on all the cases it would decide before the term ended in June, so a ninth Justice, even if he were seated quickly, would participate in very little of the Court's work until the new term opened in October.

On the other hand, unnecessary political risk might be incurred if Nixon took his fight with the Senate to the people in November and delayed another nomination until after the election. That course would make the Supreme Court a still larger political issue, particularly after the Court reopened in October, and it would not be a one-sided issue outside the South. Moreover, there were many other issues for this mid-term election and Nixon was not this year running for re-election. Also, George Wallace was not, officially, running for President in 1970. As matters now stood, Nixon had proved his good faith to the South, with two nominations. He would be campaigning in the fall for conservative Republicans in the North and South. If he personally made the Haynsworth and Carswell defeats a political issue to the extent of postponing a third nomination, Northern conservatives might think him unreasonably obstinate and Northern liberals would accuse him of insensitivity in dragging the Supreme Court deep into political mire.

The conclusion then seemed obvious. The Haynsworth and Carswell defeats would be an issue in the fall and Nixon and Mitchell would do all they could to change the Senate, and in the meantime the President would swallow hard. He would be reasonable. Nixon and Mitchell would offer the Senate liberals a compromise, or the appearance of compromise which probably was all that was necessary. They would give the liberals a Northerner, and no more. They would nominate a Republican strict constructionist from the North to fill the Fortas vacancy and they would look to the November elections to change the Senate and to a time beyond November to nominate another Southerner to the Supreme Court. Nixon and Mitchell could wait. The President would not run again until 1972, and if Nixon and Mitchell were right in believing they spoke for the majority of the American people, they could wait until 1976. By then they would have one, maybe two, perhaps three more Supreme Court vacancies to fill. William O. Douglas was seventy-one years old now, sitting on the Court with an electronic heart pacer in his chest and with perhaps other vulnerabilities implanted in his years. Hugo Black was eighty-four and although he had no apparent heart trouble, he had had cataracts removed from his eyes and he was unsteady on his feet. John Harlan would be seventy next month and his eyesight had deteriorated. The President would not necessarily welcome Harlan's departure from the Court and Black's would evoke mixed feelings. But Douglas more than any other was keeping the spirit of Earl Warren alive.

Having decided on their political strategy, Nixon and Mitchell did not linger over the tactics of this nomination. Except that the nominee would be a Northerner, his basic qualifications would be the same as those of Burger, Haynsworth and Carswell. He would share the President's conservative philosophy, he would be a sitting Federal appellate judge with a track record, and he would not be a crony of the President. Since he would be from the North, he would have no track record at all to speak of in civil rights cases.

This time around, however, there were some differences. The first was that Nixon and Mitchell took into their confidence a third man, Warren Burger.* Burger was the Chief Justice, theoretically removed now from the President's struggles with Senate liberals, but he also was the only man Nixon and Mitchell had succeeded in placing on the Court, in three tries. The second difference was that Nixon this time decided that he personally would interview the prospective nominee. The President had not talked personally to Haynsworth or Carswell prior to their nominations. Therefore, it was arranged on Thursday afternoon, April 9, the day following Carswell's defeat, that Nixon and Mitchell would meet with the nominee the next day in the President's office at the White House.

Their plans in order, Nixon late on that same Thursday afternoon broke the public silence he had maintained for 24 hours following his defeat on the Carswell nomination. Visibly angry and appearing to reporters to be surprisingly lacking in his usual composure, Nixon entered the White House briefing room and stood before the press corps which had been called together on short notice. Mitchell was at the President's side and his face wore the same heavy-jowled sobriety.

Nixon told the press of his and Mitchell's conclusion:

> With the Senate presently constituted, it is not possible to get confirmation for a Judge on the Supreme Court of any man who believes in the strict construction of the Constitution, as I do, if he happens to come from the South.
>
> Judge Carswell, and before him, Judge Haynsworth, have been submitted to vicious assaults on their intelligence, on their honesty and on their character. They have been falsely charged with being racists. But when you strip away all the hypocrisy, the real reason for their rejection was their legal philosophy, a philosophy that I share, of strict construction of the Constitution.
>
> With yesterday's action, the Senate has said that no southern Federal

*The traditional secrecy of presidential communications with members of the Court was not violated by Nixon, Mitchell or Burger. Therefore, it is not known which took the initiative or at what point after the Carswell defeat Burger was taken into Nixon's and Mitchell's confidence. However, a White House source, on the day Nixon announced his new Court nomination, disclosed that Mitchell had talked with Burger about it, at some time prior to the public announcement. Subsequent to the nomination, secrecy became more difficult to maintain regarding Burger's communications with Nixon and Mitchell on other matters.

appellate judge who believes in a strict interpretation of the Constitution can be elevated to the Supreme Court.

As long as the Senate is constituted the way it is today, I will not nominate another Southerner and let him be subjected to the kind of malicious character assassination accorded both Judges Haynsworth and Carswell. However, my next nomination will be made in the very near future; a President should not leave that vacancy on the Court when it can be filled. My next nominee will be from outside the South and he will fulfill the criteria of a strict constructionist with judicial experience.

I understand the bitter feeling of millions of Americans who live in the South about the act of regional discrimination that took place in the Senate yesterday. They have my assurance that the day will come when men like Judges Carswell and Haynsworth can and will sit on the High Court.[1]

This was not the relaxed, confident President who had taken the press into his confidence, in May, 1969, to elaborate on his selection of Warren Burger. It was not even the less relaxed Nixon who hastily called in the press in October, 1969, to explain his nomination of Clement Haynsworth. This was a Richard Nixon who had not before been seen in the White House, a stiffly formal and very angry Nixon who had, indeed, not been seen publicly since the morning of November 6, 1962—the morning after he had lost the race to be governor of California.

On that morning, eight years earlier, Nixon also had stood before a group of reporters who were startled at his display of anger and emotion. He blamed the press for his defeat in the gubernatorial race, saying:

As I leave the press, all I can say is this: For sixteen years, ever since the Hiss case, you've had a lot of—a lot of fun—that you've had an opportunity to attack me and I think I've given as good as I've taken.

I made a talk on television, a talk in which I made a flub—one of the few that I make, not because I'm so good on television but because I've done it a long time. I made a flub in which I said I was running for governor of the United States. The Los Angeles *Times* dutifully reported that.

Some newspapers don't fall in the category to which I have spoken, but I can only say that the great metropolitan newspapers, they have a right to take every position they want on the editorial page, but on the news page they also have a right to have reporters cover men who have strong feelings whether they're for or against a candidate. But the responsibility also is to put a few [reporters] on, on the candidate they happen to be against, whether they're against him on the editorial page or just philosophically deep down, a fellow who at least will report what the man says. . . .

You won't have Nixon to kick around any more, because, gentlemen, this is my last press conference.[2]

President Nixon in his angry outburst on April 9, 1970, did not blame the press in so many words for the Carswell defeat. He was fully aware that leading Eastern newspapers on their editorial pages had strongly and repeatedly criticized the nomination. The Carswell nomination represented one of a number of major differences Nixon had with the press, and the President's deep distrust of the press was angrily, sarcastically, and repetitiously voiced for him by Vice President Agnew.

On the morning following his outburst, Nixon with Mitchell at his side talked privately for forty-five minutes in the President's Oval Office with the Northern strict constructionist they had selected. The President was satisfied. Mitchell then told the Federal Bureau of Investigation to make its customary investigation and he told Deputy Attorney General Richard G. Kleindienst to prepare and document a memorandum containing biographical information, a review of the nominee's more important judicial opinions, and a statement of all his personal financial holdings. Finally, Kleindienst was to give Republican leaders in Congress an advance briefing shortly before the President publicly announced the new nomination.

The preparations made, the White House five days later, on April 14, announced the nomination of Harry Andrew Blackmun of Rochester, Minnesota, to fill the Fortas vacancy. Blackmun was a Republican whom President Eisenhower in 1950 had appointed to the U.S. Court of Appeals for the Eighth Circuit, which has appellate jurisdiction in the states of Arkansas, Iowa, Missouri, Minnesota, Nebraska, North Dakota, and South Dakota. Blackmun was a sort of Northern Clement Haynsworth, graying and bespectacled, soft-spoken almost to the point of shyness, but he spoke in his opinions with some reason and not without compassion. Blackmun had been to Cambridge, as had

Haynsworth, and in fact they almost had been contemporaries at Harvard Law School. Blackmun, now sixty-one years old, had been graduated in 1932 and Haynsworth was a member of the Class of 1936. Blackmun also had been an undergraduate at Harvard, majoring in mathematics, and was elected to Phi Beta Kappa. Blackmun was not as rich as Haynsworth, or Fortas, but neither was he as poor as Carswell. He was not a crony of Nixon or Mitchell; he was a crony of Chief Justice Burger. It was one of those relationships between two men that had lasted since childhood. As young boys they had attended the same elementary school and Sunday school in St. Paul. Blackmun was Burger's only attendant when Burger was married in 1933. Blackmun had gone to Harvard College on a scholarship and Burger had gone to night school at the University of Minnesota and at the St. Paul College of Law. Although they both practiced law in the Minneapolis–St. Paul area in the years before and after World War II, they were not in constant touch in those years. Burger became very active in Republican politics in Minnesota and that path led to Washington in 1953. Blackmun was merely "a nominal Republican" and he continued to work in Minnesota as a lawyer until Eisenhower named him to the federal appellate bench in 1959. But Burger and Blackmun remained good friends. There was initially some mystery in 1959 as to why President Eisenhower would have given an appellate court appointment to so obscurely nominal a Republican. The generally accepted answer in Washington was that Warren Burger, by then an appeals court judge himself, recommended Blackmun to the Eisenhower Administration and President Eisenhower accepted the recommendation when a vacancy occurred on the Eighth Circuit in 1959.[3]

The strategy upon which Nixon and Mitchell had decided, and in which Burger concurred, to nominate a Northern strict constructionist to the Supreme Court worked perfectly. There were at the same time two additional developments, one major and the other minor, and the action in the three rings went forward together. The other major development that followed the defeat of G. Harrold Carswell was the decision of conservatives to press for an impeachment of Justice William O. Douglas. The minor development was the decision of Judge Carswell to resign from the U.S. Fifth Circuit Court of Appeals and take his defeat to the voters of Florida by becoming a candidate for election to the United States Senate.

William Douglas was not, to say the least, Nixon's or Mitchell's kind. An Associate Justice inevitably sits in the shadow of a great Chief Justice, but Douglas had been under attack by conservative Republicans and Southern Democrats for almost as long as Earl Warren. On the bench he was more of a civil libertarian than Earl Warren and more of an economic libertarian than his friend Abe Fortas. Douglas consistently voted in defense of the constitutional rights of blacks, the poor, and the criminally accused, but he wanted to go further than the Warren Court would go and urged, for instance, the strictest construction of the First Amendment. Douglas felt, along with Justice Black, that freedom of expression is so vital to democracy that the First Amendment must be read to prohibit government absolutely from infringing on freedom of speech (including obscene expression) and freedom of the press (including the libelous press). Douglas went further than Fortas would go in insisting on economic freedom. He urged the broadest interpretation of the antitrust laws, for example, to the end that almost all mergers of corporations that were actual and even potential competitors would be forbidden. Douglas, appointed to the Court by Franklin Roosevelt in 1939 and considered by FDR as a running mate in 1940 and again in 1944, was in sum one of the few remaining New Dealers in Washington whose liberalism, as that word is politically defined, had not been dimmed by the years. Like other younger liberals, he also was impatient. As he sat on the bench while the Court heard oral argument on some dry legal technicality, he often noisily moved books around in front of him and seemed to be paying little attention to what the lawyers were saying. It was as if he had heard all this argument before, and sometimes his opinions also seemed impatiently written.

Off the bench Douglas also was not conservative in his personal life style. He had climbed mountains and traveled most of the world. He had written no fewer than twenty-seven books.* He had written articles for popular magazines, given many lectures, promoted conservation of America's natural resources long before pollution became a popular issue, and, over the years, he had taken a total of four wives.

The current round of conservative interest in removing Douglas

*Douglas's first book was *Democracy and Finance*, published by the Yale University Press in 1940; his most recent was *Points of Rebellion* (New York: Random House, 1970). Many of his other books reflect his interest in nature and travel but some concerned constitutional issues.

from the Supreme Court had begun as early as the spring of 1969, when Abe Fortas resigned under fire. Senator Thurmond at that time voiced the opinion that Douglas also should resign. In November of that year, just before the Senate voted on the Haynsworth nomination, Representative Gerald R. Ford of Michigan, the Republican leader in the House, asserted that if Haynsworth were defeated impeachment proceedings should be brought against Douglas. The "Impeach Douglas" cries grew louder after Haynsworth was defeated, and just before the Senate voted on the Carswell nomination, Senator Robert C. Byrd of West Virginia, a Democrat who voted for both Haynsworth and Carswell, repeated that Douglas should be impeached if Carswell were defeated. Immediately prior to the Carswell vote, Representative Ford also said that Douglas "should have been impeached long ago" and after the vote Vice President Agnew concurred with Ford, saying Douglas's record should be "thoroughly examined."

Ford continued to study the matter. But he did nothing about it until the day after Nixon announced the nomination of Harry Blackmun. Then, on April 15, Ford on the House floor presented a very long "preliminary statement . . . of the law of impeachment and the facts about the behavior of Mr. Justice Douglas."

Ford, a lawyer, obviously had researched in some detail the law of impeachment. His statement reviewed the pertinent sections of Articles I, II and III of the Constitution, dealing with the powers of the Supreme Court, removal from office and impeachment procedure, but he told the House that "frankly, there are too few cases to make very good law." Nevertheless, he insisted there were grounds for the impeachment of Douglas and proceeded to define what they were, in his opinion. But his statement was more in the nature of a speech than a legal document. Ford complained about some books and magazine articles Douglas had written. He referred to a "Mr. Albert Parvin and a mysterious entity known as the Parvin Foundation," without throwing much light on the asserted mystery. He alluded even more vaguely to "gangsters," to "a bloody uprising" in the Dominican Republic, and to "young hothead revolutionaries," without being at all clear how such undesirable people and events were related to Douglas.

Ford called for creation of a House select committee to investigate whether there was probable cause to impeach Douglas, as Ford believed there was. The next day, a resolution signed by 104 House members, Republican and Democratic, was introduced to authorize creation of a select committee. But House liberals, alert now to the magnitude of the threat against Douglas, introduced their own impeachment resolution. The conservatives, in demanding the creation of a special House committee, were maneuvering to steer the Douglas investigation into friendly hands and to prevent it from falling into the grasp of Representative Emanuel Celler, the liberal who chaired the Judiciary Committee, a standing committee of the House. The liberals' resolution was worded so that like other bills dealing with the federal courts, it automatically would be referred to the Judiciary Committee and to Celler.

The liberals and Celler outfoxed the conservatives. Celler was dean of the House and at the age of eighty-two he had lost almost none of his legislative skill or his liberalism. After the liberals' resolution was referred, under House rules, to the Judiciary Committee, Celler quickly announced that he already had appointed a five-member special subcommittee of his Judiciary Committee to investigate the impeachment resolution against Justice Douglas. Celler named himself chairman of the subcommittee, which was not thereafter heard from for some months—not until after the November elections, as a matter of fact.

The Senate in Washington and the voters in Florida, however, heard much from Judge Carswell. It was less than two weeks after the Senate rejected him for the Supreme Court that Carswell announced he was quitting the Federal bench to run for the Senate. He called a press conference in Miami on April 20 and announced that if he could not help Nixon in "restructuring" the Supreme Court he would help the President to change the Senate. Carswell was flanked at the press conference by the state's two top Republican officeholders, Governor Claude R. Kirk, Jr., and Senator Edward Gurney. Gurney in January had introduced Carswell to the Judiciary Committee and had voted in the Senate for Haynsworth as well as Carswell. Kirk, a colorful, hard-driving conservative who also resisted the Warren Court's school desegregation decisions, was Florida's first Republican governor since 1876. Republicanism was on the rise in Florida and the state would have an opportunity to vote its indignation over what the Northern liberals had done to Carswell.

As Carswell opened his first political campaign since 1948, the Senate Judiciary Committee began its hearing on the nomination of Harry Blackmun. On Wednesday, April 29, at 10:45 in the morning

Chairman Eastland of Mississippi called the committee to order for the third time to consider the nomination to fill the Fortas vacancy.[4] After a leisurely two-hour lunch break the committee reconvened, and at 3:45 that afternoon the hearing on the nomination of Blackmun was finished. The conservative senators who had led the fight against Fortas—Griffin, Thurmond, Hruska—and the liberals who had fought hardest against Haynsworth and Carswell—Bayh, Kennedy, Hart—all were satisfied, impossible though that seemed less than a month earlier.

The brief, almost perfunctory hearing accorded the Blackmun nomination was astonishing. The conservatives during the battle over Fortas and the liberals in the struggles over Haynsworth and Carswell each in turn had insisted stoutly that the Senate had not only the right but the constitutional duty to investigate the ethical conduct and the philosophic disposition of the President's nominees to the Supreme Court. After Nixon announced the new nomination, the press dutifully reported, "Blackmun Facing Inquiry on Ethics; Close Questioning Expected at Senate Hearing."[5] The press reports were not without foundation. The Senate knew that Blackmun as an appellate judge had participated in the decision of several cases to which companies in which he owned stock were parties. The amounts of stock he owned were minute, but they appeared no less relevant than Judge Haynsworth's stockholdings. The Senate also knew that Judge Blackmun until 1964 had served as director of a corporation and that he still was a director of a foundation. There may have been no parallels, but the Senate had had good reason to be interested in Fortas's connections with another charitable foundation.

But neither conservatives nor liberals were inclined to question the personal finances, the judicial ethics, or the constitutional philosophy of Harry Blackmun, as they variously had investigated Fortas, Haynsworth, and Carswell. Not before and not now did the senators ask the ultimate question of whether this nominee, finally, was the most qualified man the President could find to sit on the Supreme Court and interpret the Constitution. To the contrary, Blackmun was a political compromise, a noncontroversial judge who had no taste either for resisting the Warren Court's doctrines or pressing forward constitutional rights. He was the kind of judge who was more interested in tax laws than civil rights, and when he wrote law review articles they were on such subjects as "The Marital Deduction and Its

Use in Minnesota" and "The Physician and His Estate." Senate conservatives were willing to accept their President's assurance that Blackmun on the Supreme Court would be a strict constructionist. Liberals were willing to rest with the satisfaction that they had forced Nixon to abandon the South. Anyway, the liberals also were members of a majoritarian branch of government and in 1970 the electorate, North and South, was changing.

The nomination of Harry A. Blackmun was so perfect a compromise that it accomplished the almost impossible result of uniting, for this moment anyway, Eugene J. McCarthy with Strom Thurmond. Senator McCarthy of Minnesota, who as a Democrat in 1968 had proved himself too liberal a presidential contender for his own party, introduced Blackmun, his fellow Minnesotan, to the Judiciary Committee. McCarthy was one of only three members of the Senate who had voted against all three of Nixon's earlier nomiees, Burger, Haynsworth and Carswell, and he said he was happy now to introduce a nominee "whom I can vote for."[6] Senator Thurmond also made reference to the past, saying to Blackmun "it appears that you are a man of high ethical conduct, as was Judge Haynsworth, and a man of competence, as was Judge Carswell." Thurmond was "glad," too, that Blackmun was a "strict constructionist" and one whom labor and civil rights leaders will not be able to "vent their spleen against." On this basis, Thurmond said, "I shall support your nomination."[7]

When Blackmun took his place at the witness table, the senators who sat on the Judiciary Committee already had been supplied with two documents that inventoried the personal and judicial experience of the nominee. One was the memorandum that Mitchell had directed Kleindienst to prepare. The other was from the American Bar Association's Standing Committee on the Federal Judiciary, which this time had made a more thorough investigation than it had conducted prior to stating its approval of the Haynsworth and Carswell nominations.

These documents related that Harry Blackmun after graduating from Harvard Law School had practiced law in Minneapolis for sixteen years, specializing in tax work, wills, trusts, and estate planning. In 1950 he moved to Rochester, Minnesota, to become resident counsel to the Mayo Clinic, the famous medical establishment there, and to the Mayo Foundation. He also became an officer or director of a number of other organizations which were affiliated with or outgrowths of the Mayo Clinic. One was the Kahler Corporation, which operated a hotel in Rochester. Another was the Kahler Corporation Foundation. When President Eisenhower named him to the Eighth Circuit Court of Appeals in 1959, Blackmun resigned from his position with the Mayo Clinic and its affiliates. But he remained a director of Kahler Corporation until 1964 and in 1970 he still was a director of the Kahler Foundation. These documents also showed that Blackmun owned small amounts of common stocks in each of nine large corporations, including Ford Motor Company and American Telephone and Telegraph Company, as well as some Mankato Fire Station bonds, and some United States Treasury bills, all of which he had purchased from time to time at a total original cost of $52,691.83.

Both the Kleindienst memorandum and the American Bar Association report discussed the cases to which Ford and an AT&T subsidiary were parties. The Kleindienst memorandum concluded that Judge Blackmun's stockholdings in the two companies were "microscopic."[8] The ABA report agreed that the "stock holdings are so small that in our opinion he violated no statute or canon" in participating in the decision of the cases.[9]

The two documents also surveyed Blackmun's more important opinions on the Eighth Circuit. They covered a diverse range of tax, criminal, and other matters and they often were exceedingly lengthy opinions. For example, Judge Blackmun twice wrote opinions of the Eighth Circuit, both involving Negroes convicted of raping white women in Arkansas, rejecting constitutional claims that the death penalty would not have been given white rape defendants in the same circumstances. But in another case he wrote that Arkansas could not constitutionally use straps to beat convicts. He dissented when a majority of the Eighth Circuit judges threw out a conviction on the ground that the evidence against the defendant should have been suppressed. He wrote the majority opinion when the Eighth Circuit rejected an Arkansas school district's desegregation plan which provided for the continuation of four all-black schools. He also wrote the Eighth Circuit's decision holding that a St. Louis Negro was not allowed by the Civil Rights Act of 1866 to sue a real estate developer who refused to sell him a home in a white suburban housing development. That decision was reversed by the Warren Court in the case of *Jones* v. *Mayer.*[10]

The ABA committee concluded with the unanimous verdict that

SOUTHERN POLITICS AND A NORTHERN JUSTICE

Blackmun "meets high standards of professional competence, temperament and integrity."[11] The Kleindienst memorandum suggested a similar conclusion. The liberal and conservative senators who sat on the Judiciary Committee did not look much beyond the documents submitted to them.

The conservatives asked Blackmun almost no questions at all. Senator McClellan reminded the nominee that the Supreme Court has no "right to usurp" the powers of Congress or the President. Senator Ervin expressed his conclusion that Blackmun was "willing and able" to give meaningful expression on the Supreme Court to those criticisms of the Warren Court which had been voiced in 1958 by the state chief justices. Senator Hruska said, "This committee has never abdicated its responsibility in favor of the American Bar Association or any other body, but I want to say that it is comforting to have their opinion."[12]

The liberals asked a few questions. Senator Hart asked what a strict constructionist is, and Blackmun said he did not know. Senator Bayh questioned the nominee briefly about his stock holdings and seemed satisfied with the answers. Senator Kennedy said to Blackmun, "There has been a great deal of discussion about your relationship with the Chief Justice. Could you tell us a little bit about this?"[13] Blackmun related how "we grew up together," mentioned the known fact that he was the best man at Burger's wedding, and then assured Kennedy that, despite their friendship, as a member of Burger's Court he "would have no hesitation whatsoever in disagreeing" with the Chief Justice. Kennedy apparently was alluding to the separation of powers doctrine, which had been referred to before, when Fortas was denied the Chief Justiceship and when Nixon addressed the Court on the day Burger was sworn in. Kennedy could have pursued Burger's relationships with Nixon, on one hand, and with Blackmun, on the other. He would have found that Nixon and Mitchell had taken Burger into their confidence before nominating Blackmun. And he could have found evidence that Burger and Blackmun remained close in recent years. While Blackmun as an appellate judge remained a part-time director of the Kahler Corporation Foundation, Burger as an appellate judge had remained a trustee of the Mayo Foundation.* But Kennedy did not pursue the matter.

*Burger was a trustee for about eleven years. He resigned when he became Chief Justice.

The good feeling that prevailed, between Nixon's conservative nominee and the most liberal of the Democrats on the committee, was further illustrated by a colloquy in which Senator Kennedy talked about the problems of young people and Judge Blackmun revealed that he was fondly known to one of his daughters as an "old crock."[14]

Kennedy had spoken of Earl Warren's "very unique contribution to the Court" and then asked Blackmun his view of the racial, welfare, education, police, and many other problems that still face the nation.

"I could not be the parent to three daughters who have now attained the age 20 and a little beyond, without being aware of these things which you have mentioned," Blackmun answered. "These are difficult times. I do not despair. I think they are exciting times in which to live."

Kennedy asked, "From your conversations with your daughters, could you give us any kind of a feeling as to what you believe are some of their reservations in terms of alienation from the system?"

"These little daughters of ours," Blackmun said, "I call them little even though the two younger ones are now married and the oldest is a constituent of yours—they have been in my view able, intelligent, questioning individuals. There have been times, I know, when they have regarded me as perhaps, to use the vernacular and the expression that one of them used, as an old crock, but I believe that Mrs. Blackmun and I have tried to communicate with these young people. I think we have broken through whatever barrier there is.

"I have no problem with the girls. One has to work at it and sometimes go a little farther than halfway but I believe that they feel that maybe the old man could be a lot worse than he is."

Blackmun apparently was not going to be responsive to the questions and Kennedy, deliberately or hopelessly, pursued the nominee's philosophy no further. Kennedy concluded the colloquy saying, "Certainly, I think your response in terms of the alienation of youth has been extremely helpful."

There ended the Senate's investigation into the qualifications of Harry A. Blackmun to sit on the Supreme Court. The Judiciary Committee on May 9 voted to report to the Senate that Blackmun was "thoroughly qualified" and there were no dissents.

It happened that on the night of May 9 President Nixon again was unable to sleep, as he apparently had been one month earlier after the Senate defeated the Carswell nomination. This night Nixon did not go cruising down the Potomac with Attorney General Mitchell. Nixon's sleep was disturbed by alienated young people and, just before dawn, he drove from the White House to the Lincoln Memorial to talk with youths who were the remnants of a massive antiwar demonstration which had taken place the previous day.

Between 75,000 and 100,000 young men and women, most of them white college students, had come to Washington to participate in a nonviolent demonstration, as close as possible to the White House. There had been two mass demonstrations in the capital the previous fall, on October 15 and November 15. They also were to have been staged without violence, and in large part they were, but at the Justice Department there were broken windows and its Constitution Avenue façade was pockmarked with splotches of red paint. Mitchell watched from a fifth-floor balcony inside the locked building and, after the November 15 demonstration, Martha Mitchell on a national television interview said: "I will tell you, my husband made the comment to me, looking out the Justice Department it looked like the Russian revolution going on. As my husband has said many times, some of the liberals in this country, he'd like to take them and change them for the Russian Communists."[15]

The young people who looked like revolutionaries to John and Martha Mitchell also had protested in many other places throughout the land. They had demanded an end to the Vietnam war, reforms in college administration, and black study programs on campuses from coast to coast. In Chicago the Justice Department had brought to trial eight of the radicals, on charges of conspiring to incite riots at the 1968 Democratic National Convention; the trial was the first test of the anti-riot section of the 1968 Civil Rights Act.

By May of 1970, therefore, the level of confrontation in Washington was substantially higher than it had been when youths demonstrated the previous fall. Earlier in that month of May, Nixon referred to campus radicals who opposed his Vietnam policies as "bums." Three days later National Guard gunfire killed four white students at an antiwar rally on the campus of Kent State University in Ohio. In Washington President Nixon had assigned to Attorney General Mitchell full command of all government preparations, military and civilian, for the May 9 demonstration. Mitchell prepared to "guarantee rights of free speech and assembly while ensuring the general safety and welfare of all citizens." He mobilized local and federal police, the National Guard, and the Army. Communications networks were established, supply lines planned, and mass arrest procedures written. The demonstration took place with a few more broken windows at the Justice Department, but nothing worse, and President Nixon that night was able to drive without difficulty to the Lincoln Memorial.

Three days later the Senate voted 94 to 0 to confirm the nomination of Harry Blackmun and on June 9, 1970, Blackmun took his seat on the Court. His old friend, Warren Burger, administered the oath and pleasantly said, "We look forward to many years of work together in our common calling." The Chief Justice did not define their calling and President Nixon did not come to the Court to attend the ceremony. But after it was over, Burger and Blackmun drove together to the White House for a cup of coffee and a chat with the President.

The ninth seat vacated by Abe Fortas had remained empty for one year and twenty-six days. During that time, great change had taken place outside the Court. The nature of dissent in America changed. No longer were blacks rioting and burning in the ghettos of the largest cities, and no more were Congress and the White House moving forward with major new civil rights legislation. The fears and hopes of the White House, Congress, and the nation were turned now to riotous young whites, who soon won from their government the right to vote at age eighteen. In his guarded fortress Mitchell no longer talked with blacks in the Great Hall; he and his entire executive staff arranged a series of meetings at the Justice Department to talk with clean-cut young whites and they made many trips to college campuses to promote "change within the system." Nixon and Mitchell pursued a positive policy of isolating young radicals, white and black, who persisted in violent words and deeds, and of confronting them with new law and order tactics that included electronic surveillance, "preventive detention," "no-knock" searches and seizures, and massive arrests.

The great changes were reflected, sometimes subtly, as the Senate considered the succession of nominations to fill the vacant ninth seat. The civil rights issue was debated, along with other topics, when the Senate considered the Haynsworth nomination. Carswell was rejected in part because of a racist speech he had made many years earlier. But when Nixon retreated to the North and nominated Blackmun, the civil rights issue was less clearly drawn and the nature of dissent in the streets was changing more rapidly. Senators who tried to question Blackmun about the alienation of youth almost ignored the civil rights issue, and the National Association for the Advancement of Colored People did not testify at the hearing.

Senators also are members of a majoritarian branch, and eventually Congress and the White House would make their peace with the great majority of dissenting whites. Blacks, however, would have to look still and again to the Supreme Court and they would see that a strict constructionist from the North bears a striking resemblance to one from the South.

# CHAPTER 13

# Retribution and Recklessness

As Justice Blackmun was slipping comfortably into his black robe at the Supreme Court, G. Harrold Carswell's campaign against the United States Senate for denying the same privilege to him was encountering unexpected difficulty in Florida. Carswell was stumping the state under the motto, "This time the people will decide," and making speeches such as one at a Kiwanis Club luncheon where a band was playing "Dixie" and Carswell rose up to say, "I truly believe that I stand before you as one Republican who can sing 'Dixie' with conviction." He told the Florida voters that the "ultra-liberals" in the Senate had not solved their own school, racial, and narcotics problems in the North, "and yet they have the audacity, if you please, and I might even suggest the hypocrisy, to try to export their brand of government all over this nation."*

White middle-class audiences cheered but anyone could see that Carswell as a political campaigner had grown a bit rusty since 1948. Reporters were writing that his handshaking was stiff, his collars seemed too big, and, ironically, that his speeches often sounded like legal opinions. He sometimes blurted malapropisms, such as, "When I'm senator from Florida, the present level of mediocrity in the Senate, whatever it is, will be raised."** Also, there was a question whether Carswell really could mount an effective campaign in Florida by running against Northern liberals who represented other states in the Senate. A radio and television announcement, for instance, urged voters to "send him to Washington to do battle with Senate liberals like Kennedy, Fulbright, and Birch Bayh."

*Wall Street Journal, July 30, 1970, p. 1.
**New York Times, July 13, 1970, p. 38.

On top of those difficulties, Carswell faced an unfortunate problem within the Republican Party in Florida. Carswell had the support of Governor Kirk and Senator Gurney, and all three apparently had assumed that the party could be united behind Carswell's candidacy. But Representative William Cramer, a Republican who had represented his Florida district in Congress for sixteen years, refused to unite. Cramer also wanted to be the party's candidate for the seat from which Democratic Senator Spessard Holland was retiring, and his claim to the Republican nomination was particularly strong because, some time before the Senate refused to confirm Carswell for the Supreme Court, President Nixon had assumed there would be no other worthy Republican contenders and personally had urged Cramer to be the Republican candidate in the Senate race in Florida. So Carswell now was caught in the middle of a Republican power struggle in the state, and he had to beat Cramer in a primary election in September before he could run against the Democratic nominee for the Senate seat in the November general election. The primary campaign really offered Florida Republican voters little choice because Cramer was as conservative as Carswell and both were for Nixon and against school busing, obscene movies, and riotous young people. But Cramer, a tough and seasoned political campaigner with a grass-roots political organization, won the election with a substantial 62.7 per cent of the votes cast in the Republican primary. Carswell thus did not help Nixon in the Senate or the Supreme Court, his judgeship was gone, and the best Nixon could do was to name him to a part-time job that paid no salary on an obscure agency in Washington with a ponderous name, the Administrative Conference of the United States.

But Nixon, assuming a stance that was not inaccurately described as vengeful, in the fall did take his fight with the liberal Democrats and effetist Republicans to the people in Florida and twenty-two other states. Vice President Agnew campaigned in thirty-two states and together Nixon and Agnew transformed the mid-term elections into a contest that approached a national referendum on the Nixon Presidency, even though the Supreme Court vacancy had been filled. It was a risky venture, as Nixon and Mitchell certainly knew. There was risk enough because mid-term elections, more than elections when the President is running, tend to turn on hundreds of different local issues and personalities. The results inevitably are less than crystal clear, insofar as national trends are concerned, and the party in control of the White House frequently loses seats in Congress in a mid-term election.

But Nixon and Agnew plowed in anyway, spreading before the voters the issues that implicitly and explicitly had been fought over in the Senate. There were, of course, other national issues in the 1970 elections, such as unemployment and Vietnam, and there were gubernatorial and House as well as Senate races. Nixon could not campaign against Earl Warren and Ramsey Clark as he had done in 1968. He had not in 1968 and he did not in 1970 campaign against civil rights as such. In 1970, as in the earlier election, Nixon made law and order the big issue and he and Agnew were hard-line campaigners again against campus rioting, school busing, and the coddling of criminals. On election eve Nixon bought prime-time television to tell the nation that America's dissenters were not "romantic revolutionaries." Dissenters, he said, "are the same thugs and hoodlums that have always plagued the good people. Our approach, the new approach," he asserted, "demands new and strong laws that will give the peace forces new muscle to deal with the criminal forces in the United States."

In the elections the next day the Republicans suffered net losses of nine seats in the House of Representatives, ten governors' chairs, and control of about two dozen state legislatures. But the Republicans scored a net gain of two seats in the United States Senate. Washington pundits interpreted the results as a horrendous defeat for Nixon. The President interpreted them as an enormous success, "ideologically," and Nixon was closer to being right.

Nixon lost some races, politically and ideologically. In Florida Republican Cramer was defeated for the U.S. Senate by his Democratic opponent, a moderate named Lawton Chiles. A liberal Democrat named Adlai E. Stevenson III in Illinois defeated a Nixon Republican, Ralph T. Smith, for the late Everett McKinley Dirksen's seat in the Senate. In California a liberal and young Democrat named John V. Tunney ousted Senator George Murphy, a conservative Republican, from his Senate seat. Albert W. Watson, a conservative Republican handpicked by Richard Nixon and Strom Thurmond, was defeated in his bid for the governorship of South Carolina by a moderate Democrat, John C. West. And in Minnesota voters returned Nixon's 1968 presidential opponent, Hubert Humphrey, to the U.S. Senate; Humphrey defeated Clark MacGregor, the Republican endorsed personally by Attorney General Mitchell, for the Senate seat of retiring Democrat Eugene McCarthy.

But Nixon also won some, and his successes were ideologically more significant than his losses. Nixon, Agnew, and Mitchell had given the Senate their highest priority, and Agnew had singled out as "radic-libs" Senators Gore of Tennessee, Goodell of New York, Tydings of Maryland, Hart of Michigan, Kennedy of Massachusetts, and Proxmire of Wisconsin. Gore's sponsorship of Fortas for the Chief Justiceship and his votes against confirmation of Haynsworth and Carswell became major issues in the Tennessee race, and he was defeated by a Republican strongly backed by Nixon and Agnew, William E. Brock III. Goodell was a Republican, but a liberal, who also had voted against Haynsworth and Carswell; he was defeated by James L. Buckley, the New York Conservative Party candidate who campaigned with the tacit support of Nixon and Agnew. Tydings was a liberal Democrat who, though a member of the Judiciary Committee, had not assumed a leadership role in the fights against the Haynsworth and Carswell nominations; but he voted against Haynsworth and Carswell, and was defeated for re-election by his Republican opponent, J. Glenn Beall, Jr. And, in Alabama, George C. Wallace was returned on a landslide to the governor's chair, scoring an ideological victory and a political defeat for Richard Nixon. Nixon and Agnew did not defeat Hart, Kennedy, or Proxmire, but they did not expect to beat these particularly popular Democrats.

The most impressive evidence of Nixon's claim to ideological victory in 1970, however, was not his net gain of two seats in the Senate. It was the perceptible movement of many candidates and voters toward the right on the law and order issue, in its full context; if Nixon's victory was not complete in the partisan political sense, it was rendered incomplete largely because many liberal Democratic and effetist Republican candidates had met the Nixon-Agnew-Mitchell challenge by moving closer to the President's position on the burning issues of youthful protest and civil liberties.

The November election over, the President returned to the White House, Congress returned to the Capitol, and Representative Emanuel Celler's special subcommittee issued its final report on the matter of Justice William O. Douglas.

The conservatives' attack on and the liberals' defense of Douglas turned out to be an interesting, but relatively unimportant, chapter in the battle for control of the Supreme Court. It was too obviously an exercise in political retribution, in both its offensive and defensive aspects. It was almost a comic opera, in which conservatives sought to avenge the defeats of Haynsworth and Carswell and the liberals succeeded almost in rectifying the destruction of Abe Fortas. The Republicans who started it were no match at all for the Democrats who ended it. Emanuel Celler outfoxed the Republicans all the way and in the end succeeded even in accusing Attorney General Mitchell of refusing to contribute to the determination of the profound question of whether Justice Douglas should be tried for "high crimes and misdemeanors."

Celler was the judge; Representative Ford, the House Republican leader, was the chief prosecutor; the defense was given a helping hand by a lawyer named Ramsey Clark, the predecessor of John Mitchell and the archenemy of Richard Nixon. Douglas had retained, to represent him before the Celler subcommittee, a New York lawyer named Simon H. Rifkind, whose prestigious law firm was to the Democratic Party much what Nixon's and Mitchell's old New York firm had been to the Republican Party, a place of welcome for political luminaries who temporarily or otherwise were out of office.* After his dismissal by President Nixon, Ramsey Clark had become a member of the Rifkind firm, in charge of its Washington office. Clark did much of the leg work in defense of Douglas, although Rifkind retained top billing and made the required public presentations on Douglas's behalf. One of the documents Rifkind presented to the Celler subcommittee was an expensively handsome and specially prepared eighty-page booklet which was titled, as if to goad the conservatives more, "Readings from the Works of William O. Douglas." It contained excerpts from many of Douglas's writings, ranging from his first book, published in 1940, to an article he had written for the *Ladies' Home Journal* in 1964, and it demonstrated that among Justice Douglas's

---

*Rifkind's firm was Paul, Weiss, Goldberg, Rifkind, Wharton & Garrison. Simon Rifkind for many years had been associated with Democratic figures in New York and Washington. President Franklin Roosevelt had named him to the federal bench, from which he subsequently resigned to return to private practice. President Kennedy had named him to a panel which exhaustively studied railroad labor problems, and Rifkind at one time represented Kennedy's widow. The Goldberg in the firm's name of course was Arthur Goldberg. Another member was Theodore C. Sorensen, former special counsel to President Kennedy.

other merits were his reverence for God, the flag, "the right to bear children," and, last but not least, "judicial restraint."

The writing of twenty-seven books appeared to be a record for any Justice in the history of the Supreme Court, but it was not in itself an impeachable offense. Neither was the writing of articles for the *Ladies' Home Journal.* But the title of Douglas' latest book, *Points of Rebellion,* was alone enough to make conservatives deeply suspicious. Representative Ford, in the bill of particulars against Douglas he had presented to the House on April 15, 1970, said the book was evidence of the seventy-one-year-old Justice's "espousal of hippie-yippie style revolution." Worse, if possible, was the fact that an excerpt from *Points of Rebellion* had been purchased by *Evergreen* magazine and published with an accompanying cartoon that depicted a very full-jowled Richard Nixon dressed as King George III.[1] The excerpt and cartoon were immediately preceded in the pertinent issue of *Evergreen* by a five-page portfolio of more than a dozen sepia photographs of women in various horizontal positions, very full-breasted and very nude. Representative Ford thought the Justice's book might be "drivel," and he was quite certain the photographs were "hard-core pornography."

Douglas off the bench practiced what he preached on the bench about freedom of speech and of the press, and his energetic individualism often had frightened conservatives and sometimes also had given pause to the more tradition-minded liberals. Justice Douglas for years in his writings and speeches had been attacking, not always with great care, such honored institutions as the Army Corps of Engineers and the Federal Bureau of Investigation. Some of his attacks had appeared not only in *Evergreen* but also in magazines such as *Playboy* and *Avant Garde.* There were various other instances where his choice of forums was inappropriate for a member of the Supreme Court. For example, after *Points of Rebellion* was published, Douglas helped to promote sales of the book, like any other struggling author, by making himself available one Saturday for free autographs in the book department of Woodward & Lothrop, a downtown Washington department store that prominently advertised his appearance in the local papers. He chose his friends not from among the leaders of the American Bar Association or the academic community, with whom members of the Supreme Court might be expected to mingle in private life; rather, he found friends in such liberal places as the Fund for the Republic and its adjunct, the Center for the Study of Democratic Institutions, in California and in unstuffy haunts like Jimmie's Cafe, a comfortable, old sandwich and beer pub on Pennsylvania Avenue, near the Supreme Court, in Washington.

Another aspect of Justice Douglas's private life was his four marriages. Representative Ford did not specifically mention the four wives in his recitation of charges against Douglas. But Washington in many ways resembles a small town when it gossips about the private lives of its official residents, and the Douglas marriages had been talked and written about for years. Of course they were part of the life of the Justice and were woven inextricably into the background of the move to impeach him.

Douglas's first wife and the mother of his two children was Mildred Riddle. They were married in 1923, before Douglas graduated from Columbia University Law School, and the marriage lasted for thirty years until it was ended by divorce. It was then that Douglas at the age of fifty-five embarked on his series of marriages that made the conservatives frown and everybody talk. About a year after his divorce, he married the former Mercedes Hester, a younger research assistant to the Justice who was the attractive daughter of a one-time sheriff of Tallulah, Louisiana. She divorced him on July 31, 1963, and the Supreme Court's press office announced a few days later, on August 5, that Douglas on that day had married Miss Joan C. Martin. The third Mrs. Douglas was a very attractive twenty-three-year-old government worker whom Douglas reportedly had met a bit earlier when he was lecturing at Allegheny College in Meadville, Pennsylvania, where she was a student. The third marriage lasted until she filed for divorce in late 1965, charging Douglas with personal indignity. Six months later, at the age of sixty-seven, when most men have retired, Douglas married a pretty twenty-three-year-old blonde with a pixie haircut named Cathleen Heffernan, of Portland, Oregon, and they went off on a camping and hiking honeymoon in Douglas's home territory in the Pacific Northwest, saying they planned a second honeymoon as soon as they could get visas to Red China. Douglas had been talking about going to the Chinese mainland since about 1950. But he was far, far ahead of his time, until President Nixon decided to make the trip in 1972. Their common interest in Red China was a happy coincidence, because it was about the only thing they shared.

Representative Ford's bill of particulars against Douglas rested essentially on five charges, vague though they were, that Representative Celler's subcommittee had to deal with.[2] First, Ford alleged, as the liberals had against Haynsworth, that Justice Douglas had participated in the decision of cases from which he should have disqualified himself because of personal interests; for instance, said Ford, there were several obscenity cases against magazines which had published articles by Douglas and for which he presumably had been paid. Second, Ford alleged that Justice Douglas while a member of the Supreme Court might have been paid to give legal advice, a practice forbidden by law. Third, the Republican leader took issue with Douglas's new book, *Points of Rebellion,* because, Ford declared, in it Douglas "and his young hothead revolutionaries" encouraged violence. Fourth, Ford took very particular exception to the issue of *Evergreen* magazine in which appeared the excerpt from *Points of Rebellion,* accompanied by the cartoon depicting Richard Nixon as George III and preceded, Ford had told the House, by "hard-core pornography." Finally, he alleged that something was amiss in the $12,000 a year Douglas had been drawing as president of the charitable foundation whose principal asset was a mortgage on the Hotel Flamingo and its gambling casino in Las Vegas, Nevada.

Before these allegations could be dealt with, however, the prosecution and the defense had to face the threshhold question of what is an impeachable offense? As Ford had acknowledged, there had been so few impeachment proceedings, and still fewer convictions, in American history that there really was very little legal or factual precedent. Concerning the Supreme Court and inferior courts, the Constitution said merely that justices and judges "shall hold their Offices during good Behavior."[3] Relative to impeachment generally, it said the House "shall have the sole Power of Impeachment"[4]—a process similar to an indictment voted by a grand jury. The Constitution said the Senate "shall have the sole Power to try all Impeachment. When the President of the United States is tried, the Chief Justice shall preside: And no Person shall be convicted without the Concurrence of two thirds of the Members present."[5] It said that the penalty "in Cases of Impeachment shall not extend further than to removal from Office," although a removed official subsequently could be tried in an ordinary criminal court.[6] Finally, the Constitution said, in reference at least to members of the executive branch, that "The President, Vice President and all civil Officers of the United States, shall be removed from Office on Impeachment for, and Conviction of, Treason, Bribery, or other High Crimes and Misdemeanors."[7] As with so many other parts of the Constitution, the sections concerning impeachment raised more questions than they answered, when applied to a concrete set of facts.

Representative Ford insisted that what the Constitution meant was that "an impeachable offense is whatever a majority of the House of Representatives considers it to be at a given moment in history." His loose construction, however, was immediately attacked by two lawyers who should have been Ford's friends. Fred Rodell, a professor who had taught Ford at Yale Law School, wrote a scathing letter to the editor of the New York *Times* in which he asserted that Ford's standards required the impeachment also of Judges Haynsworth and Carswell and insisted that Ford's effort against Douglas alone "lays bare not only the strictly political motivation of his move but also the blatant and patent intellectual dishonesty of my old student and one-time friend, Representative Gerald Ford."[8] The second lawyer who attacked Ford's position was Representative Paul N. ("Pete") McCloskey, Jr., the ex-Marine who was a Republican thorn in Nixon's side. McCloskey, from California, had been in the House for three years, compared with Ford's twenty-two years of service. Nevertheless, McCloskey on the floor of the House made a speech attacking the Republican leader, asserting that Ford's interpretation of the Constitution "would do grave damage to one of the most treasured cornerstones of our liberties" by subjecting the entire federal judiciary to fears of the threat of executive or legislative disfavor. He said he was not defending Douglas, but insisted that his study of the precedent that existed suggested that a successful impeachment had never been brought except for judicial misconduct, on the bench, or criminal behavior off the bench.[9]

The Celler subcommittee decided that impeachment for "high crimes and misdemeanors" did not necessarily require a showing of criminal conduct, on or off the bench, but it did require "a showing of misconduct which is inherently serious in relation to social standards."[10] But the interpretation was not really necessary. The subcommittee on December 16, 1970, released a tome of 924 pages on its investigation of Justice Douglas, but the conclusion of the majority was stated in three lines: "Intensive investigation of the Special Subcommittee has not disclosed creditable evidence that would warrant preparation of charges on any acceptable concept of an impeachable offense."[11]

In the 924 pages was buried a variety of interesting tidbits. For instance, Douglas's income tax returns showed that he had been so busy that he actually had been making more off the bench than on. In the ten-year period 1960–69, his Supreme Court salary was $389,-749.26. In the same period his writing and lecturing brought in $377,-260.19 and in addition he received $96,680.00 from the Parvin Foundation.[12] His book and magazine writing business was indeed so substantial that he employed the services of a literary agent.[13] Random House thought well enough of his literary talents to give him a $10,000 advance against royalties on *Points of Rebellion*.[14] But strangely, it would seem, Douglas in 1968 found it necessary to ask his friend Albert Parvin for a loan to buy two lots in front of the Douglas lodge at Goose Prairie, Washington.[15]

Among other tidbits, the Celler volume disclosed that President Johnson had spent three hours one evening in June, 1966, listening to Douglas discuss plans for an international convocation in Geneva at which Douglas apparently hoped to build bridges between the United States and the governments of North Vietnam and possibly Red China also.[16] And the document revealed a private letter, dated May 12, 1969, in which Douglas wrote to Albert Parvin that some unnamed force was pursuing a "strategy . . . to get me off the Court."[17]

Mostly, however, the tome contained pages upon pages of reproduced letters and other papers from the files of Douglas, Parvin, and others that seemed to bear only marginally on the charges Representative Ford had outlined. With this overwhelming stack of papers, the Celler subcommittee disposed of the charges, one by one. It concluded that Douglas had neither participated in cases from which he should have disqualified himself nor given legal advice. The subcommittee decided that Ford and his conservative friends had quoted parts of *Points of Rebellion* out of context and it went to the trouble of supplying the context. The subcommittee also found that the Justice had nothing to do with the dirty pictures in *Evergreen* magazine, because, it said, the publisher had sold the excerpt from the Douglas book to *Evergreen* without Douglas's consent. Finally, the subcommittee disposed of Douglas's involvement with the Parvin Foundation.

Many wealthy men, of course, set up foundations to which they can make tax-free contributions. Presidents, including Nixon as well as

Johnson, have them.[18] At least three other members of the Supreme Court had or used to have connections with foundations. Albert Parvin was a wealthy businessman who had established the Parvin Foundation in 1961 and assigned to it a portion of the proceeds of the mortgage he held on the Hotel Flamingo in Las Vegas.[19] Parvin was the president of a Los Angeles concern, Parvin-Dohrmann Company, which also acquired interests in certain Las Vegas hotels and gambling casinos. Parvin, according to the Celler report, admired Douglas's writings and consequently Douglas became president and a director, serving in those positions from the inception of the foundation until May 21, 1969. Other directors included Parvin; Robert F. Goheen, president of Princeton University; and Robert M. Hutchins, president, and Harry S. Ashmore, executive vice president, of the Center for the Study of Democratic Institutions. The Center, an institution with a notoriously liberal reputation, was located in Santa Barbara, California. It sponsored seminars in which many prominent persons participated; Warren E. Burger, as a federal appellate judge, once participated.[20]

The ties between the Center and the Parvin Foundation were quite close. According to the Celler report, the foundation provided some financial support to the Center, and Douglas, while president of the foundation, also held office with the Center. But the foundation's major purposes were to sponsor Parvin Fellowships for young men from Africa, the Middle East, and Asia at Princeton and the University of California at Los Angeles. In time it began to branch out, with, for example, educational programs to teach illiterate adults in the Dominican Republic how to read and write. In time also, the Celler report said, the foundation became the subject of an investigation by the Internal Revenue Service, and Justice Douglas as president of the foundation recommended that it retain the services of an expert tax lawyer.[21] The lawyer who was retained, in 1966, was Carolyn Agger, who in private life was, of course, the wife of then Justice Abe Fortas. Douglas, according to the Parvin Foundation, resigned in May, 1969, because of "too heavy a work load"; the foundation denied that there was any relationship with the resignation of Abe Fortas from the Supreme Court that same month, following the disclosure that Fortas had agreed to accept an annual stipend from the Wolfson Family Foundation.[22]

Those were the facts, as found by the Celler subcommittee. The majority of its members found in the facts no evidence that would warrant impeachment proceedings against Douglas. It disposed of the issue of Douglas's acceptance of $12,000 annually in "compensation" by concluding that he had performed no legal services for the foundation and therefore violated no law. No mention was made of Fortas's agreement to accept $20,000 annually from the Wolfson Foundation, and no effort was made to explain why Fortas's conduct was wrong and Douglas's right. Representative Ford in making his charges on the House floor had recited also the names of some of the nation's best known hoodlums whom he linked in one way or another with Las Vegas hotels and casinos. But Douglas through his lawyers denied flatly any personal associations or relations with hoodlums, and the Celler subcommittee majority concluded that nothing in the "files of this investigation supports these charges."

The majority was composed of the three Democrats on the subcommittee, Celler, Byron G. Rogers of Colorado, and Jack Brooks of Texas. The two Republicans who completed the subcommittee were Representatives William M. McCulloch of Ohio and Edward Hutchinson of Michigan. Hutchinson alone dissented,, saying the subcommittee had amassed a huge array of documents and done little to find out what they all meant. McCulloch abstained, which was about the best he could do for his old friend Manny Celler. McCulloch had been in Congress only twenty-three years, compared with Celler's forty-eight, but McCulloch was the senior Republican on the Judiciary Committee, and in Congress seniority sometimes takes precedent even over party.

Celler's investigators had examined more than half a million documents, according to the chairman, from which they selected 287 for reproduction in the final report. The subcommittee apparently had taken no testimony under oath. It had held no public hearings. The conservatives cried "whitewash" and objected that Douglas had been let off without so much as a reprimand. To which Celler replied: "I am sure all fair-minded people after studying . . . this mountain of evidence . . . will agree that there is no basis for impeachment of Associate Justice Douglas. Should we strain to dredge all of the Seven Seas?"

Celler had drowned the charges against Douglas in a sea of paper. The investigation was over and the public, having no way of really of knowing whether Douglas had been more than indiscreet, had been treated only to a bit more than it had learned concerning the full and true nature of Fortas, Haynsworth, Carswell or Blackmun. But the liberals had won this round; the conservatives would not force Douglas off the Court, not as long as Celler remained in the House.

Douglas was a tough old man who had no intention of giving Nixon his seat to fill. Weaker and younger men had fled but Douglas, the morning after Celler released his report, called a press conference at the Supreme Court building. His purpose was to announce that he of course had no intention of resigning, if perchance the Republicans still hoped he might. He placed himself in the spot where Earl Warren had stood in the spring of 1968 in the East Conference Room and said the Celler subcommittee "has now performed its constitutional duties and I will try to continue to perform mine."

Now it was Douglas's turn to be magnanimous toward his enemies who had tried to have him impeached. Without being asked, he spoke about the two men Nixon had placed on the Court; Burger and Blackmun, of course, were nowhere in sight. "We have a fine Chief Justice and it is a pleasure to work with him. Our newest member, Harry Blackmun, is what the mountain men I knew in the Far West would call a 'stout fellow.' There's no higher compliment."[23] Douglas had been around a long time—ever since the Supreme Court was last turned around, by Franklin Roosevelt. Now the breath of Richard Nixon was hot on Douglas's neck.

CHAPTER 14

# Promises and Threats

Impeachment is the only method the Founding Fathers provided in the Constitution for removing an obstinate Justice from the Supreme Court, but it is a "bungling way, an impractical thing, a mere scarecrow." President Jefferson came to that conclusion when the Senate acquitted Justice Samuel Chase, a mere eighteen years after the Constitution was written.* President Nixon might very well have shared Jefferson's frustration one hundred and sixty-five years later, when the conservative effort to impeach Justice William O. Douglas collapsed under the weight of Representative Celler's mighty tome that dismissed the charges against Douglas. The trouble with impeachment, as a practical matter, is that the case against a member of the Court invariably becomes confused with and inseparable from the concurrent attack on the Court itself, as the charges against Chase inevitably were confounded by Jefferson's hostility toward the Marshall Court and the case against Douglas was umbilically joined to Nixon's campaign against the Warren Court.

Nixon now had been in office nearly two years. He entered the White House under the most auspicious of circumstances, with Earl Warren's retirement in his pocket. His selection of Warren Burger was proving to be most satisfactory. But the additional good fortune of Abe Fortas's resignation had turned to bitter disappointment with

*Jefferson was quoted by Senator Robert P. Griffin, who had led the successful fight to prevent President Johnson from naming Abe Fortas as Earl Warren's successor. Griffin quoted Jefferson later, after Fortas resigned under threat of impeachment. U.S., Cong., Senate Committee on the Judiciary, *Nonjudicial Activities of Supreme Court Justices and Other Federal Judges,* 1970, p. 39.

the defeat of Clement Haynsworth and G. Harrold Carswell, and the Senate's confirmation of Harry Blackmun was a political defeat for Nixon and the South, even if Blackmun distinctly was an improvement over Fortas from an ideological point of view. And now, almost on the eve of Christmas, 1970, Justice Douglas, the leading proponent of libertarianism remaining on the Supreme Court, was freed of the threat of impeachment and audaciously was offering to make peace with Burger and Blackmun.

The Presidency of Richard Nixon offered hope to white Southern conservatives who had signed the Southern Manifesto but who had had no hope of reversing the trend of Supreme Court decisions ordering racial integration in the South. The Nixon Presidency offered hope also to conservatives everywhere whose tolerance of political and racial dissent and violence was at an end and who wanted law and order. The President, of course, could not tell the Supreme Court how it must interpret the Constitution, and Burger and Blackmun were only two of nine members of the Court. But there had been dissenters within the Court when Warren was Chief Justice and they now could fall in behind Burger. From without the Court, the emerging chief justiceship of Warren Burger did indeed appear to be the vehicle that could carry the hopes of the President and his constituency forward. Burger clearly was not the aloof, withdrawn Chief Justice that Warren had been. He was making speeches and engaging in other activities that brought him into contact with the President, the Attorney General, others in political positions, and with newspapermen even, all of whom Warren had kept at arm's length. These contacts frequently resulted from the new Chief Justice's particular interest in court administration, as opposed to adjudication and judicial philosophy, and in his evident determination to use his position to promote efficiency in the federal and state court systems and to encourage speedier trials. For instance, early in January, 1971, a picture of Burger with Nixon appeared in newspapers across the country, recording an event of substantial importance to the Chief Justice. One of Burger's earliest off-the-bench projects had been to promote the training and use of court "executives," who would help judges to be more efficient. The picture showed the President, with the Chief Justice standing at his side, signing into law a bill authorizing eleven such executives for the federal circuit courts of appeal.

Yet Chief Justice Burger's influence on the Supreme Court, where it counted most, fell far short of fulfilling the hopes of Nixon's conservative constituency, South and North. Burger and Blackmun were making their presence felt in some cases, certainly, but in others the new Chief Justice was unable to command a majority and therefore the strict constructionist viewpoint did not prevail. The impression over-all was that Nixon had not succeeded in gaining control of the Court and in reversing the trend of its constitutional decisions.

Also early in January, the Court heard oral argument in a case that was particularly revealing of the difficulty Nixon faced in obtaining revision of constitutional interpretations, even in the law and order area where constitutional rights are not absolute and where the Warren Court's decisions were most vulnerable. The case grew out of a raid that was made on a morning in November, 1965, by six agents of the Federal Bureau of Narcotics. The agents entered the New York apartment of Webster Bivens and arrested him for alleged drug violations. They manacled Bivens in front of his wife and children, threatened to arrest the entire family, and searched the apartment from one end to the other. Eighteen months later Bivens brought suit in a federal court seeking damages of $15,000 from each of the agents. He alleged that the arrest and search were conducted without a warrant and without probable cause, that the agents acted with unreasonable force and subjected him to great humiliation. The question before the Supreme Court was whether the Fourth Amendment, which says "The right of the people to be secure against unreasonable searches and seizures, shall not be violated," allows an individual to sue federal agents who have violated that right. More broadly, the question was whether the Court, as the final interpreter of the Constitution, should sanction damage suits as a deterrant to federal police misconduct, inasmuch as neither Congress nor the Constitution explicitly provided lawsuits as a remedy for official violation of the Fourth Amendment.

When the Court in the spring of 1971 decided the case, it held 6 to 3 that federal agents can be sued when they engage in unlawful searches and seizures.[1] So compelling was the result that it joined the Court's liberal leaning Justices, Brennan, Douglas and Marshall, with its moderate-to-conservative members, Stewart, White, and Harlan. Justice Brennan wrote the majority opinion. John M. Harlan, although a man of conservative views, wrote in his concurring opinion, "The judiciary has a particular responsibility to assure the vindication of constitutional interests such as those embraced by the Fourth

Amendment." The dissenters were Burger, Blackmun, and Black. Justice Black was moving toward the right in certain of his opinions, including those involving law and order questions, and moving not at all from his liberal position in certain others. Justice Blackmun was voting as the Chief Justice voted and in his dissent said that the majority decision "will tend to stultify law enforcement." Chief Justice Burger wrote a strong dissent that looked both to the question at hand and beyond. He said, as had the government in its defense of the six narcotics agents, that the Court should not create "a damage remedy not provided for by the Constitution and not enacted by Congress." Burger also used the occasion to broadly attack the exclusionary rule, a constitutional doctrine followed by the Supreme Court for fifty-five years, which holds that evidence obtained in violation of the Fourth Amendment must be suppressed in criminal trials despite its probable reliability and its undoubted value to the prosecution. Burger agreed that there should be some means of enforcing the Fourth Amendment against what he said were the "honest mistakes" of police, and he shed judicial restraint to suggest such means to Congress. But he insisted that the exclusionary rule had extracted from society a high price in the form of "thousands of cases in which the criminal was set free because the constable blundered." Subsequently, J. Edgar Hoover, director of the Federal Bureau of Investigation, wrote an editorial applauding Burger's position and saying, "There is no benefit in a doctrine which continually releases patently guilty criminals to prey again upon society because of inadvertent 'blunders' by hard-pressed law enforcement officers."[2]

The conflict between the Bill of Rights and Nixon's demand for law and order returned many times to the Supreme Court and in the spring of 1971 the same 6-to-3 majority that decided the *Bivens* case ordered the state of Wyoming to free one Harold Whiteley, who had been sentenced to life imprisonment after he was found guilty of breaking and entering Shively's Hardware and the Rustic Bar, and of being a habitual criminal. The majority opinion, this time written by Justice Harlan, held that Whiteley's conviction could not stand because police had searched and arrested him without a warrant, in violation of his Fourth Amendment rights.[3] The Court's conclusion was to Harlan constitutionally "fundamental and obvious," for to rule otherwise would encourage police to ignore the Fourth Amendment. Black's intemperate dissent, to which Burger and Blackmun agreed, said the decision was "one of those calculated to make many good people believe our Court enjoys frustrating justice by unnecessarily turning professional criminals loose to prey upon society."

The Fourth Amendment obviously does not frustrate "justice." Its very purpose is to shield the otherwise defenseless citizen from the overwhelming official power of the police. This clash of individual rights with public law and order, in which the Warren Court's definition of justice still prevailed, was evident also in one of the many cases growing out of the Vietnam war and youthful resistance to the draft. A young man named Paul Robert Cohen had walked quietly down a corridor of the Los Angeles County Courthouse and was arrested and sentenced to thirty days' imprisonment for disturbing the peace. His offense was wearing a jacket bearing the words "Fuck the Draft."[4] Justice Harlan, writing again for the same majority that decided the *Bivens* and *Whiteley* cases, reversed the young man's conviction. Under the precedent of Court decisions dating back to 1931, Harlan said, Cohen's conduct must be regarded constitutionally as individual expression and it therefore was protected by the First Amendment. The Constitution would not permit Cohen to be punished for asserting on his jacket his opinion of the "inutility or immorality of the draft," Harlan wrote. Blackmun, joined by Burger and Black, dismissed Cohen's conduct as an "absurd and immature antic," deserving of no constitutional protection.

Research into the matter, while admittedly incomplete, indicates that the *Cohen* case marked the first time the four-letter expletive appeared in United States Reports, the bound volumes of nearly two hundred years of Supreme Court decisions. Its appearance now was particularly unfortunate, coming at the time of a President who held Sunday worship services and prayer breakfasts in the White House, attended by and on one occasion at least addressed by the new Chief Justice.

The Court, of course, could have refused to review Cohen's conviction in the first place and thus denied him the protection of the Constitution. Having taken the case, it could have dismissed it by holding, as it has on a number of occasions, that *certiorari* had been "improvidently" granted. Or, it could have upheld Cohen's conviction by going around precedent; that is, it could have "distinguished" between Cohen's case and prior First Amendment decisions in similar cases. Burger, soon after he came to the Supreme Court, said quite frankly in a dissenting opinion that he would not necessarily be bound by precedent, especially in law and order cases. "I am bound to reject the thesis that what the Court said lately controls over the Constitution," he asserted.[5] But Justice Harlan, a man of deep intellectual as well as personal conservatism, resisted such winds of change and helped to steady the Court, for so long as he lived. In another 1971 decision, in which Burger's view prevailed, Harlan in a dissenting opinion wrote that, even though "I have often protested past decisions" in the area of the law at issue (involving maritime liability in this instance), "I must in good conscience regard the issue in this case as having been decided" a decade earlier. The earlier decision "cannot justly be distinguished from the case before us," Harlan asserted.[6]

The Court many times in history has departed from precedent and at some times it explicitly has reversed prior constitutional decisions. It has done so without injury to itself or to the nation when there has been demonstratively good and intellectually sound reason for change. But change that reflects no more than a new Justice's personal predilictions or the momentary political climate outside the Court is "disquieting, both in its abrupt break with the past and in its consequences for the future."[*]

Early in the spring the Chief Justice took time out from the Court's work of deciding cases and controversies to attend with the President an unusual gathering in the historic town of Williamsburg, Virginia. Nixon, inspired by Burger's intense interest in judicial reform, came to Williamsburg to lend his prestige to the National Conference on the Judiciary. Nearly six hundred federal and state court judges and court administrators attended, and it was the first such gathering in history. Even though the separation of powers doctrine dictates against camaraderie between the President and the Chief Justice, the assembled jurists witnessed a historic event as Nixon and Burger shared the same platform and spoke almost with one voice.[**] Each addressed the conference on the need for greater efficiency in the federal and state court systems, but as they talked it became quite clear that efficiency meant sending more criminals to prison and keeping them there longer. It meant, in other words, that the courts,

[*]Harlan, dissenting in Fay v. Noia, 372 U.S. 391, 448 (1963).
[**]The American Bar Association, still at this time on very friendly terms with Nixon, admiringly observed that the President and Chief Justice "were as one." ABA *Journal*, vol. 57, May 1971, p. 421.

and primarily the Warren Court, were to blame for lawlessness and violence in America.

Nixon declared, as he had in many political speeches, that the most "fundamental civil right of every American is the right to be secure in his home and on the streets."* The President called on the nation's judges "to reverse the trend toward crime and violence, to reinstill a respect for law in all our people. A system of criminal justice that can guarantee neither a speedy trial nor a safe community cannot excuse its failure by pointing to an elaborate system of safeguards for the accused," President Nixon asserted. Following the President to the podium, the Chief Justice declared that criminal courts and prisons are "suffering from a severe case of deferred maintenance. As a consequence, perpetrators of most criminal acts are not detected; those who are apprehended, arrested and charged are not tried promptly; and third, the convicted persons are not punished promptly. A growing number of law breakers jeopardize cities and towns and life and property of law-abiding people."** Burger called for speedier justice, enlisting in his cause not only the nation's federal and state judges but also the country's entire legal establishment, through its American Bar Association.

But, back in Washington, Nixon's campaign to change the Court ran into more and greater trouble. Indeed, on April 20, 1971, Nixon's campaign crashed headlong into the tremendous force of great constitutional precedent, and into John Harlan and Justices like him, present and past. So thunderous was the collision that Nixon lost, momentarily, even his new Chief Justice.

The issue was the ancient one of racial equality. The Warren Court had held unanimously in 1954, in *Brown* v. *Board of Education,* that segregation of black from white children in schools in Southern and border states, where segregation was mandated by state laws, violated the Constitution.[7] All of the Court's decisions since 1954 requiring the racial integration of schools had been unanimous. In 1955 the Court had held that desegregation must proceed "with all deliberate speed."[8] In 1964, it said that schools must be integrated "forthwith."[9] And in 1968 it demanded that school authorities come forward with desegregation plans "now."[10] Not only were the Court's decisions unanimous,

*In a speech delivered March 11, 1971.
**In a speech delivered March 12, 1971.

but Presidents Eisenhower, Kennedy, and Johnson had used their authority to enforce the Court's doctrine when it was physically challenged, as it was by Governor Faubus of Arkansas in 1957 and by Governor Wallace of Alabama in 1962. Congress, with the Civil Rights Act of 1964, had authorized the federal government to file school desegregation suits and to provide technical assistance to Southern school boards in their preparation of desegregation plans.

Yet, in 1971 the promise of the 1954 decision was not fulfilled and the law still was not obeyed, because school boards resisted integration, because the legal and technical resources of the federal government were brought to bear with less than total commitment to racial equality, and because many whites evaded integration by moving out of the increasingly black cities to suburban school districts in which few Negroes could afford housing. When Nixon became President, many thousands of black children still attended all-black schools and when the Warren Court finally demanded desegregation "now," the question that remained unresolved was, *how?*

The Warren Court had spoken indirectly to the question in 1968, when it held that the Civil Rights Act of 1866 allowed a black man to sue a real estate developer who refused to sell him a house in the white suburbs.[11] Congress also had spoken when it enacted the Civil Rights Act of 1968, making racial discrimination in the rental and sale of housing unlawful. But if racial integration of the educational process in 1971 remained illusory, housing integration was a black mirage.

If, then, housing patterns made it impossible to racially integrate neighborhood schools, the only possible way to achieve desegregation "now" was to transport a sufficient number of white and black children to schools outside of their neighborhoods in order to achieve a racial mix in all of the schools within a local school system. The answer, in short, was busing. Yellow school buses were a familiar sight in rural America, where the one-room schoolhouse had long since disappeared and children were being transported over substantial distances to consolidated schools. Until such time as whites lived with blacks in the same urban neighborhoods and could attend the same neighborhood schools, why should the yellow buses not be used to transport children for the purpose of achieving racial integration? A number of lower federal courts in the South, and a few in the North where desegregation suits also were being brought, ordered local school authorities to prepare busing plans in order to achieve desegregation "now." It was a temporary solution, theoretically, that should neither detract from nor contribute to the educational process itself, so far as white children were concerned. The fundamental rationale of the school desegregation doctrine was that integration would help black children to learn.

Nixon as a candidate could not and did not repudiate the Supreme Court's fundamental 1954 desegregation decision, popular though that explicit position might have been to some Southern voters, and as President he swore to uphold the Constitution. But in 1970, when Governor Kirk of Florida ordered Manatee County children to ignore a court-ordered integregation plan, the President and his Attorney General did not speak out. In 1971 Nixon and Mitchell again said nothing when Governor Wallace of Alabama ordered a white pupil, who had been assigned to a predominantly black school twenty-two miles from her home, transferred to a school closer to her home. Kirk and Wallace eventually bowed to the courts, but the President's silence left great confusion inside the government over what the Nixon Administration's position on school desegregation was or should be. In the course of the debate Leon Panetta resigned as the civil rights officer of the Department of Health, Education and Welfare and other civil rights enforcement officials left the Department of Justice. Eventually, the debate produced a long position paper that in many respects was ambiguous but that clearly stated Nixon's strong opposition to busing as a means of achieving racial balance in the nation's schools. Nixon, of course, also nominated Haynsworth and Carswell to the Supreme Court, and after they were defeated he assured the South still that its "day will come on the High Court." If Nixon's position was ambigious to some, it was contended by the National Association for the Advancement of Colored People to be "anti-Negro."*

The Supreme Court itself had not yet decided whether busing was required by the Constitution, but the entire question of how school desegregation was to be achieved "now" was scheduled for oral argument early in the Court's term that opened on October 5, 1970. On August 31, more than a month before the term began, Burger evidenced his acute awareness of the sensitivity of the busing issue in the world outside the Court. He called into his office for a most unusual,

*Bishop Stephen G. Spottswood, chairman of the NAACP, in his keynote address to the association's annual convention, Cincinnati, Ohio, June 29, 1970.

off-the-record talk the reporters assigned to the Court by the Associated Press and United Press International. Burger talked about why the Court had delayed hearing the issue earlier and insisted that various desegregation devices, such as pairing of schools and zoning, were involved, even though busing had become a sort of code word for the whole problem. He said he recognized that the Court's decision would have great impact in the North as well as the South and noted that some Southern governors had held press conferences to urge the Court to resolve the busing controversy promptly. Finally, he explained that he had singled out the AP and UPI reporters because their stories on the Court's decision would be used by newspapers and broadcast stations across the nation. Burger wanted the decision to be reported accurately, and he added that some members of the court felt that some reporters had not read the Court's prior school desegregation decisions with complete accuracy.

The Court heard oral argument on a group of school cases on October 12. It handed down its decision the following spring, on April 20, 1971. On that Tuesday the weight of precedent carried the Supreme Court to the conclusion that busing is "required as one tool of school desegregation. Desegregation plans cannot be limited to the walk-in school."[12] Not only were Burger and Blackmun carried along, but the Chief Justice wrote the unanimous opinion of the Court. Earl Warren had written the 1954 decision, and Burger either believed or was convinced that he should write this opinion, which in many ways was the most important since 1954 on the school issue. In the light of later developments, Burger's agreement to speak for the Court begs explanation. No official explanation is available, because the deliberations of the nine members of the Court are secret. But it is obvious that many of the Court's major constitutional rulings have been the product of give and take among the Justices, and this process may well have produced on April 20 the unanimous opinion bearing Burger's name. Harlan and perhaps Black may have impressed on Burger the great significance of unanimity and of his authorship of the Court's opinion. In exchange for Burger's agreement, the Court's liberals may have accepted a decision that was less than rigid in requiring that children be bused to racially integrate the schools.

In the leading case of *Swann* v. *Charlotte-Mecklenburg Board of Education,* the Court was dealing with a North Carolina school district with 21,000 black students, two thirds of whom still were attending twenty-one schools which ranged between 99 per cent and 100 per cent black. The Burger opinion held that courts may require busing of students "as one tool of school desegregation." Burger reasoned that busing was not, in itself, anything new, since "bus transportation has been an integral part of the public education system for years, and was perhaps the single most important factor in the transition from the one-room schoolhouse to the consolidated school." But the Chief Justice was not inflexible. He held that busing could be avoided where "the time or distance of travel is so great as to risk the health of the children or significantly impinge on the educational process." More importantly, he held that the Constitution does not require that total racial integration be achieved within any school district, by busing or any other means.

The opinion thus rejected as an integregation standard the concept of "racial balance," under which each school within a district would have a white-black student ratio reflecting the racial mix of the local population as a whole. Racial quotas can be "a useful starting point" in formulating school desegregation plans, but quotas are not an "inflexible requirement." Indeed, Burger added, "some small number" of all-black and all-white schools may remain within an integrated school system. Finally, Burger made clear that the Court's opinion did not apply to the North, where schools also were racially segregated and whites had fled to the suburbs sometimes to avoid some state-imposed integration plans, but where segregation had in years past never had been required by state law.

The White House made no immediate reply to the Supreme Court, perhaps because it was too startled or because it was not sure precisely how much busing the decision required. In any event, Nixon already had made known his opposition to massive busing of students for purposes of school integration. He also had said, in another policy statement that also was the product of long deliberation within the Administration, that while he would enforce existing laws against racial discrimination in housing, he would not try to force the white suburbs to accept low-income housing projects. The month following the Court's decision on school busing, Nixon toured the Deep South for the first time since the 1970 mid-term election campaign. In Birmingham, Alabama, he shared a platform with Governor Wallace and expressed "utter contempt for the double, hypocritical standards" of Northerners who criticized the South for failing to integrate its schools.

If the President's position on school integration seemed to the public, in the South and North, to be less than crystal clear at the moment, it was clear enough to those in Washington who were immediately concerned. "There just won't be very much in the way of creative enforcement" of the Supreme Court's decision, said a government official who had assumed that his job was enforcement of school desegregation.[13] The public reaction of the U.S. Civil Rights Commission, a watchdog agency created by Congress in 1957, was that Nixon was "seriously undermining" desegregation efforts and leading the nation onto a "collision course."

Richard Nixon and John Mitchell in the spring and summer of 1971 were in fact steering multiple courses that would lead to constitutional collision with the Supreme Court. As the nature of unrest, dissent, and violence changed, Nixon and Mitchell also were changing, and America was not greening.

This spring and summer, there were no more black riots on the scale of those that had ignited spontaneously in recent years in the ghettos of Watts, Detroit, Washington, and many other cities. Perhaps blacks had spent their energies, for the moment, but the civil rights movement still was moving forward. The effects of the Court's busing decision had not yet spread widely, and sometimes there was violence in places where courts had ordered busing. Whites threw fire bombs at school buses in Pontiac, Michigan, and in Lamar, South Carolina buses bringing black children to a newly integrated school were attacked by a mob of screaming whites, armed with ax handles and baseball bats. Still, integration was progressing peacefully in hundreds of other communities. Moreover, college campuses had grown more quiet as Nixon withdrew more American troops from Vietnam, and there were no more massive campus protests after National Guardsmen killed four white students at Kent State in the spring of 1970.

The nation seemed to be moving toward more peaceful times, at home and abroad, apparently as rapidly as its diversity of blacks and whites, doves and hawks, all under one President, would allow. Nixon was withdrawing, but had not withdrawn, from Vietnam. He was in favor of slowing, but not stopping, school integration. He announced that he would enforce laws against housing discrimination but said he would not force white communities to accept low-income housing that blacks could afford. He announced a "Philadelphia Plan" to increase black job opportunities in the building trades, but as unemployment rose to 5.5 per cent in the nation at large it swelled to 35.5 per cent among black youths, according to the U.S. Bureau of Labor Statistics. He was not against gun control, and he was not for it.

Nixon's policies were intentionally ambiguous; they were the policies of a President who had entered office without a popular majority or a clear mandate, and who did not attempt to lead the entire nation so much as he tried to protect and enlarge his political constituency. He addressed his various policies to all Americans, white and black, young and old, rich and poor, and without question he succeeded in communicating with substantial numbers of blacks, young people, and poor people, without seriously offending his constituency of white, older, and more affluent Americans. Dissent and violence in America did decline.

But they declined also because Nixon practiced what he preached about law and order. Nixon, with the assistance of Agnew, Mitchell, and, on occasion, Mrs. Mitchell, also pursued a calculated policy that was intended to isolate whites and blacks who persisted in demonstrating their dissent. The President, for example, declared that campus radicals in the East who opposed his Vietnam war policies were "bums," and he flew out to the friendlier Midwest where, at the University of Nebraska, he invited other young people to join him in an "alliance of the generations." The radicals, white and black, were identified and prosecuted as threats, real or imagined, to the national security. They and their followers who still demonstrated were dealt with harshly, with massive arrests and similar techniques that were used in Washington and recommended to police throughout the country.

To some extent, policies and practices that caused people to fear, particularly after the killings at Kent State and Jackson State, contributed along with the promises to the appearance of more peaceful times, on the campuses and in the ghettos. For instance, the Federal Bureau of Investigation created a network of paid informers who infiltrated not only radical organizations such as the Black Panthers and Students for a Democratic Society but also the NAACP. Mitchell utilized the wiretaps and electronic surveillance devices that Ramsey Clark as Attorney General had refused to use. Under Mitchell's direction the FBI tapped and bugged black and white dissenters, without obtaining court warrants; Mitchell took the position that warrants, as required by the Constitution, were unnecessary because domestic dissenters were a threat to the nation's internal security and therefore could be tapped and bugged at will, under executive authority alone, just as Russian spies were kept under FBI surveillance. There was evidence that many local police departments, following the federal lead, were engaging in surveillance of political dissenters and multiplying many times over the use of wiretaps and electronic bugs in the United States. Grand juries, both federal and state, were summoned to investigate and indict radicals, and at times newspaper reporters, including a black New York *Times* newsman named Earl Caldwell, were subpoenaed to tell the grand juries what they had learned, as reporters, concerning Black Panthers and other radicals. The same month Nixon flew to the University of Nebraska, a federal grand jury in Harrisburg, Pennsylvania, indicted the Reverend Philip F. Berrigan, a Catholic priest, and others on charges of conspiring to kidnap presidential adviser Henry A. Kissinger and to blow up the heating systems of government buildings in Washington; the purpose of the alleged conspiracy reportedly was to protest the Vietnam war. Ramsey Clark became one of the defense attorneys representing the Harrisburg defendants.

As Nixon and Mitchell thus cleared the streets and campuses with threats and promises, violence became less spontaneous and assumed aspects of guerrilla warfare. In March, 1971, a bomb exploded in the United States Capitol, and during the twelve months that ended June 30 there were 1,858 explosive and incendiary bomb incidents in the country, according to the newly established National Bomb Data Center.[14] The FBI did not solve the Capitol bombing so quickly as it had discovered the Harrisburg conspiracy, and later that March radicals rifled the Bureau's office at Media, Pennsylvania, and distributed to newspapers and antiwar members of Congress stolen documents that graphically portrayed the FBI's surveillance activities. It was revealed that the Army was maintaining its own domestic surveillance program, with thousands of files, not only on long-haired youths but also on some United States senators who did not actively support Nixon's Vietnam policies. Sniper attacks on policemen patrolling their beats in black ghettos increased, and Nixon, with J. Edgar Hoover at his side, proposed legislation to give each murdered policeman's family $50,000. He proposed to Congress also a pretrial detention bill, patterned after the law already obtained for the District of Columbia, to allow all federal judges to hold in jail, pending trial, persons who were suspected of crimes and believed to be dangerous to the community. By executive order Nixon revived the Subversive Activities Control Board, an agency rendered impotent by the Warren Court's decisions upholding the constitutional rights of alleged subversives. Without order, Mitchell revived the Internal Security Division of the Justice Department and named as its director a law and order man named Robert C. Mardian. And in Philadelphia voters elected as their mayor a tough former police commissioner named Frank L. Rizzo.

It was in this atmosphere of escalating violence and reaction that Mayday, 1971, arrived in Washington. The antiwar demonstrations of this spring began early. Two demonstrations were staged in April. Vietnam veterans, who demonstrated first, concluded their rally by throwing their combat medals over the barbed wire that guarded the Capitol steps. The second attracted perhaps 200,000 persons, most of them young whites but some of them middle-aged, who marched down Pennsylvania Avenue to urge Congress to end the war. The rallies were peaceful, despite Mitchell's predictions of violence. Many of the youths stayed over for the Mayday demonstration, sponsored by a number of antiwar organizations which banded together as the Peoples Coalition for Peace and Justice. The demonstrators, again overwhelmingly white, planned to sit in the streets and disrupt the flow of morning traffic carrying government workers to their jobs. With Mitchell as usual in command of a network of local and federal police and military forces and again predicting violence, authorities during the night of May 2 raided the demonstrators' encampment, scattering 30,000 youths and arresting more than 200. After dawn broke on Monday, May 3, some of the youths straggled back into the downtown streets, but they were quickly dispersed by police and hardly a bureaucrat failed to arrive at his desk. A few of the youngsters tossed tacks onto the pavement, some went home, and many just milled about. Some had beards, some could not yet shave, and most looked as if they should be back in school in Ashtabula or Dubuque or Scarsdale. But Mitchell and the police defended the city, sweeping the streets with massive arrests. Girls with long hair, bearded and beardless young men, older men in business suits, and a number of graying and bald bureaucrats who happened on the streets were hauled off to temporary detention centers. People were arrested merely for standing still on the sidewalks, as police threw away the arrest forms on which in normal times they enter the cause of arrest. In three days more than 12,000 persons were arrested and often held for a day or longer without being able to phone their lawyers, or even their parents. Almost all of the cases ultimately were dropped (the first 3,949 that came before the District of Columbia Superior Court resulted in only 79 convictions) and Nixon recommended Mitchell's tactics to other cities across the nation. Mitchell, who this time did not need his wife to speak for him, compared the Mayday demonstrators to Hitler's Brown Shirts. The New York *Times* editorialized with the most vicious kind of name calling that could be summoned against Mitchell, saying the Attorney General may be an expert in "marketing municipal bonds," but he "understands very little about law and liberty in a free society."[15]

And it was in this atmosphere that the first of many constitutional questions raised by escalating dissent and repressiveness arrived at the Supreme Court. The New York *Times* on June 13, 1971, had begun to publish excerpts from the Pentagon Papers, a top-secret study prepared under auspices of the Defense Department, that elaborately and candidly traced the origins of United States involvement in the Vietnam war. A few days later the Washington *Post* also began to publish excerpts. Daniel Ellsberg, a former Defense Department official, publicly admitted giving the classified study to the press and he was promptly indicted by a federal grand jury. Mitchell immediately filed suits to prevent the *Times* and *Post* from further publication of the Pentagon Papers. The government had never before in history attempted to restrain any publication and the lawsuits alleged no violation of a law passed by Congress. Instead, the suits asserted that the Pentagon Papers secrets would endanger "national security" if published and that therefore the President had authority to stop publication under the implied powers which the Constitution vested in him as commander in chief of the armed forces and as the nation's chief executive.

The case presented the most sensational clash in history between the First Amendment's right of press freedom and a President's claim of inherent power to stop the press. The Court decided it on June 30 and handed Nixon a stinging rebuke. It ruled 6 to 3 that the First Amendment would not allow the government to restrain publication of the Pentagon Papers.[16] Justices Black, Douglas, Brennan, White, Stewart, and Marshall voted against Nixon. Chief Justice Burger and Justices Harlan and Blackmun were for him. Each of the nine wrote separate opinions.

Justice Black, now eighty-five years of age and departing from the liberal viewpoint on criminal rights issues, remained adamantly strict constructionist concerning the First Amendment and he wrote the strongest opinion. Black could imagine "no greater perversion of history" than Nixon's assertion that the First Amendment was something less than an absolute bar on government interference with press freedom. Black continued:

> The press was protected so that it could bare the secrets of government and inform the people. Only a free and unrestrained press can effectively expose deception in government. And paramount among the responsibilities of a free press is the duty to prevent any part of the government from deceiving the people and sending them off to distant lands to die of foreign fevers and foreign shot and shell. In my view, far from deserving condemnation for their courageous reporting, the New York *Times*, the Washington *Post*, and other newspapers should be commended for serving the purposes that the Founding Fathers saw so clearly.

Justices Douglas and Brennan concurred. Justices Stewart, White, and Marshall agreed that the government had not proved a case for restraining publication of the Pentagon Papers, but they also evidenced a certain amount of sympathy for Nixon's predicament, saying that publication of government secrets might be restrained if Congress passed a law for that purpose.

The Chief Justice and Blackmun in dissent could see no good reason for all the "pressure and panic and sensationalism" and thought the newspapers should be enjoined while the government developed its case further and the courts pondered. Justice Harlan wrote the strongest dissent. In this case there was no substantial precedent to be respected and Harlan's innate conservatism required respect for presidential authority in the field of foreign relations. Harlan would have restrained further publication of the Pentagon Papers, pending more complete judicial review, but he also expressed in his carefully worded dissent the view, disturbing to liberals, that judicial authority under the Constitution to review presidential actions in the area of foreign relations is "exceedingly narrow."

The case was the last decided by the Supreme Court in its 1970–71 term, and it turned out to be the last in which both Black and Harlan participated.

During the summer recess the work of the Court stopped and its members, except the Chief Justice, went to the moutains or the sea-shore. Burger, on the other hand, undertook several assignments that, while not necessarily required of a Chief Justice, shed further light on his particular concept of the position. There were two major incidents with which Burger made news in the summer of 1971.

In July Burger attended the annual meeting of the American Bar Association, as was his habit. The ABA in 1971 divided its meeting into two parts, and Burger was a most prominent partici-pant in both. The lawyers conducted the regular business of the association in New York and then traveled to England (the trip, of course, being tax-deductible) to revisit the Magna Carta memorial at Runnymede and share professional interests with their British counterparts. The ABA has about 150,000 members, but only the more interested and generally the older, wealthier, and more conservative members regularly attend the annual meet-ings. Nearly 6,000 were interested and wealthy enough to attend the sessions in New York and London.

It was to this audience that Chief Justice Burger in New York addressed his second annual State of the Federal Judiciary message. (The first of these speeches, rather presumptiously titled after the presidential State of the Union addresses, was delivered before the ABA meeting a year earlier.) Burger pressed onward with his many proposals for improving the efficiency of the courts and the speed of trials, but there also was a cantankerous note to his speech. He criti-cized the courts for "the excessive writing of opinions," and he was quite upset with a "small minority" of lawyers who practice their profession with what Burger said was excessive vigor.* While groups of antiwar and black lawyers quietly demonstrated in a corridor out-side the hall where he was speaking, Burger called on the ABA to exercise "more stringent discipline" over such lawyers. Inasmuch as courtroom unruliness of lawyers was no substantial current problem or issue, except for some of those lawyers who lately had been defend-ing black and white radicals accused of crimes arising out of political dissent, Burger's speech nicely complemented, within the Chief Jus-tice's sphere of expertise, the Nixon Administration's law and order policies. Before the ABA recessed its New York meeting, its assembly

*Before the ninth annual meeting of the American Bar Association, New York, July 5, 1971.

also debated and defeated a resolution calling for immediate withdrawal of all American troops from Vietnam.

A week later, in London, Chief Justice Burger was joined by Attorney General Mitchell. They set the theme of the American Bar's revisitation to the historic home of the common law. It might have been an occasion of rededication to the Magna Carta and to the rights of man, but it was not. It became a professionally and politically embarrassing attack on the Warren Court. Burger began by delivering a speech titled "The Role of the Advocates in Criminal Justice," in which he again attacked "unprincipled and unrestrained" defense lawyers and held that American law schools "teach lawyers to think brilliantly but fail to teach them how to behave properly."* The British system, Burger said, was much better. With Burger seated on the dais close by, Mitchell delivered his speech, which was a blunt attack on the United States Supreme Court for its criminal rights decisions handed down when Earl Warren sat as Chief Justice. Mitchell said, "We face in the United States a situation where the discovery of guilt or innocence as a function of the courts is in danger of drowning in a sea of legalisms."** These legalisms consist of "the hydra of excess proceduralisms, archaic formalisms, pretrial motions, post-trial motions, appeals, postponements, continuances, collateral attacks, which can have the effect of dragging justice to death and stealing the very life out of the law," Mitchell declared. He quoted Burger's own criticism of the Warren Court and, adding his voice to the Chief Justice's attack on defense lawyers, Mitchell said, "Too often the trial attorney acts as though he is representing an issue rather than a client." The courts must discipline such lawyers and "recognize that society, too, has its rights, including the right to expect that the guilty will be corrected. The judiciary has been too preoccupied in the exhilarating adventure of making new law and new public policy, and this function has outdistanced the more sober task of judging guilt and innocence," Mitchell concluded.

Burger's and Mitchell's speeches were enthusiastically applauded, and then Lord Widgery, the Lord Chief Justice of England, addressed the lawyers gathered in the Great Hall of Grosvenor House. In the spirit of the occasion, Lord Widgery declared that it was "startling and unacceptable" that the Warren Court should have read the

*In London July 16, 1971.
**In London July 16, 1971.

United States Constitution to mean that police cannot question criminal suspects without warning them of their right to counsel. Finally, Edward L. Wright of Little Rock, Arkansas, then president of the ABA, took his turn to "go on record," saying he also believed the Warren Court had been wrong. Each succeeding speaker had drawn from the audience a longer round of applause.

The second strange interlude of the summer came after Burger returned to Washington and found the school busing problem back on his desk. It also was on the President's desk, where it had sat since Burger in April had delivered the unanimous opinion of the Court in the *Swann* case.

Early in August Nixon loudly broke the silence he had maintained since April on the school busing issue. During the interval the staff people at the Department of Health, Education and Welfare and at the Justice Department who were responsible for school desegregation enforcement had prepared a plan to integrate the schools of Austin, Texas. It had been a routine case. The Justice Department in 1970 had filed suit in a Federal district court charging that the Austin school system illegally segregated students by race. Local authorities had responded by proposing a desegregation plan that would have racially mixed black, brown and white students one week out of every four. The HEW staff, following the Supreme Court's decision in the *Swann* case, presented to the district court a counter plan, calling for integration every day of the school week, under a school clustering plan that would require some but not a great deal of busing. The plan seemed to HEW officials to conform with the Supreme Court's decision, authored by Burger.

The Austin plan, however, was of more than routine interest. It was the first plan to be proposed by the HEW staff after the *Swann* decision and thus was being watched as indicative of Nixon's position. Early in August, Nixon broke his silence by publicly repudiating the Austin plan, which innocently had been prepared by his own civil rights staff at HEW. At the same time, Nixon restated his position, saying, "I am against busing in school desegregation cases," and underscoring it with the announcement that he was instructing both the HEW and Justice Departments to "work with individual school districts to hold busing to the minimum required by law."

Before the month of August was over, Burger spoke from the Supreme Court on the busing issue.

After his return from London Burger, as circuit justice for the

Fourth Circuit Court of Appeals, was presented by the Board of Education of Forsyth County, North Carolina, with an application for a stay of a federal district court order requiring the county, in conformity with the Supreme Court's decision in the *Swann* case, to "achieve the greatest possible degree of desegregation." The district court's order required the board of education to bus an estimated 16,000 students in addition to the 18,000 pupils it already was busing each school day.

Burger on August 31 handed down his decision which, largely for technical reasons, denied the stay. In doing so, however, he wrote a ten-page opinion which was unusual, to say the least. The Chief Justice, alone, attempted in the ten pages to explain what the Court as a whole had said in the *Swann* decision concerning busing. The district court's action in the Forsyth County case, Burger wrote, "suggests there may be some misreading" of the *Swann* decision.[17] The Supreme Court had not required a "fixed racial balance or quota," he explained. "Nothing could be plainer, or so I had thought, than [the Court's] disapproval" of the quota test in busing cases, Burger wrote. He emphasized that, inasmuch as the Supreme Court had rejected complete and final desegregation, as would be required by the racial balance or quota test, it also had rejected busing on a scale that would risk children's health or the quality of their education.

Supreme Court decisions are routinely sent to all federal judges. But the unusual nature of this decision, emphasizing what the Constitution did *not* require, was carried still further by the Chief Justice. When the printed decision arrived in judges' chambers across the nation, it carried an extra, typewritten notation: "For the Personal Attention of the Judge." The notation on some of the copies of the decision, but apparently not on all, was followed by the initials "WEB."

Warren Earl Burger was an activist, of a kind that had not been seen in the position of Chief Justice of the United States in many, many years. He was the nominee of a President who had attacked the Supreme Court with a greater vengeance than Presidents of many previous years. Yet, Nixon still had not gained control of the Court.

His time, however, was now at hand.

214

CHAPTER 15

# Politics and Professionalism

August, 1971, was not typical in any way of this month of malaise in Washington. President Nixon transcended the heat, humidity, and boredom that normally settle on the capital at the end of summer, first, by declaring his strong opposition to school busing, and then, in the middle of the month, announcing an economic reform plan more revolutionary than any since the New Deal, when Franklin Roosevelt had laid out his plans to rescue the nation from the Great Depression. Members of Congress, bureaucrats, and lobbyists left the seashore and the mountains to hear Nixon's plans for rescuing the country from the Great Inflation. Apollo 15 astronauts David Scott and James Irwin were exploring the moon this month. Governor Wallace of Alabama was announcing that he would become a presidential candidate in 1972. And Justices Hugo Lafayette Black, eighty-five years old, and John Marshall Harlan, seventy-two, were seriously ill in Bethesda Naval Hospital, just outside Washington. The events of the next several months left the impression that Nixon, who had prepared so carefully for his first two vacancies on the Supreme Court, now was so busy with state and political affairs that he was wholly unprepared for two additional vacancies created, as the first two were not, by natural causes.

Black and Harlan appeared in good health when the Court had last sat, on June 30, and had handed down its nine opinions in the Pentagon Papers case. Their opinions were diametrically opposed, and each was the strongest and most lucid presentation of the two philosophies that divided the Court that day. The careers of both men, as they had grown older and continued to sit on the Court through that June, were reason to give pause to those who espouse in theory the notion that all men and women should be subject to mandatory retirement at a uniform age.

No two men or women who share a fundamental belief in the Constitution, a deep respect for the function of law, and an intellectual capacity to interpret both ever will be in complete agreement on all of the meanings of the Constitution. If ever nine members of the Court are consistently in agreement, they will indeed be puppets on a string pulled by the President. Black and Harlan frequently disagreed, with each other and with Presidents. Black was from Clay County, Alabama, and once had been a Democratic politician as well as a lawyer. Harlan had been a patrician Wall Street lawyer in New York. The independence of both stood as a barrier to political control of the Court, in a sense more frustrating to the President than the predilections of the most liberal holdovers from the Warren Court.

Black would never retire, and give Nixon another vacancy, until forced to do so by ill health. In February, 1971, on his eighty-fifth birthday, he invited reporters to his office with the understanding he would talk about almost anything, except cases before the Court. He chatted about his family tree, a branch of which went back to the first Justice John Marshall Harlan, and about the occasional game of tennis he still played with his wife. Speaking of history, he said, "Chief Justices come and Chief Justices go." Black himself had sat with five Chief Justices. He had served on the Court for thirty-four years, longer than all but two others in history, John Marshall and Stephen J. Field. He said in February that he had "no plans to retire" and would let life take its course.

In the spring of 1971, there had been rumors in Washington that Harlan would retire. They were based, presumably, on his deteriorating eyesight. There were other stories that Harlan was determined not to retire; it was said that he was deeply disturbed by the conservative political attacks on the Supreme Court and that he had expressed his concern privately to Attorney General Mitchell. The latter seems to have been the more valid. No retirement letter had arrived on Nixon's desk when Harlan entered the hospital in August. Quite probably, Nixon and Mitchell until then had been given no reason to anticipate or hope for Harlan's retirement.

Harlan entered the hospital on August 16 for treatment of what was thought to be a strained back and he did not notify Nixon of his retirement until September 23, after it was confirmed that he was suffering from spinal cancer. Black entered the same hospital on August 28, for treatment of what his office termed "an inflammatory condition of the blood vessels." He notified Nixon of his retirement on September 17 and died eight days later, after suffering a severe stroke. Black was buried at Arlington National Cemetery in an unfinished pine casket, after the Reverend Duncan Howlett delivered a eulogy at Washington Cathedral, saying that Black "had little patience with the so-called strict constructionists." Nixon and Mitchell sat impassively in a front pew.[1] Harlan died on December 29 and was buried in Weston, Connecticut, where the family for many years had maintained a summer home.

The departures of Black and Harlan gave Nixon, in his first term in office, the rare opportunity to name a total of four members of the Court. President Franklin Roosevelt had waited through his entire first term before an opportunity came to name one member. But Nixon fumbled again and in the scramble that ensued the President became even more distempered than he had been when Carswell was defeated. This time, however, Nixon's fumbles were recovered not by his enemies in the United States Senate but by his supposed friends in the American Bar Association.

The ABA is not a political organization, but it enjoys a unique relationship with politics and politicians. It is substantially more than just another trade association and its only peer as a professional organization is the American Medical Association. Its strengths, both professional and political, go down to the grass roots level, as do those of the AMA. The ABA is a federation of all the state bar associations and some 1,700 local bar associations. There are about 350,000 lawyers in the United States, and roughly half of them are members of the ABA. The ABA is less conservative than the AMA, but the Bar Association nonetheless is fundamentally conservative and the two dozen or so older and richer lawyers who have worked their way to the top rungs of association leadership tend to be the most conservative. But the ABA is a unique American institution because it can count among its members judges, legislators, governors, and, on occasion, Presidents. In 1970 the President, the Vice President, four members of the Cabinet, sixty-seven U.S. senators, a majority of the members of the House of Representatives, and uncounted federal bureaucrats and state office holders were lawyers.[2] Not all retained membership in the ABA, but many did. President Nixon and Attorney General Mitchell had never been active in the association, when they were practicing lawyers, but they were members.*

The ABA hierarchy and the Supreme Court can share a very special relationship, if it suits the purposes of both. A close relationship suited neither when Earl Warren was Chief Justice. Warren had been a member of the association but had never been active in its affairs. In the summer of 1957 he participated as Chief Justice when the ABA met in London, and paid its respects to the Magna Carta and shared professional interests with the British Law Society. A special committee of the American Bar Association on this occasion in London issued a report sharply critical of the Warren Court's decisions upholding the constitutional rights of individuals accused during the McCarthy era of disloyalty. After Warren returned home, he quietly resigned his ABA membership.[3]

The American Bar Association did not meet again in London until 1971, and once more the association lent itself to an attack on the Warren Court. Presumably it was coincidence, or maybe Justice William O. Douglas was right, after all, when he insisted that he could see a certain affinity between President Nixon and George III.[4] In any event, the 1971 assault on the Warren Court, launched after Warren had left both the ABA and the Court, was not so much an ABA project as the work of Chief Justice Burger and Attorney General Mitchell. Burger and Mitchell recognized full well the strengths of the American Bar Association, as well as its weaknesses, and both sought to create a very special relationship with the association and its leaders.

Burger, as a federal appellate judge and ABA activist, had served as chairman of a special ABA Committee on Standards for the Administration of Criminal Justice. Its ambitious task was to prepare uniform, national rules governing the conduct of police and judges in criminal cases. Almost as soon as Burger became Chief Justice, he sought and received the ABA's cooperation in his plans for speedier and more efficient criminal justice. Early in 1970, for example, Chief Justice Burger and Bernard G. Segal, then president of the ABA, held

*Mitchell joined the ABA in 1941. Nixon joined in 1951, when he was in the Senate, and resigned in December, 1969, when he was President. The resignation had no apparent significance, other than to avoid the appearance of any conflict of interest.

a joint news conference at the Supreme Court to announce the establishment of a training program for federal and state court "executives," the efficiency experts who were hired by the U.S. appellate circuits under the legislation Nixon signed, as Burger approvingly watched, early in 1971. The ABA in New York, London, and elsewhere provided a platform from which Burger propounded his many plans for improved judicial administration, and the association created another special committee to help him obtain the necessary legislation and appropriations from Congress. From those platforms Burger also began his attack on the "small minority" of unruly lawyers, and soon ABA leaders almost in chorus were demanding disciplinary action against exceptionally vigorous defenders of Black Panthers and antiwar protesters.

Mitchell's principal joint venture with the ABA was less noisy and more profound. The Attorney General agreed to give the ABA's Standing Committee on the Federal Judiciary what amounted to a veto power over potential Supreme Court nominees. Specifically, Mitchell agreed, on July 23, 1970, to submit privately to the ABA committee the names of persons whom the President would consider when Court vacancies occurred in the future. The committee privately would give Mitchell its comments on their professional qualifications. This rather startling arrangement, under which the American Bar Association was to share the President's constitutional power to fill Supreme Court vacancies, was initiated by the ABA committee. The arrangement was made after the Senate had defeated Nixon's nominations of Clement Haynsworth and Harrold Carswell, and at that disastrous moment Mitchell and the ABA concurred, but for different reasons, that something must be done. The arrangement first began to operate when Nixon and Mitchell proceeded to try to fill the seats left vacant by Hugo Black and John Harlan. It ended there also.

Presidents of course share many of their prerogatives with powerful groups and individuals outside the White House, and usually the arrangements are more covert and subtle than those with the ABA. The Bar Association publicly announced the agreement with Mitchell when it was reached in 1970. The names Mitchell submitted and the committee's responses were to be private, but secrecy was not regarded as indispensable; Mitchell's understanding merely was "that the committee will make every effort to keep these names confidential" and the committee agreed to "do its best," adding however that its investigations "may result in public speculation as to the prospective nominee."[5] As a practical matter, Mitchell quite apparently did not expect the committee to find his prospective nominees anything but entirely qualified, and under those circumstances there would be no need for secrecy. Indeed, the publicity would strengthen political and popular support for nominations which the President would submit to the Senate.

There were good reasons for Mitchell's expectations. The ABA had approved all of Nixon's nominees thus far, including Haynsworth and Carswell, after those nominations had been sent to the Senate. Moreover, the Federal Judiciary Committee was a select group within the ABA, consisting of a chairman plus one member from each of the eleven federal judicial circuits. All twelve were corporate lawyers, bank directors, and men of equal prominence in the bar. The chairman was Lawrence E. Walsh, a Republican and a Wall Street lawyer with a string of excellent credentials. Walsh earlier had held executive positions under Governor Thomas E. Dewey of New York. President Eisenhower in 1954 named him a federal district judge in New York and he resigned in 1957 to serve until 1960 as deputy attorney general in the Eisenhower Administration. In 1969 he had been President Nixon's personal representative to the Paris peace talks with the North Vietnamese, with the rank of ambassador. Beyond all that, Mitchell's expectations reflected the continuing warmth of the relationship between himself, Nixon, and Burger, on one hand, and the leadership cadre of the ABA, on the other.

Mitchell's assessment was not entirely incorrect; the Walsh committee was not a hotbed of liberals who would find fault with Nixon's strict constructionists, as such. But the Attorney General failed to appreciate the nature of the problem the Haynsworth and Carswell affairs caused the ABA, and thus did not fully understand the reasons why it proposed the pre-nomination screening arrangement. Simply put, Mitchell failed to recognize that the Walsh committee had resolved never again to submit to the embarrassment it suffered in the Haynsworth and Carswell matters.

The committee's problem was, in a sense, of its own making. The ABA was not required to express its opinion concerning any federal judicial nominations; it wanted the job. If on balance its role served the public interest in keeping the worst possible nominees off the bench, it also served to augment the power and prestige of the ABA.

The problem the ABA faced in 1970 had evolved over some years. After World War II the ABA committee had begun to submit its comments on federal judicial nominations to the Senate Judiciary Committee, but this arrangement allowed the association to give its views only after the President had made a nomination and thus had publicly committed himself to it. In 1953 the ABA worked out a new arrangement with President Eisenhower's Attorney General, Herbert Brownell, Jr., under which it was able to comment before prospective nominations were sent to the Senate. Brownell agreed to give the ABA committee an opportunity to comment on the professional qualifications of prospective nominees to federal district and appellate courts but not to the Supreme Court. This arrangement continued under each succeeding President, including Nixon.

Appointments to lower federal courts are different, judicially and politically, than Supreme Court nominations. In long-standing practice, nominees to the lower courts are picked by the one or two senators who represent the state in which the vacancy occurs and who belong to the same political party as the President; the President has more leeway if his party holds no Senate seat representing the state where the vacancy exists.* Under these circumstances, the ABA committee can stop and has stopped the nomination of wholly unqualified judges. Since lower court appointments rarely are of more than regional public interest, the secrecy of the ABA's recommendations is easily maintained. The Supreme Court is different because it alone, as the court of last resort in the judicial branch, writes law; because the President does not by hoary tradition give his power of nomination to individual members of the Senate, although senators urge their favorites on the President; and because High Court nominations are of intense, national public interest.

Beginning in 1956 with Eisenhower's nomination of Justice Brennan and continuing through President Johnson's nomination of Abe Fortas to be Chief Justice in 1968, Attorneys General agreed to give the ABA a peek at potential Supreme Court nominees. Generally, the ABA Judiciary Committee was given about twenty-four hours' notice of an impending nomination. The short period of time prevented news leaks and was satisfactory to the Attorney General. But it was unsatis-

*For a description and criticism of the process, by a former Attorney General, see Nicholas deB. Katzenbach, *New York Law Journal*, November 3, 1971, p. 1.

factory to the ABA. The committee attempted initially to make a reasonably complete investigation and to apply to Supreme Court nominees the same elaborate classification used in rating lower court nominees: "exceptionally qualified," "well qualified," "qualified," or "not qualified." The rating always was limited to professional qualifications, and has never been applied to the ideology or politics of a prospective nominee to a lower court or the Supreme Court. But the ABA found that twenty-four hours was not long enough to investigate even the professional qualifications of a potential Supreme Court nominee, and its efforts yielded little more than rubber stamp approval of the names submitted to it.

When Richard Nixon became President, he announced that he would continue to consult with the ABA committee on lower court nominations but would not give the Walsh committee even a peek at his Supreme Court nominations. Therefore, the committee continued its ratings but reported them to the Senate Judiciary Committee, after Nixon made his nominations. By then the committee had reduced its ratings to two: "highly acceptable from the viewpoint of professional qualifications" and "not qualified."

When Nixon nominated Warren E. Burger to succeed Earl Warren as Chief Justice, the Walsh committee reported to the Senate Judiciary Committee that it found Burger "highly acceptable" professionally. After Nixon in 1969 nominated Haynsworth to fill the Fortas vacancy, the Walsh committee conducted a more extensive investigation. It had found Haynsworth "well qualified" when Eisenhower nominated him to the Fourth Circuit Court of Appeals in 1957. From its more extensive investigation, the Walsh committee concluded that Judge Haynsworth was "highly acceptable" professionally for the Supreme Court; after further disclosures were made during the Senate hearing about the Judge's stock holdings, the ABA group took another look and still concluded that he was highly acceptable. After Nixon in 1970 nominated Carswell, the Walsh committee changed its ratings to simply "qualified" or "not qualified." It had found Carswell "well qualified" when Eisenhower had named him to a federal district court in 1958 and when Nixon elevated him to the Fifth Circuit in 1969. It reported to the Senate Judiciary Committee that Carswell was "qualified" for the Supreme Court, and after the hearing disclosed among other things the Judge's 1948 speech advocating white supremacy, the Walsh group met again and decided once more that the nominee was qualified for the Supreme Court. When Nixon finally nominated Harry Blackmun to fill the Fortas vacancy, the ABA committee changed signals again, and adopted the ratings: "meets high standards of integrity, judicial temperament and professional competence," "not opposed," or "not qualified." The Walsh committee gave Blackmun a most extensive investigation and the highest rating.

The Senate's refusal to confirm Haynsworth and Carswell rested on a variety of ideological, political, and professional considerations, but the ABA's effort to disassociate itself from all but the professional considerations was fruitless. So far as the public was concerned, the ABA had endorsed Nixon's defeated nominees. The ABA was ridiculed by some and accused by others of being a tool of white political conservatives. Its prestige suffered, and it was embarrassed.

Inside the Walsh committee, there were second thoughts concerning its role, even before the Senate voted on the Carswell nomination. But it was too late to turn back after the Senate committee's new disclosures concerning Carswell, or so the Walsh committee felt, since it by then three times had found Carswell qualified. So the Walsh group found Carswell qualified a fourth time, but simultaneously determined never to repeat its blunders. It therefore took two steps. After the Fortas vacancy finally was filled with the nomination of Blackmun, the Walsh committee sought and obtained Mitchell's agreement to submit to it in the future the names of prospective Supreme Court nominees, and to allow the committee sufficient time to conduct a thorough investigation of their professional qualifications. Secondly, the committee decided that it would not approve nominees on the "mere absence of specific fault. Excellence [would be] required, as measured against a national standard rather than a local standard. As to sitting judges, more than pedestrian judicial experience [would be] required. In the absence of judicial experience, only a record of exceptional professional accomplishment and national prominence in the legal profession could justify an appointment to the Supreme Court."[6] Those were the ABA's new standards for the Supreme Court, requiring excellence and rejecting mediocrity. They were the standards that were in effect when Nixon and Mitchell proceeded to fill the seats left vacant by Hugo Black and John Harlan. The trouble was that, while the ABA had raised its standards, Nixon and Mitchell had not changed theirs.

Their differences, which eventually burst into public view to the further distress of the ABA, quickly became apparent within the ABA and the Justice Department. Some time before Black or Harlan became ill, Mitchell asked the Walsh committee for its recommendations concerning the possible nomination of Representative Richard H. Poff to be a judge on the U.S. Fourth Circuit Court of Appeals, which covers North and South Carolina, Maryland, Virginia, and West Virginia, and on which Judge Haynsworth sat. Poff, a Virginia Republican, had been on Nixon's and Mitchell's list of Supreme Court candidates since the President nominated Burger. At the moment there was no Supreme Court vacancy, but Judge Albert V. Bryan of the Fourth Circuit had notified the President of his intention to retire, as soon as a replacement was nominated and confirmed, and it was commonplace enough for Presidents to name selected individuals to appellate courts as stepping-stones to the Supreme Court. Poff was presented to the ABA, secretly of course, merely as a potential replacement for Judge Bryan. But the Walsh committee refused to consider him just for the appellate court and insisted on applying its new standards for Supreme Court nomination. By these standards it appeared that Poff would be found either "not qualified" or "not opposed" but would not be given the top rating of "meets high standards of integrity, judicial temperament, and professional competence." The ABA committee's objection was that Poff, before he entered Congress in 1952, had had only four years of trial experience; it refused to accept his time in Congress as evidence of a "record of exceptional professional accomplishment and national prominence." The Walsh committee informed Mitchell or Deputy Attorney General Richard G. Kleindienst of the committee's likely conclusion, but events overtook Poff's circuit court candidacy and he was never formally rejected by the ABA group for that position.

In early September, after Justice Black had entered the hospital, Mitchell asked Lawrence Walsh to come to Washington. At the meeting, which was not announced to the public or the press, Mitchell ran down a list of names for possible nomination to the Supreme Court, asking Walsh what rating, in his opinion, the ABA committee likely would give to each of the individuals. When Mitchell reached Poff's name, Walsh repeated that the congressman was unlikely to get more than "not opposed," or maybe "not qualified." Mitchell also recited the name of Lewis F. Powell, Jr., a Richmond, Virginia, lawyer and former ABA president, and Walsh's response was that Powell probably would get the highest rating. The list included William H. Rehnquist, Mitchell's assistant attorney general in charge of the Justice Department's Office of Legal Counsel, and Walsh also reacted positively to Rehnquist's name. Mitchell mentioned the name of Herschel Friday, and Walsh's face went blank, apparently because he knew almost nothing about Friday.

The meeting did not strike Mitchell or Walsh as unusual. Mitchell, having agreed to consult with the ABA committee before making any Supreme Court nominations, seemed to feel it was his privilege to sound out the committee chairman. Walsh had been willing to keep Mitchell and Kleindienst informed of the progress of the committee's investigations of possible nominees for lower court judgeships and to give them his appraisal of the possible outcome. There was no reason not to extend this informal exchange to potential Supreme Court nominees.

There were no commitments on either side at the early September meeting, but soon thereafter Mitchell privately asked the Walsh committee to begin its investigation of Poff for the Black vacancy. Poff appeared from Mitchell's point of view to be the ideal nominee, and Nixon strongly favored the Virginian. Poff would have fulfilled the President's promise, delivered at the Carswell defeat, to nominate a Southerner. Moreover, Poff had established his reputation as a tough law and order man and a critic of the Warren Court. He had been instrumental in preparing the Republican Party's position on the issues of crime and violence in 1968. Poff also had established a reputation as a Southern conservative on racial issues. He had been a signer of the Southern Manifesto of 1956, in which one hundred senators and congressmen pledged themselves to a reversal of the Warren Court's initial school desegregation decision, and he had voted against every major civil rights bill Congress passed after the Warren Court's breakthrough. Finally, from Nixon's and Mitchell's viewpoint, Poff at the age of forty-eight was young enough to begin a new career on the Court and old enough to have gained substantial support and respect among his colleagues in Congress. He had been in the House for ten terms, he was the second highest ranking Republican on the House Judiciary Committee, and he was endorsed for the Supreme Court even by the Democratic chairman of that committee, Emanuel Celler, the senior liberal in the House and Justice Douglas's good friend.

Therefore Poff's confirmation by the Senate seemed reasonably sure, and the White House let it be known publicly that Richard Poff was its choice to succeed Hugo Black.

Nixon's assessment of Poff was, of course, based on essentially political and ideological considerations. Meanwhile, the ABA was proceeding with its quite different assessment of his professional qualifications, by interviewing lawyers, law professors, and judges for their opinions and knowledge of Poff. Kleindienst, still pursuing Mitchell's effort to convince the ABA that Poff met its standards, submitted to the Walsh committee a long memorandum arguing that Poff did indeed stand tall, professionally and nationally. Walsh still was telling Kleindienst that Poff was unlikely to get the desired rating, because of his "relatively short experience in the actual practice of law."[7] The ABA committee did not insist that a lifetime of trial experience was the only valid evidence of exceptional professional accomplishment, but it refused to accept membership on the House Judiciary Committee as testimony of professional merit.

On Saturday, October 2, Walsh and his committee members met in New York to consider the final results of the ABA investigation of Poff and, apparently, to cast their votes. After the meeting had been underway for four hours, Walsh received a telephone call from Kleindienst in Washington, who said that Poff had requested that his name be withdrawn as a Supreme Court nominee. Mitchell phoned Nixon, who was spending the weekend at his home in Key Biscayne, Florida, and the President's press secretary told reporters that Poff's decision was "entirely his own." The press secretary added, "The President always had and still does have great respect for Congressman Poff, for his abilities, for his record in the Congress serving on the Judiciary Committee. The President feels that Congressman Poff was highly qualified. Now there is one less highly qualified individual to be considered."

The Walsh committee disbanded in New York, without making any formal report to Mitchell on Poff's professional qualifications. Poff himself announced to the press that he had withdrawn because "it appears that the confirmation process would be protracted and controversial." It would have been controversial, without question. After the White House had let it be known that Poff was the President's choice to succeed Black, civil rights and labor leaders declared their opposition, and women's liberationists voiced disappointment that

Nixon was not going to put a woman on the Court. Yet, the support Poff could have had from fellow members of Congress probably would have nullified the black, labor, and women's lib opposition. Therefore Nixon probably was correct in suggesting that the ABA committee tipped the balance against Poff. Representative Celler was more direct. "Where the hell do they get off that a candidate must have judicial experience," Celler declared. The Walsh committee had not demanded judicial experience, but Celler was not deterred. "The President is making a grievous blunder by submitting anything to the American Bar Association," he asserted.[8]

Nixon and Mitchell soon would arrive at the same conclusion, if they had not already. The President sincerely wanted Poff on the Court and was surprised and unprepared when he withdrew. The pressures of time and politics were pressing in, and the President's patience was wearing thin. Nine days earlier Harlan had sent a short, typewritten note, notifying Nixon of his retirement, effective immediately. With Poff's withdrawal Nixon now had two vacancies to fill and his press secretary said the President was "not close" to making any decision. The following Monday morning, October 4, the Court opened the new term, with its flags at half staff and two seats empty.

The political and patronage pressures on Nixon were becoming intense. To avoid such pressures, Presidents often have tried to announce simultaneously a Supreme Court retirement and a nomination and perhaps Nixon's original aim had been to name Poff when Black retired. Now, however, senators and representatives, Republicans and Southern Democrats, and other favor seekers were after Nixon and Mitchell. Particularly with two empty seats, Nixon could not dismiss the demands of the women's liberation movement for Court representation, as Senator Eastland of Mississippi had during the Carswell hearings, when he kept saying "Thank you ma'am," and nothing more, to Betty Friedan of the National Organization for Women. Nixon had no choice but to name a Southern conservative to one of the seats. He had promised he would, and now that promise would be related in the South to his emphatic opposition to school busing, stated only two months ago. But Nixon and Mitchell had no intention of picking a Southerner whose nomination would incite another difficult fight with the Senate. The Haynsworth and Carswell nominations had served their political purpose at the time. Nixon still had to maintain his credibility in the South, but not at the expense of his dignity or his credibility among conservatives and moderates elsewhere. The white South could not alone reelect Nixon; he would run in 1972 on his total record, as the President who brought peace and security, at home and abroad, not as the leader of a geographical or political faction that represented a minority of the nation's voters.

Such were the conflicting political, ideological, and professional considerations that Nixon faced and had to resolve under pressure. Nixon and Mitchell still felt, as they had when they picked their nominees to fill the Warren and Fortas vacancies, that they could not name a close personal or political friend. They still insisted on a "track record" evidencing agreement with the President's view that the Court should take a strict, narrow view of its role in government. Their first problem was to find a Southerner who met their requirements and could not be rejected by the Senate. The obvious solution was to name a member of the Senate, if not the House. But the ABA committee already had said it would not accept legislative experience as evidence of professional stature. Nixon and Mitchell were not quite so circumscribed in filling the second vacancy, but here too they required a strict constructionist who would meet with the approval of the ABA and the Senate. These were the pressures, and Nixon reacted to them by doing "reckless things," in the judgment of one who was intimately involved.

The first thing Nixon did was to decide for himself that Senator Robert C. Byrd of West Virginia could and should be his Southern conservative on the Court. The idea apparently was planted in Nixon's mind by Senator Russell Long of Louisiana. The President had had breakfast with Long, the chairman of the Senate Finance Committee, within a few days after Poff's withdrawal. The breakfast presumably had been arranged so that the two could talk about Nixon's economic program, his welfare proposals, and other legislative matters in which Long's support was of great importance. But Long spent thirty-five minutes promoting Byrd for the Supreme Court.[9]

Byrd of course was a Democrat and West Virginia is not in the Deep South. But Byrd had voted for both Haynsworth and Carswell and, while he had not voted against civil rights legislation as consistently as Poff, his over-all record in the Senate was unmistakably conservative. Being a member of the Senate, his chances of confirmation were substantially greater than those of Poff had been. Specific evidence of Byrd's good standing among his fellow senators was that in January, 1971, he had beaten Senator Edward M. Kennedy for the position of assistant majority leader. It may or may not have been relevant to Byrd's consideration for the Supreme Court, but Nixon and Mitchell always worried much more about Kennedy than any other potential Democratic presidential contender for 1972, excepting always, of course, George Wallace. In any event, Byrd's nomination would have pleased Senator Long and the prospect that Long would return the favor, by supporting Nixon's legislative proposals, reportedly was the reason that John Connally, Nixon's Democratic Secretary of the Treasury, endorsed Nixon's plans for Byrd.

Nixon decided, without delay following his breakfast with Senator Long, that Byrd met his qualifications for the Supreme Court. Word quickly leaked from the White House that Byrd would be named and Nixon on Friday, October 8, encouraged public speculation by taking an airplane ride to West Virginia. He flew to the Mountain State Forest Festival at Elkins, West Virginia, with Byrd and Representative Harley O. Staggers, a West Virginia Democrat, as his guests on the presidential plane. Politicians in West Virginia believed Byrd was going to the Supreme Court until the moment, nearly two weeks after the plane ride, that Nixon publicly announced his final Court selections. In fact, Nixon's mind was changed within a few days after the ride.

The President's mind was changed by his Attorney General and chief political adviser. Perhaps Mitchell had his own reasons for opposing Byrd. Certainly he recognized, as Nixon did, that Byrd probably would have been confirmed, simply because he was a member of the Senate, if that was the only consideration. But Mitchell checked with the ABA committee and received the expected reply that Byrd probably would not get the committee's highest rating. Byrd was neither a giant in the legal profession nor a legislator of national stature; he was known in the Senate for the attention he paid to small details, legislative and political. He was a lawyer. He had earned his law degree from American University in Washington in 1963, five years after he became a senator, and he had never practiced law. He had been in the House and then the Senate for a total of nineteen years, and he was a junior member of the Senate Judiciary Committee.

Nixon thought all this was enough. Mitchell either felt it was not enough or in his judgment there was a risk that the Senate might not confirm Byrd in the face of possible ABA opposition. When Mitchell told Nixon of the difficulties of the situation, the President's reaction was as angry as it had been after the Carswell defeat. His words, expressed this time in the privacy of the Oval Office, yet more characteristic of Lyndon Johnson than Richard Nixon, were: "Fuck the ABA." But Nixon rarely, if ever, acted against the advice of Mitchell and the President abandoned Byrd.

More than a week now had passed since Poff's withdrawal. Nixon had said nothing publicly, although he had made the flying trip to West Virginia. Mitchell, however, had been busy searching for Court nominees and Nixon, after he abandoned Byrd, apparently took a hand in the search. They settled on their next move, and on Tuesday, October 12, Nixon broke his public silence. He announced to the press that he would fill the two Court vacancies the following week.

When Lawrence Walsh heard the news in New York, he telephoned Kleindienst. Mitchell had forwarded no names for investigation by the ABA committee, and Walsh was concerned that Nixon either was going to bypass the ABA or cut short the time it would have to investigate. There was no reason for concern, however. Nixon's new candidates, or at least one of them, had been picked with the American Bar Association in mind and Kleindienst called Walsh back shortly and submitted to the committee not two names, but six.

The six were Herschel H. Friday, Mildred L. Lillie, Senator Byrd, Judge Paul H. Roney, Judge Charles Clark, and Sylvia Bacon.

Kleindienst left no doubt in Walsh's mind, however, that Herschel Friday and Mrs. Lillie were the leading candidates. He told Walsh that the ABA should concentrate its investigation on those two and consider the other four less intensively. Kleindienst also told Walsh that the President wanted to announce the two nominations before Friday, October 22, when the Senate would begin its Veterans Day recess. The following day, Wednesday, Kleindienst called Walsh again to tell him to limit the ABA investigation to Friday and Mrs Lillie.

The other four, drawn from Mitchell's list of more than a dozen names, apparently were on the initial list because the harassed President had not made up his mind sooner. Byrd's name, however, was on the list of six because Nixon, after having encouraged the senator and the public to believe he would be nominated, could not now ignore him. Sylvia Bacon as the second woman on the list added a desirable balance, but her name was not added promiscuously. A graduate of Vassar and Harvard Law School, she had worked on legislative matters at the Justice Department when Ramsey Clark was Attorney General and she had drafted anticrime bills for John Mitchell. Nixon seven months earlier had named her a judge in the District of Columbia. Only forty years old, Sylvia Bacon still could be nominated to the Supreme Court at some future time. Judges Roney and Clark rounded out the list at an even half-dozen. They were Southerners, and their presence on the list demonstrated the seriousness of Nixon's promise to place a Southerner on the Court. Nixon had named both to the U.S. Fifth Circuit Court of Appeals. Roney, who was fifty, and Clark, who was forty-six, also remain Supreme Court timber as long as Nixon remains in the White House.

Of the six, Herschel Friday and Mildred Lillie were the least known nationally, and Nixon and Mitchell put the pair at the top of their list.

Herschel Friday was the President's strict constructionist from the South who, Nixon and Mitchell believed, could meet the exacting standards of the American Bar Association. There were other Southern conservatives who also could have met the ABA's standards, but the name of Herschel Friday stood out above the others because he was recommended to the President and the Attorney General by Chief Justice Burger and Justice Blackmun.

Burger and Blackmun, more than fully aware of the Court vacancies, put forward Friday's name apparently without knowing, or without caring, that history regards Justices' intervention in the nomination process to be a violation of the separation of powers doctrine. Nixon and Mitchell, it would seem, accepted the suggestion gladly, inasmuch as Burger's lifetime friendship with Blackmun had proved to be an excellent recommendation when the President and Attorney General were desperate for a nominee to fill the Fortas vacancy. Mitchell, therefore, called Herschel Friday in Little Rock, Arkansas, to tell him that he was the President's first choice. Friday was greatly astonished and greatly pleased.

Friday, forty-nine years old, was a successful Little Rock lawyer and an experienced trial attorney. He was a partner in the firm of Smith, Williams, Friday & Bowen, one of the largest in Arkansas. He was an active member of the American Bar Association and had served in successively higher positions in the organization, although he was not a member of its ruling hierarchy. He had known Harry

Blackmun well for many years and had argued many cases before Blackmun when Blackmun sat on the Eighth Circuit Court of Appeals. He also knew Burger but less well. Their relationship stemmed principally from Burger's activity, as Chief Justice, in the affairs of the ABA. Friday's practice included some municipal bond work in Arkansas and he had worked with Mitchell on several bond matters, back when Mitchell was a leading bond lawyer in New York.

His acquaintanceship with Mitchell may have helped, but Friday was selected to go to the Supreme Court because he was recommended by Blackmun and Burger. To Nixon and Mitchell the recommendation seemed entirely right. Friday was a genial, disarming individual, an Arkansas lawyer who probably would get on well with members of the Senate Judiciary Committee. He was a Democrat, which also should help. So far as the ABA was concerned, his professional background included not only extensive trial experience but also his work within the association. He had been a member of the ABA's House of Delegates between 1954 and 1968. In 1968 he had been elected to a term which had not yet expired as a member of the Board of Governors, the association's top policy making body. He also was a fellow of the American Bar Foundation, and he had been to the recent ABA meetings in both New York and London. In London a photographer had snapped a picture of Mr. and Mrs. Friday with Attorney General and Mrs. Mitchell, all on their way to the same reception. (The picture was printed in the ABA *Journal* in September, just before Friday was selected for the Supreme Court, of course giving rise to suspicions that Mitchell personally had selected Friday for the Court. But the picture and the proposed nomination were a coincidence; the *Journal* editors wanted to print a picture of Mrs. Mitchell and this was the best one they could find.)

Most important, however, in Nixon's and Mitchell's view, was the fact that Friday was from Arkansas, and Arkansas was more Southern than West Virginia. In addition Friday was experienced in school desegregation litigation and had argued a number of school cases before Judge Blackmun on the Eighth Circuit. Friday had represented the Little Rock School Board since late 1958. He became counsel to the board after Governor Faubus defied the court order requiring racial integration of the city's high schools and federal troops came to Little Rock to enforce the order. In the summer of 1971 he still represented the school board in desegregation litigation. As recently as July a federal district court had handed down a decision which noted that Little Rock "has been in the courts for some sixteen years," that it had not yet submitted an acceptable plan to integrate its elementary schools, and that "the problem is that the schools simply cannot be integrated without a massive transportation of students of all grade levels."[10] Friday of course was representing his client, not arguing his personal view of school desegregation, but his experience could not have escaped Blackmun, Burger, Mitchell, and Nixon.

Mildred Lillie was Nixon's woman strict constructionist for the Supreme Court. There was substantial political and public pressure on the President to nominate a woman, and Nixon had no aversion to being the first President in history to name a woman to the highest tribunal. He apparently agreed with the women's liberationists that, if America's blacks and Jews were entitled to a seat, certainly the time had come when women were similarly entitled. The Senate would find it politically difficult to reject a woman. Nixon's problem was to find one who would meet his qualifications and those of the ABA.

Had the President adjured politics and ideology, he could have selected from a reasonably broad field of women in private law practice, law schools, government positions, and on courts. But, because he insisted on a track record evidencing a judicial philosophy similar to his own, he looked principally to the courts and therefore his choices were quite limited.* For instance, there were but five women judges in the entire federal court system, and four of them had been appointed by Democratic Presidents. Four additional women judges sat on District of Columbia courts, where vacancies also are filled by

*The nine women judges in the federal and District of Columbia court systems and the dates of their appointments were: Shirley H. Hufstedler, U.S Ninth Circuit Court of Appeals, appointed September 12, 1968, by Johnson; June L. Green, U.S. District Court, District of Columbia, appointed June 7, 1968, by Johnson; Constance Baker Motley, U.S. District Court, Southern District of New York, appointed August 30, 1966, by Johnson; Sarah T. Hughes, U.S. District Court, Northern District of Texas, appointed October 5, 1961, by Kennedy; Cornelia G. Kennedy, U.S. District Court, Eastern District of Michigan, appointed October 7, 1970, by Nixon; Catherine B. Kelly, D.C. Court of Appeals, appointed March 28, 1957, by Eisenhower and reappointed June 8, 1967, by Johnson; Joyce Hens Green, D.C. Court of General Sessions, appointed March 11, 1968, by Johnson; Sylvia A. Bacon, D.C. Court of General Sessions, appointed October 15, 1970, by Nixon; Normalie Holloway Johnson, D.C. Court of General Sessions, appointed October 15, 1970, by Nixon.

presidential appointment, but two of them had been appointed or reappointed by Democratic Presidents. Thus, of these nine women judges, Nixon had appointed only three. Nixon thought well of Sylvia Bacon, but she as well as the other two had been in office only about one year, not long enough to meet his or the ABA's qualifications.

As in the case of the other Supreme Court vacancy, many hands were eager to help the President and Nixon accepted a recommendation that came from within his circle of friends and admirers. A number of them, at the White House and the Justice Department, were from Nixon's home state of California, and they were almost unanimously of the view that Mrs. Lillie was precisely the kind of woman he was looking for. She had been a judge for nearly twenty-five years. She now was the highest ranking judge in California, one of the largest and politically most important states in the country. At the age of fifty-six she had acquired substantial judicial experience and still was not too old for nomination to the Supreme Court.

Mildred Loree Lillie, a native of Ida Grove, Iowa, had earned her bachelor and law degrees at the University of California at Berkeley. She had practiced law until 1947, when the state's Republican Governor Earl Warren appointed her to the municipal court of the city of Los Angeles. She was promoted to the Superior Court of Los Angeles County in 1949, and in 1958 another Republican governor, Goodwin J. Knight, elevated her to the District Court of Appeals in Los Angeles, where she still sat, one step below the California Supreme Court.

Over those years Judge Lillie acquired "a strong reputation as a law and order lady, and she is tough on criminal convictions," one prominent California lawyer now serving the Nixon Administration in Washington commented privately. "Any number of communications came into Mitchell's office backing Lillie." In fact, Mitchell had met her on a recent California visit. Nixon at least knew of her.

By those means, Herschel Friday and Mildred Lillie became Nixon's complementary pair of candidates for the seats left vacant by Hugo Black and John Harlan. Their names were not frivolously submitted to the ABA committee, nor was their selection a Machiavellian scheme to deceive the ABA. Under the professional standards the Walsh committee applied when it approved Burger, Haynsworth, Carswell, and Blackmun, the President's selection of Friday and Mrs. Lillie most likely also would have been accorded the ABA's endorsement for the Supreme Court. Indeed, all of the six individuals on Mitchell's list represented some amount of professional accomplishment and under those standards all probably would have won approval. But Burger and Blackmun were no better prepared than Nixon and Mitchell to accept the ABA's new, higher standards.

When Kleindienst on Tuesday, October 12, gave Walsh the list of six names, ten days remained until Friday, October 22, the deadline the President had set for his public announcement of the two nominees. Nixon made his deadline, but not with Herschel Friday and Mildred Lillie. In the interim, ABA investigators, college professors, FBI agents, newspaper reporters, and of course Nixon, Mitchell, and Kleindienst, engaged in a great chase that was closer in resemblance to the script for a Marx Brothers movie than to the constitutional process of Supreme Court nomination. The public saw little more than the opening and closing episodes, but what in fact transpired bore no resemblance at all to the statecraft of Niccolo Machiavelli.

The opening episode, in which the White House, the ABA committee, and hordes of reporters participated, consisted of the public disclosure of all six names within twenty-four hours after Kleindienst privately gave the list to Walsh.* First, after Nixon on Tuesday publicly announced his intention to fill the vacancies the following week, White House sources, not with complete candor, told reporters, who asked that three of those under consideration were Senator Byrd and Judges Roney and Clark. Reporters were able to learn the identity of the other three from the many lawyers, law professors, and judges who were being questioned about the qualifications of the candidates, and thus all six names soon were being headlined and broadcast throughout the nation. This rather large leak in the ABA investigative procedure, however, was not disturbing to Mitchell and Kleindienst or, it would appear, to Nixon. Walsh on Tuesday had told Kleindienst that, as a practical matter, the ABA committee could not undertake a full-scale investigation of all six, questioning dozens of persons familiar with their professional qualifications, without the names becoming public in short order. Kleindienst replied to Walsh that the

*Five of the names appeared on the Dow Jones News Service wires on Wednesday afternoon, as the result of the efforts of a young woman reporter, Nina Totenberg, who later claimed that, "A little sexism in the pursuit of a story is a virtue." Shortly thereafter, all six names began to appear in various newspapers.

risk was "acceptable" and public disclosure would not be undesirable.[11] His optimism seemingly reflected Nixon's and Mitchell's conviction that their candidates were of Supreme Court caliber and therefore would win ABA approval.

After Kleindienst on Wednesday, October 13, told the ABA committee to narrow its investigation to Friday and Mrs. Lillie, the Walsh group intensified its interviews concerning the professional qualifications of the pair. The FBI was making its investigation, on Kleindienst's orders, of their personal and business lives. Newspaper reporters, looking toward the now familiar routine of Senate confirmation hearings, were inquiring of civil rights and labor leaders for their opinions of the potential nominees. And a number of the law school professors who had been so critical of the Carswell nomination were researching Judge Lillie's court opinions in California and otherwise examining the professional and other qualifications of Mrs. Lillie and Herschel Friday.

As the ABA investigation progressed, Walsh in New York kept Kleindienst in Washington informed "of significant information as it was received."[12] By Friday afternoon Kleindienst's and Mitchell's optimism was fading and the Attorney General hastily called in about a dozen reporters, from the New York *Times,* Washington *Post,* and other leading news media, for what was supposed to be an off-the-record, background news conference, but that also soon became public information.[13] Mitchell, unusually testy that afternoon, seemed to feel that an Eastern establishment of newsmen, professors, and lawyers again was ganging up on the President's nominees. Yet, the message he sought to convey to the reporters was that he and the President were bound to no one and nothing, not to Herschel Friday, Judge Lillie, or the ABA.

On Monday, October 18, Mitchell's fears became more concrete. Walsh called Kleindienst to say that, on the basis of the ABA investigation thus far, in his judgment neither Friday nor Mrs. Lillie would be given the top professional rating and there was a substantial likelihood that Mrs. Lillie would be found "not qualified" for the Supreme Court. That same morning newspapers were carrying stories datelined Cambridge, Massachusetts, about the research that Harvard Law School Professor Laurence H. Tribe had been conducting into the judicial opinions of Judge Lillie. Tribe, apparently in communication with academic associates on the West Coast, was quoted as saying that

Judge Lillie's decisions had been overturned by the California Supreme Court with "extraordinary frequency," and, therefore, in Tribe's opinion, she "lacks the distinction" to serve on the United States Supreme Court.

The Justice Department responded quickly on Monday to Tribe's criticism in two ways. First, Assistant Attorney General Rehnquist telephoned Walsh and then dispatched to the ABA committee a three-page memorandum insisting that Judge Lillie's record of reversal by the state supreme court was about the same as the reversal rate of all California appellate court judges. Second, an FBI agent, acting on Kleindienst's instructions, visited Tribe's office at Harvard. According to Tribe, the agent asked "clearly improper" questions concerning the reasons for his interest in Mrs. Lillie and his conclusions about her professional qualifications.[14]

On Tuesday morning the twelve members of the ABA committee gathered in New York to begin final consideration of the professional qualifications of Friday and Mrs. Lillie. Mitchell had been informed that the committee was meeting and that it intended to take its final vote before it adjourned. By Tuesday evening, after the committee had debated and discussed the proposed nominations at length, Walsh called Mitchell to report that Friday's stock also was sinking. Walsh said that, although no vote had been taken yet, there was an increasing likelihood that Friday would be found "not qualified," instead of "not opposed."[15] Mitchell then asked whether the committee could give a prompt report on Lewis F. Powell, if his name were submitted, and Walsh said he believed it could. At Mitchell's request Walsh then agreed to keep his committee in session the following day.

That evening in Washington Nixon and Mitchell conferred in what later was described as a mood of "near desperation." It was agreed that Mrs. Lillie, and the opportunity to nominate a woman, must be abandoned. Herschel Friday was to be saved, if at all possible. They weighed the advantages of pairing Friday with a Northerner. Arlin M. Adams, a Philadelphian whom Nixon had appointed to the U.S. Third Circuit Court of Appeals, was discussed and then dropped, perhaps because he had been on the appellate bench only a little more than a year and therefore probably lacked the judicial experience the ABA demanded. With no other realistic alternatives left, among the strict constructionists on their list, Mitchell put in a telephone call to Richmond, Virginia, and offered a nomination to Powell. Later this same evening the President himself called Powell and urged him to accept the nomination. Powell accepted.

On Wednesday morning, as the ABA committee reconvened in New York, its members and everyone else, other than Nixon, Mitchell, and Powell, proceeded on the assumption that the nominees still were to be Friday and Mrs. Lillie. In Cambridge Dean Albert M. Sacks and thirty-four faculty members of the Harvard Law School were preparing to issue a statement, saying that "at least three" of the six names on the original list were "plainly unqualified" and adding, "We are left with the conviction that the President has approached his task improperly, giving too much weight to factors which should have been subordinated to an overriding goal of locating candidates of the highest quality." In New York Walsh did not hear further from Mitchell, so the ABA committee continued with its discussion of Friday and Mrs. Lillie and proceeding to the voting. Shortly after five o'clock Walsh telephoned the results to Mitchell. Eleven of the votes held Mrs. Lillie "not qualified" for the Supreme Court, and there was one vote for "not opposed." On Herschel Friday six votes were for "not qualified" and six were for "not opposed"; inasmuch as committee practice required at least eight votes to report a candidate other than "not qualified," the official verdict on Friday was "not qualified."

Mitchell asked Walsh to canvass the votes again on Herschel Friday. The ABA committee reopened its discussion, to be certain that there would not be a change of two votes in Friday's favor. There were not. The committee members remained long enough to complete rough drafts of the formal reports finding Friday and Mrs. Lillie not qualified to sit on the Supreme Court, and at six-thirty the members left Walsh's office in New York and headed for airports or hotels or wherever business or pleasure took them.

The President now was left with Lewis Powell, whose name had not formally been submitted to the ABA committee, and without Herschel Friday. His deadline for announcing the two nominees was less than forty-eight hours away. Without waiting any longer, Nixon and Mitchell, between six-thirty on Wednesday and noon on Thursday, agreed to dump the American Bar Association, as the President had wanted to do when the ABA rejected Congressman Poff, and without further communication with New York they selected for the second vacancy the strict constructionist who was most obviously and closely at hand, William Hubbs Rehnquist.

It is not known at exactly what hour Nixon and Mitchell made up their minds. But if they went to bed Wednesday night without making final decisions, they waited no longer after they saw the late edition of the Washington *Post* on Thursday morning. The front page of the paper reported, boldly and unequivocally, the votes that the Walsh committee had cast the evening before on Friday and Mrs. Lillie. Walsh was sorely embarrassed, Mitchell was extremely angry, and the diligent *Post* reporter who disclosed their secret, John P. MacKenzie, was not talking. Nixon's words on this occasion are unrecorded, but at noon on Thursday the White House announced that the President would announce his nominees on national television at seven-thirty that evening.

In West Virginia politicians still were believing that Nixon was going to announce the nomination of Senator Byrd. In Washington all sorts of rumors, including one that Nixon was going to defy the ABA and nominate Herschel Friday and Mrs. Lillie, were being circulated and printed. In Cambridge the most authoritative sources were reporting that Judge Irving R. Kaufman, a tough law and order man on the Second Circuit Court of Appeals, would be named. In New York a puzzled and troubled Lawrence Walsh, having good reason to fear that Nixon either was going to defy or ignore the ABA, tried all of Thursday afternoon to reach Kleindienst by telephone and was told that Mitchell would call him. But Mitchell did not call. Less than five minutes before Nixon went on the air, Walsh finally reached Mitchell and for the first time learned that the nominees would be Powell and Rehnquist. Mitchell also read quickly from a letter he already had written, to Walsh and Leon Jaworski, then president of the ABA. The letter, which the Justice Department released to the press before it was delivered to Walsh or Jaworski, terminated Mitchell's agreement to clear prospective Supreme Court nominees with the American Bar Association.[16]

Nixon's decision to announce the nominations on prime-time national television was itself evidence of the personal turmoil he had endured and of the political importance he placed on the Court. It was the first time he had announced a Supreme Court nominee on television, and thus taken the issue directly to the people, since his choice of Warren Burger to replace Earl Warren in 1969. In introducing Powell and Rehnquist, he told the television audience that he firmly believed the members of the Court "should, above all, be among the very best lawyers in the nation," and he gave his assurance that Powell was a lawyer of "excellence" and Rehnquist "rates at the very top." Both are Phi Beta Kappas, he said. But the President did not limit his remarks to their professional qualifications. Both are "judicial conservatives," he added. Being an old judicial conservative himself, he said, as if to remind Powell and Rehnquist and the nation of what he now expected: "I believe the peace forces must not be denied the legal tools they need to protect the innocent from criminal elements."[17]

The sentence said far more than Nixon intended, about himself and the entire chaotic, unhappy series of events in the nomination of Hugo Black's and John Harlan's successors. The nomenclature of the judicial branch of government is not ordinarily considered to include "tools," and the purpose of the Bill of Rights most certainly is *not* to provide the police with tools. But the form as well as the substance of Nixon's approach to the Supreme Court was not ordinary. Ideology and politics were his paramount considerations, and long after Powell and Rehnquist were seated, Nixon, Mitchell, and Kleindienst still believed that the ABA committee had turned down Herschel Friday and Judge Lillie because it did not like their ideology or their politics. Their belief was demonstrably unfounded. Powell and Rehnquist both had track records that ideologically were substantially more impressive than those of Friday and Mrs. Lillie, but Powell's and Rehnquist's professional accomplishments were such that Lawrence Walsh, at his private meeting with Mitchell in early September, could say that both probably would be approved by the ABA. Moreover, after the ABA committee indicated its unwillingness to approve Congressman Poff for the Supreme Court and Poff withdrew, Walsh wrote a personal letter to Mitchell, strongly urging that the President nominate Powell. Walsh's suggestion was not at that time accepted, because Nixon's approach to the Court took him first to Senator Byrd and then, on the recommendation of the highest judicial authority, to Herschel Friday. In addition Powell's age was against him, until Nixon became desperate.

Mitchell's letter to Walsh and Jaworski, dated October 21, the day Nixon announced the nominations of Powell and Rehnquist, said that the agreement allowing the ABA to investigate Supreme Court candidates was being canceled because of the public disclosure of the President's intended nominees. Quite obviously, however, the new leaks also provided Mitchell with a convenient excuse for ending the agreement. The experiment turned out to have had quite the opposite of its intended effect of strengthening Nixon's hand in Senate confirmation debates, and it was one of the very few mistakes made by Attorney General Mitchell, as the President's chief legal and political adviser.

Even this publicly performed, closing episode seemed paradoxical. Mitchell and the ABA parted, but as friends. Nixon displayed none of the temper he had shown after the Senate defeated Carswell. The day after his television address, he made a speech before a Republican women's group in which he gently chided the ABA. "When the ABA's jury of twelve decides on the qualifications of individuals that the President submits for consideration, the jury should at least have one woman on it," Nixon said.[18] On this occasion he also made a promise: "There will be a woman on the Court in time." The Republican ladies cheered, but Nixon's promise did not ring with the angry determination that had made his similar promise to the South, after the Carswell defeat, sound so real. Mitchell's letter to Walsh and Jaworski also was not angry in tone, and it did not end the older arrangement under which the ABA committee evaluated candidates for federal district and appellate courts. Mitchell and Walsh still called one another by their first names, and, on the day Powell and Rehnquist were sworn in, the two had a private talk and agreed that the agreement concerning Supreme Court nominees might be reactivated at some future date. There was in fact no good reason for Mitchell and Nixon to be angry with the ABA as they had been with the Senate; Powell and Rehnquist ideologically and politically, if not professionally, met all their qualifications. There were very good reasons not to engage publicly in any acrimonious exchange with the ABA. The American Bar Association had welcomed Mitchell and Burger to its platforms and demonstrated its usefulness to Nixon. The Southern Strategy never contemplated the alienation of any group so large and fundamentally conservative as the ABA, and no such result was indicated now.

With the nomination of Lewis Franklin Powell, Jr., Nixon fulfilled his promise to the South. Powell was a Virginian whom the Northern liberals in the Senate would find very difficult to oppose. William Rehnquist's chances of confirmation were less certain. But it also appeared unlikely that the liberals could muster against him that combination of political, ideological, and professional opposition that had defeated Carswell and Haynsworth.

Powell was older, wealthier, and more fundamentally conservative than any of Nixon's prior Supreme Court nominees or potential nominees. He had had substantially more experience in school desegregation matters than Herschel Friday and therefore was better equipped to address himself to the school busing issue. Nixon and Mitchell evidently had hoped that Friday's membership on the ABA Board of Governors would provide added weight to the evidence in his favor. Powell was a past president of the ABA and stood on the highest rung of professional achievement and respect. He had never been a judge, but nevertheless had an extensive record, accumulated over many years of public service. His record demonstrated an ideological conservatism that extended to substantially more public issues than any of Nixon's prior nominees and candidates had reached.

Powell was born in Virginia and graduated from both the Washington and Lee Law School and Harvard Law School. He had practiced law in Richmond since 1931, and since 1937 as a partner in the firm of Hunton, Williams, Gay, Powell & Gibson. He had served as president of the ABA in 1964 and 1965, and during his presidency started several significant projects, one of which was the program, later headed by then Judge Warren Burger, to improve national standards of criminal justice. Powell also had served as president of the American Bar Foundation, and the American College of Trial Lawyers, and he was an Honorary Bencher of Lincoln's Inn in London. He was a director of a number of large corporations and a trustee of Colonial Williamsburg, Incorporated. He had been chairman of the Richmond Public School Board and president of the Virginia State Board of Education in the years following the Warren Court's 1954 school desegregation decision. Powell and Jaworski were two of the nineteen members of the crime commission appointed by President Johnson in 1965, and they were two of the four members who did not agree entirely with the commission's report that emphasized poverty and the other social causes of crime. The four appended to the commission's 1967 report their view that the Warren Court shared the blame for crime in America, saying, "The scales have tilted in favor of the accused and against law enforcement."[19] Powell had spoken out on student unrest, condemning the "license, discord and even anarchy on the campus."[20] He had written an article in which he said it was "sheer nonsense" for liberals to accuse the Nixon Administration of repression, because of its wiretapping, massive Mayday arrests, and indictments of Black Panthers.[21] The article was reprinted in the FBI *Law Enforcement Bulletin*. Powell also had helped to write an attack on the opponents of the President's defense policies. He was one of the sixteen members of the so-called Blue Ribbon Defense Panel, which reported to Nixon in 1970 on Defense Department procurement and research policies; seven of the members, including Powell, signed a supplemental statement which went beyond the panel's purposes and consisted of a lengthy, almost emotional criticism of "the mounting hostility of segments of the public towards the military, the defense establishment, and 'the military-industrial complex.' "[22] Lewis Powell, as Nixon's Supreme Court nominee, now was sixty-four years old, but "better ten years of Powell than thirty with someone less qualified" for the Supreme Court, Nixon said.

Rehnquist was only forty-seven. He was born in Milwaukee, Wisconsin, earned a masters degree at Harvard, a law degree at Stanford University, and had acquired his conservative record, in ways even broader than Powell's, in the service of Nixon, Mitchell, and Senator Barry Goldwater of Arizona. After Rehnquist left Stanford, he was a law clerk to Supreme Court Justice Robert H. Jackson, a complex and talented man who was a liberal on some issues and a conservative on others. In 1953 Rehnquist moved to Phoenix, Arizona, where he practiced law until 1969 and formed what the senator termed a "long and close association" with Goldwater. He did not become the leading lawyer in Phoenix or a leading member of the ABA, but he became a Goldwater Republican and when Nixon became President in 1969, Rehnquist and a number of other Goldwater lieutenants, including Kleindienst, moved to Washington. Rehnquist became a top assistant to Mitchell as head of the Justice Department's Office of Legal Counsel. The office gives legal advice to the Attorney General and through him to the President, and thus Nixon called Rehnquist "the President's lawyer's lawyer." This is not to say that Nixon or Mitchell always consulted their lawyer before they engaged in wiretapping, electronic surveillance, massive arrests of Mayday crowds, or the attempt to stop publication of the Pentagon Papers. But Rehnquist, in congressional testimony and speeches, defended the legality and constitutionality of all of these actions and many more. Concerning the Mayday arrests, he said in a speech, "The authority of the nation to protect itself against violence is held to outweigh the normal right of any individual detained by governmental authority to insist on specific charges of criminal conduct being promptly made against him."* Detention in jail, for limited periods, of "dangerous" criminal suspects, before they are brought to trial, is, "I believe entirely consistent with the spirit and the letter of the Constitution," he said in another speech.** At the London meeting of the ABA, Rehnquist said, "The invasion of privacy entailed by wiretapping is not, I think, too high a price to pay for a successful method of attacking crime."† Before congressional committees he defended presidential actions ranging from Nixon's executive order that breathed new life into the Subversive Activities Control Board to Nixon's action in ordering American troops to attack Communist sanctuaries inside Cambodia.

Despite the professional eminence of Lewis Powell and the government position held by William Rehnquist, Kleindienst instructed the FBI to investigate. This time agents in at least a half-dozen cities questioned law professors and lawyers who had opposed the President's prior nominees, and an agent twice asked Professor Tribe in Cambridge whether he was doing any study of Powell and Rehnquist similar to his investigation of Mrs. Lillie. Later Harvard President Derek C. Bok complained to Kleindienst that lawyers and scholars are likely to find such FBI interrogation "seriously intimidiating," and Kleindienst replied that the FBI had conducted "numerous interviews" relative to Mrs. Lillie, Powell, and Rehnquist, and any assumption that intimidation was intended "is completely unjustified."[23]

The Senate Judiciary Committee opened hearings November 3 on the Powell and Rehnquist nominations. Two months earlier Lawrence Walsh privately had told Mitchell that both probably would meet with the ABA committee's approval, if nominated. After they were nominated, the Walsh committee made its investigations, at the invitation of the Senate committee, and on November 3 Walsh reported that his committee unanimously found that Powell "meets, in an exceptional degree, high standards of professional competence, judicial temperament, and integrity and that he is one of the best

*At Appalachian State College. Boone, North Carolina, May 5, 1971.
**Before the Arizona Judicial Conference, Tempe, Arizona, December 4, 1970.
†At a panel discussion on "Privacy and the Law in the 1970s," London, July 15, 1971.

qualified lawyers available for appointment to the Supreme Court."[24] The Walsh Committee found Rehnquist "qualified." Nine of its members agreed that he "meets high standards of professional competence, judicial temperament, and integrity," while the other three, Walsh said, "would not oppose the nomination, but [are] not ready to express this high degree of support."[25]

Throughout the Senate hearings and floor debate, there never was serious doubt that Powell and Rehnquist would be confirmed, and when the final votes were counted, the Senate's conclusions were much the same as those reached by the ABA.

All, or almost all, of the familiar faces were back in the Judiciary Committee hearing room. Joseph Tydings of Maryland of course had been defeated for re-election since the last time around, when the Senate confirmed Justice Blackmun. But Tyding's place on the committee had been taken by another Democratic liberal, the new, long-haired Senator John V. Tunney of California.

Powell's nomination was supported by ten other former presidents of the ABA, by a number of law school deans, and many lawyers and friends. Senator Eastland, the committee chairman, called the names on the long list of those who had come to the hearing to appear in Powell's behalf, and when he came to the name of Joseph Tydings, he looked up, took his cigar out of his mouth, and said, "I haven't seen you in a long time." After Eastland, Ervin, McClellan, Thurmond, and the other conservatives on the committee paid their respects to Powell, Tunney joined Senators Bayh, Hart, and Kennedy in questioning him. The liberals asked Powell about his substantial holdings of corporate stocks, a subject they had pursued at great length with Haynsworth. Powell replied, "Obviously I have some problems."[26] He proposed to solve them by not participating in any cases that came to the Court involving companies whose shares he owned, and the liberals were satisfied. They questioned him at greater length concerning the writings and speeches in which he had criticized campus disorder and antiwar dissent. Powell did not back away from his criticisms, and he answered by saying, "I believe in the federal system, and that both state and federal courts must respect it, according to the Constitution. I have a deep respect for precedent."[27] Such words, spoken by Carswell, could be challenged; the same words, spoken by Powell, could not be challenged. The liberals moved on, asking Powell about his role in school desegregation, as head of the Richmond and Virginia school boards. From his answers they concluded that Powell had kept the Richmond schools open at a time when white resistance to desegregation closed other schools in Virginia; therefore, if Powell had not done as much as he might to press for racial integration, he had done enough.

The Judiciary Committee unanimously voted to recommend confirmation of Powell, and the Senate on December 6 confirmed him by a vote of 89 to 1. Senator Fred R. Harris alone dissented. The Oklahoma Democrat later said Powell "does not have the kind of exemplary record in the field of civil liberties that I'd like to see in a man appointed to the Supreme Court."[28]

Senator Goldwater, instead of a galaxy of former ABA presidents, hovered over the Rehnquist nomination. Goldwater, in a chair immediately behind Chairman Eastland, sat through most of the Judiciary Committee hearing, although the senator from Arizona was not a member of the committee. The conservative members of the committee might have been expected to question Rehnquist rather closely, inasmuch as some of them from time to time had questioned Nixon Administration policies that Rehnquist had defended, in his role as the President's lawyer's lawyer. For example, he had appeared a number of times before Senator Ervin's constitutional rights subcommittee, and Ervin on one occasion had declared that Nixon's preventive detention program "smacks of a police state." Even Senator McClellan, a law and order advocate before Nixon, had warned the President to "take care" that his anti-crime proposals be kept "within the framework of the Constitution."[29] But these Southern conservatives now were praising Rehnquist, not questioning him; they could argue with him when no more was at stake than the Republican President's initiatives in specific areas, such as preventive detention and electronic surveillance, but now the future of the Supreme Court and of racial desegregation in America were at stake. Sam Ervin's substantial reputation as the Senate's resident authority on constitutional law had never extended to the constitutionality of racial discrimination.

The Judiciary Committee liberals attempted to make the point that Rehnquist's speeches and congressional testimony since 1969 raised serious doubts about his commitment to the Bill of Rights. Senator Kennedy in particular pressed Rehnquist on the issue of the massive Mayday arrests. Rehnquist was chain smoking cigarettes, but he gave not an inch. "I could not fault" the police on arrest procedures, he said, and added that if any changes were to be made in the future he would recommend "more adequate" detention facilities.[30] More often, however, Rehnquist successfully frustrated the liberals by asserting, time and again, that he could not answer their questions about such matters as electronic surveillance, wiretapping, and the Pentagon Papers, because as the President's lawyer's lawyer his relationship with his clients was privileged and therefore private. He thus insisted that, as a Justice Department official, his duty was to Nixon and to Mitchell rather than to the public, and on this curious ground he refused to answer. The liberals tried harder, by turning up evidence tending to show that Rehnquist, when he had been practicing law in Arizona, had resisted local and state desegregation measures. But the nominee blunted this line of questioning by saying that, after racial antidiscrimination laws had been passed, he thought they had worked out rather well. He stated that he remained opposed to large-scale busing for the purpose of racially integrating school systems, and this statement drew no substantial argument from the liberals.

Rehnquist's nomination was opposed by Clarence Mitchell and Joseph Rauh, both testifying for the Leadership Conference on Civil Rights; by the Black Congressional Caucus, composed of thirteen Negro members of the House of Representatives (who also opposed Powell); and by Andrew J. Biemiller, legislative director of the AFL-CIO. But this kind of ideological opposition was not joined, as it had been in the Carswell debate, by a great outpouring of professional opposition. To the contrary, the professional support offered by the ABA was augmented in unexpected ways. For example, Representative Paul N. McCloskey strongly testified in Rehnquist's behalf. McCloskey had told his fellow Republicans in the House that they could not impeach Justice Douglas, and more recently he had declared himself a candidate for the Republican presidential nomination in 1972, in opposition to Nixon. But he testified before the Judiciary Committee in support of Rehnquist, saying that he had gone to Stanford with Rehnquist and "I believe him to be a man of the highest character, integrity and professional ability."[31]

The committee recommended by a vote of 12 to 4 that Rehnquist be confirmed. The dissenters were Bayh, Hart, Kennedy, and Tunney. On the Senate floor Edward Brooke of Massachusetts, still the Senate's only black member, spoke passionately against Rehnquist's casual

# CHAPTER 16

# Out-Wallacing Wallace

The Founding Fathers were unduly optimistic. They, or some of them, assumed two hundred years ago that when the President would have occasion to nominate members of the Supreme Court, by and with the advice and consent of the Senate, partisan politics and political ideology would be laid aside. Nominees would be considered on their merits alone. The senators might well disagree with the President's judgment of the merit of a nominee and refuse to consent, requiring the President to select another nominee, "in their estimation more meritorious than the one rejected. Thus it could hardly happen that the majority of the senate would feel any other complacency towards an appointment, than such as the appearances of merit might inspire, and the proofs of the want of it, destroy."*

Some Presidents in American history have placed great emphasis on integrity, ability, and accomplishment in nominating members of the Court; others have placed their emphasis almost wholly on ideology and politics. At times the Senate has insisted on a more meritorious nomination, and at other times it has obfuscated meritoriousness.[1] President Madison in 1811 attempted to place a mediocre nominee, Alexander Wolcott, on the Court, to counterbalance the judicial activism of Chief Justice Marshall and to subordinate the doctrine of constitutional supremacy to states' rights. The Senate refused to accept Wolcott. It was the Senate, however, that placed great weight on ideology and little on meritoriousness in 1916, when it refused for five months to vote on President Wilson's nomination of Louis D. Brandeis and then confirmed him by a vote of 47 to 22,

*Alexander Hamilton, *The Federalist,* No. 66.

with twenty-seven senators abstaining, as the first Jew to sit on the Supreme Court.

More than mere lip service is paid still to the merit of Supreme Court nominations, as the Senate, the American Bar Association, and ultimately President Nixon himself demonstrated. But politics and ideology also have played a major part in all of the struggles in history between Presidents and Senates over the Court. The relative weight accorded each has depended upon the personality of the President, the political composition of the Senate, the constitutional assertiveness of the Court, and the current state of what Chief Justice Marshall described as "the various crises in human affairs."

Richard Nixon came to the presidency at a time once more of racial crisis in America, compounded by the use his predecessors had made of their power as commander in chief to wage wars undeclared by Congress and thus unmandated by the branch closest to the people. Nixon's party did not control the Senate. The Warren Court had been the most activist since the Marshall Court. Nixon's four opportunities to nominate members of the Court, brought to him by Johnson's cronyism, Fortas's acquisitiveness, and the natural departures of Black and Harlan, posed a direct confrontation between those political and ideological forces in the Senate and the nation that were set against racial equality in America and those that supported or acquiesced in racial desegregation.

In this crisis and these times, Nixon selected his candidates for the Supreme Court with more emphasis on politics and ideology, and less on meritoriousness, than any President in this century and perhaps any in history.

After the Senate had rejected Nixon's two Southern jurists, Haynsworth and Carswell, for the Fortas vacancy, a member of John Mitchell's Department of Justice privately surveyed the judicial wreckage and saw in it political gain: "Nixon finally out-Wallaced Wallace. He played to all the fears of the South and gained its affection."

In much the same vein, Mitchell in an appearance on a national television program said he had "not the slightest" regret over having recommended Haynsworth or Carswell to the President. The nominations were not a mistake, Mitchell insisted, because both "were eminently qualified jurists as their records on the bench showed, and I think both of them would have made fine Supreme Court justices."[2]

The American Bar Association, as well as the Senate, disagreed with Mitchell, however. "One clear lesson we have learned," Lawrence Walsh said, after his ABA committee had found Haynsworth and Carswell qualified, "is that the American public is deeply concerned with the well-being of the Supreme Court. The people want a Supreme Court of which they can be proud. The professional qualification of a nominee is only one of several factors which contribute to its image of integrity, fairness, and justice. In some ways it is among the least dramatic factors, yet the teaching of the public reaction to the last two nominations is that the people are as concerned with the high professional quality of this Court as they are with its political and ideological leaning."*

The ABA thus raised its standards above the level of mediocrity, and Nixon's and Mitchell's selection of Poff, Byrd, Friday, and Lillie failed to qualify. Mitchell then dumped the ABA, and Walsh said the tumult of October, 1971, "showed the value of the committee's advisory process."³ Indeed it had.

This is not to say, of course, that Burger, Blackmun, Powell, and Rehnquist were the most eminently meritorious Supreme Court nominees to be found in the land, or that Nixon named them without reference to politics and ideology. All four were political conservatives whose ideologies Nixon believed, with good reason, to be a mirror image of his own conservative ideology.

The Founding Fathers were not so optimistic as to expect that the Senate could do more than reject a sufficient number of the President's nominees to effect a compromise, even on grounds of merit. Lawrence Walsh never claimed that the ABA could or should attempt to evaluate a nominee's political or ideological qualifications and never expected that the profession could force the President to nominate the most meritorious man or woman to the Supreme Court. Walsh said, "The wide range between a nomination which is ideal in terms of professional qualifications and one which is so bad that it should be actively opposed is likely to place the Association regularly in a position of supporting a nomination less than ideal."**

The American Bar Association, in its official *Journal*, editorially criticized Nixon's narrow, political approach to Supreme Court nomi-

*In a speech at the Law Day Ceremony, Vanderbilt Univeristy Law School, Nashville, Tennessee, April 10, 1970.
**In his speech at Vanderbilt University Law School, April 10, 1970.

nations, even after Lewis Powell, one of its own most eminent leaders, was confirmed. The ABA said:

> Among recent Presidents Mr. Nixon has been the most outspoken of his intention to change the court through the use of the nomination power. He made it an issue in his campaign with his criticism of the Court's decisions in the field of criminal law and procedure, and he iterated that criticism when he referred to law enforcement people as "peace forces" who had been weakened and denied their rightful "legal tools" by Supreme Court decisions.
>
> The inevitable result of this policy is to restrict the field of persons from whom nominations are to be made—a restriction that serves the nation and the Court poorly because it excludes those who, while outstanding candidates, might not adhere to the President's views of certain decisions and, more's the pity, those who have undoubted stature but have not committed themselves on the issues the President holds important and who would be able to approach the future shaping of the law as the cases and needs arise free from a doctrinaire conviction that certain decisions must be changed.
>
> President Nixon indicated his keen appreciation of the importance of the Supreme Court in his radio-television appearance in October when he said: "Presidents come and go, but the Supreme Court through its decisions goes on forever."
>
> Without intending in any way to reflect on Lewis F. Powell, Jr., or William H. Rehnquist, let us hope that President Nixon will broaden the sights through which he looks for nominees for the Court.[4]

The great mystery, then, of Nixon's and Mitchell's tortuous journey to find Powell and Rehnquist, going from Poff to Byrd to the list of six topped by Friday and Mrs. Lillie, was no mystery at all.

The standards that Nixon and Mitchell applied in selecting Supreme Court nominees were, first and foremost, politics and ideology, as defined by their own positions on the issues of criminal justice and racial equality. The standard that the American Bar Association applied was meritoriousness, as defined by personal integrity, judicial temperament, and professional competence. The Washington press corps is fully accustomed to politics and ideology as the standards that ordinarily are dominant in the nomination of dozens of lesser officials, and the press is admittedly cynical. The role played by the ABA was in part an accident of history, resulting from Mitchell's mistake in allowing the association to investigate his Supreme Court candidates and from the Carswell debacle, that may never be repeated. But lawyers who are admitted to practice before the courts of this country have a special obligation to judicial merit, and the ABA has a special obligation to the Supreme Court, even if the opportunity to meet that obligation came by accident. Little wonder then that, looking in from the outside, the press was confused and the public was baffled.

It is a commonplace that Presidents use the power of nomination to fill up vacancies in the great departments of government, in ambassadorships, on regulatory agencies, and in many other federal offices lower than the Supreme Court, for a variety of political and personal reasons that often have no positive relationship with the competence or integrity of the officeholder. Political, personal, and ideological premises of course have a place in the appointment by the President of officeholders who serve in the executive branch, at the pleasure of the President, and who are responsible to him. Rarely has the Senate refused, on any grounds, to confirm these nominees. Theoretically, under our Constitution, appointments to lower federal courts as well as to the Supreme Court are to be made on the basis of merit alone. In practice, political and ideological considerations also play a large part, because of presidential desire or the demands of the ancient system of senatorial courtesy, whether a Democrat or a Republican is in the White House, and despite the ABA. President Johnson, for example, made a total of 181 nominations to federal courts of all levels, and 170 of his nominees were Democrats. President Nixon in his first two and one-half years in office made 116 such nominations, of whom 109 were Republicans.*

*The compilations, from records of the Justice Department, represent the totals of confirmed nominations and a small number of recess appointments for these federal courts: Supreme Court, Court of Customs and Patent Appeals, Customs Court, Court of Claims, Circuit Courts of Appeal, and District Courts.

The totals for each of these Presidents are as follows (Nixon covering the period January 20, 1969, through June 8, 1971):

|  | DEMOCRAT | REPUBLICAN | NEITHER |
|---|---|---|---|
| Roosevelt | 203 | 8 | 0 |
| Truman | 129 | 13 | 0 |
| Eisenhower | 8 | 176 | 3 |
| Kennedy | 113 | 11 | 2 |
| Johnson | 170 | 11 | 0 |
| Nixon | 7 | 109 | 0 |

All Presidents have looked upon Supreme Court nominations as opportunities of the highest order, in terms of politics, ideology, or, on occasion, meritoriousness. Some, including Harry Truman, seem to have viewed Court nominations as the ripest of political patronage plums. A number of Presidents, including Lincoln and Grant, nominated the best of their personal friends. But no President took cronyism so far as Lyndon Johnson did, by creating a vacancy for Fortas and then sending to the Senate in a single package the nominations of Fortas to be Chief Justice and Thornberry to be an Associate Justice. Nixon, as the beneficiary of Johnson's cronyism, was precluded from naming his own cronies and therefore was forced to look elsewhere for nominees who would fulfill his political and ideological ambitions for the Court. His search led to Carswell, who, Dean Pollack of Yale said, "presents more slender credentials than any nominee for the Supreme Court put forth in this century," and then to Poff, Byrd, Friday, and Mrs. Lillie. When Carswell was defeated, Pollack and others suggested names of Southerners whom the Senate and the American Bar Association, even under its higher standards, almost certainly would have accepted. They suggested John R. Brown of Texas and John Minor Wisdom of Louisiana, both judges who sat as Carswell did on the U. S. Fifth Circuit Court of Appeals; Frank Johnson, a federal district court judge in Alabama, and Lewis Powell of Virginia. Brown, Wisdom, and Johnson, however, did not have records of resistance to the forward movement of racial desegregation or to the other constitutional doctrines of the Warren Court, and therefore they would not have "out-Wallaced Wallace." Powell's ideological and political record was more acceptable to Nixon and Mitchell, but his professional record as well as his age were against him, until after the President blamed the Senate for defeating Carswell and campaigned against the Senate in 1970, and until the ABA in 1971 forced Nixon to turn in desperation to Powell.

All of the nominations Nixon made and intended to make were part of his great and historic struggle to gain control of the Supreme Court after Earl Warren retired. Nixon fought with the Senate on primarily political and ideological grounds, familiar to both. He fought with the ABA on the ground of merit, which was to Nixon unfamiliar and hostile. If the ABA, in its opinion, did not force the President to abandon his narrow political and ideological grounds, its victory nonetheless was more substantial than that of the Senate, in terms of the ultimate stake of control of the Court. The Senate forced Nixon only to the North. The ABA forced him onto the higher ground of "exceptional professional accomplishment and national prominence." The ABA was not presumptuous enough to assume that it could prevent the President from placing control of the Court in conservative hands, even if it had been so inclined. Rather, it assumed, along with the Founding Fathers, that meritorious nominees are more likely to be meritorious Justices than nominees selected primarily because of their politics or ideological beliefs. History bears out the further assumption that nominees selected primarily on the basis of merit are more likely to be independent Justices, and perhaps great Justices.

Nixon at various times talked of greatness on the Supreme Court, and he recited the names of three men he considered to have been "great," Holmes, Brandeis, and Cardozo.* The three names are on almost every list that has been compiled of great Justices of the past, and it appears not accidental that none came from a lower federal court or the other kinds of places where Nixon sought a record that reflected his own conservative ideology. All three came to the Supreme Court from careers of great distinction in the legal profession. Holmes came from the Massachusetts Supreme Judicial Court, where as chief justice he was an acknowledged legal scholar and judge. Brandeis came from an active and controversial career as a lawyer, student of the law, and Zionist. Cardozo had been chief judge of the New York Court of Appeals, and there was substantial agreement among his professional peers that he was at the time the best qualified man in the nation to succeed to Holmes's seat on the Supreme Court.

Studies that have been made of the professional and personal backgrounds of Holmes, Brandeis, Cardozo, and other past members of the Court who are considered to have been great offer further evidence that Nixon looked in the wrong places for greatness. Such studies suggest that experience on a lower federal court is one of the least likely contributors to greatness. The appellation is more likely to be associated with Justices who were born in the Northeast, went to highly regarded law schools, were not Protestants, had no judicial experience prior to appointment to the Supreme Court, and were

*Nixon first named the three in the course of his meeting with the press on May 22, 1969, the day following his nomination of Warren Burger.

frequent dissenters.* There have been some judges on lower federal courts of outstanding accomplishment, including, certainly, Learned Hand, but not many; the able judges on lower federal courts may be too much overshadowed by the Supreme Court or, more likely, the hoary political system that permits senators often to name such judges may in general preclude judicial eminence.

Some students of the Supreme Court, and some Court nominees, have suggested that the nominee and the Justice are not necessarily the same, that the stature of the Court and the lifetime tenure conferred on its members by the Constitution breed an independence that frustrates the efforts of any President to control the Court or remake it in his own image. Such efforts, it is said, are "self-defeating; the nominee's position is not always the subsequent Justice's position, and a given 'judicial philosophy' does not always produce a given result."⁵ Or it is said, as it was by Abe Fortas, that a nominee's political alliance with a President is immaterial, because the President will leave office and the Justice will remain. The evidence usually put forward of Presidents' frustration with Justices they nominated consists of Theodore Roosevelt's displeasure with Justice Holmes's votes in antitrust cases, in which Roosevelt had a very special interest, and Dwight Eisenhower's uneasiness concerning various decisions of the Warren Court.**

Many things go into the making of a Justice, including the professional, ideological, and political qualifications of the nominee. If all Justices were uniformly predictable, the Supreme Court would be little more than an extension of the executive branch and its constitutional independence would have no meaning. The Court, constitutional precedent, and lifetime tenure can breed in some Justices an independence of presidential politics and temporal ideology.

*See, Stuart S. Nagel, "Characteristics of Supreme Court Greatness," *American Bar Association Journal*, vol. 56 (October 1970), pp. 957–59. The Nagel study was based on Felix Frankfurter's 1957 list of nineteen Justices who Frankfurter considered to have been preeminent, and on John Frank's 1961 list of twenty-three.

**After hearing of the Court's decision in the *Northern Securities* case, 193 U. S. 197 (1904), Roosevelt said of Holmes: "I could carve out of a banana a judge with more backbone than that." Quoted in Catherine Drinker Bowen, *Yankee from Olympus: Justice Holmes and His Family* (Boston: Little, Brown and Company, 1944), p. 370.

Eisenhower and Warren shared a "mutual disenchantment." See, John D. Weaver, *Warren: The Man, The Court, The Era,* op. cit.

But history does not support the notion that the nominee who was selected first for his political or ideological beliefs suddenly, on donning a black robe, becomes a supremely independent Justice. Those Presidents who have had both the determination and the opportunity to change the Court have been able to nominate entirely predictable Justices, particularly when the President's party has controlled the Senate. The most political Presidents have been able to influence the Court's decisions long after they have gone from office. The American Bar Association has made no claim that it can protect the Court absolutely from presidential politics, much less insure greatness on the Court. "The political and ideological views of the Justices may have a more profound effect upon the decisions of the Court than their professional capabilities," the ABA has said.*

All Presidents are politicians. But some Presidents are known to history primarily as political Presidents or as ambitious politicians. Franklin Roosevelt was a President of great political strength whose nominees and Justices shared with the President belief in those issues that were important to him. Warren G. Harding was an ambitious politician and weak President who was prevailed upon to select nominees for their politics and ideology, and whose Justices also continued to sit long after he departed.

On the other hand, the strengths of Theodore Roosevelt, who appointed Holmes, were more in his own independence than in his politics. Brandeis was named by Woodrow Wilson, who is not known to history primarily as a political President or an ambitious politician. Cardozo was nominated by Herbert Hoover. And Earl Warren was nominated by Dwight Eisenhower.

It made no difference to Holmes, to the Court, or indeed to history that the Justice's votes in antitrust cases disappointed Theodore Roosevelt. Holmes's position on antitrust matters in fact is considered by many legal scholars, judges, and economists of today to have been wrong.** But Justice Holmes's place in history does not rest on his

*Lawrence Walsh, in his speech at Vanderbilt University Law School, April 10, 1970.

**For instance, Holmes, speaking for a unanimous Court in Federal Baseball Club v. National League, 259 U. S. 200 (1922), held that the business of organized baseball was not subject to the Sherman Antitrust Act. Judge Henry J. Friendly of the Second Circuit Court of Appeals, wrote in 1970: "We freely acknowledge our belief that *Federal Baseball* was not one of Mr. Justice Holmes' happiest days." See Salerno v. American League, 429 F. 2d 1003 (1970).

antitrust decisions. It rests on his dissents in civil liberties cases, and on the fact that his dissents often later became a basis of majority opinions, and thus the law of the land. Some of Warren's opinions without doubt also will be read objectively in the future as having been wrong. But Warren's place on any list of great members of the Court similarly is made secure by his opinions in civil liberties and individual rights cases.

President Nixon very frankly selected nominees for their politics and ideology and, less frankly, suggested they would be something else when they became Justices. He said he was nominating men who "share my conservative philosophy," and he also said he did not mean that, once on the Court, they should agree with him "on every issue. It would be a total repudiation of our constitutional system," Nixon said, "if Judges on the Supreme Court were like puppets on a string pulled by the President who appointed them. When I appointed Chief Justice Burger, I told him that from the day he was confirmed by the Senate, he could expect that I would never talk to him about a case that was before the Court."[6]

Nixon could not, and did not, dedicate himself to changing the Court without intention of influencing its decisions. The Court is empowered by the Constitution to speak only through its decisions on cases and controversies brought before it. Nixon, therefore, could not possibly have meant that he had no intention of changing the Court's decisions; he had made that intention abundantly clear ever since the 1968 presidential campaign. What he apparently meant was that, having selected nominees who thought as he did on the law and order, racial, and other contemporary political issues, he would not speak to them about specific cases because there would be no need to speak to them as Justices. It must be assumed, particularly from the Court's unanimous decision on school busing in 1971, that the President did not talk with any member of the Court about the decision of a specific case. But Nixon, Mitchell, and Burger communicated frequently, in public and quite apparently at times in private, concerning the most controversial issues, if not cases, before the Court, and they created the appearance of one or more Justices, like puppets on a string pulled by the President who appointed them.

The separation of powers doctrine, like many another tenet of the Constitution, does not easily lend itself to television specials or newspaper headlines, especially in an era of growing presidential power in the fields of economics and foreign affairs. But Nixon's habit of commenting at every opportunity on the Supreme Court and the issues before it drew the attention of the troublesome American Bar Association. The ABA *Journal* commented editorially that the President's declared intention to change the Court applied to "apparently both its judicial outlook and its decisions." Nixon's running commentary on the Court "places an unfair burden on the President's nominees, for they go forth with the appearance of bearing Presidential commissions to perform certain deeds of judicial transformation and are questioned accordingly," the editorial said.[7]

The questioning began early, when Nixon in 1969 shattered precedent by addressing the Supreme Court, not in the context of a specific case but on the occasion of the swearing in of Warren Burger to succeed Earl Warren as Chief Justice. Burger the following year launched his many faceted program to improve federal and state court administration and to speed criminal justice, and Mitchell provided much of the financing.* Burger's many speeches calling for disciplinary action against lawyers whom he accused of courtroom "incivility" were widely interpreted in the legal profession as criticisms of attorneys who were defending antiwar protesters and Black Panthers, the groups Nixon and Mitchell were attacking and isolating. Burger played some role when the President nominated his old friend, Harry Blackmun, to the Court. Nixon and Burger in 1971 shared a platform at Williamsburg, from which the President repeated his familiar political line, saying the Courts must "reverse the trend toward crime and violence," and Burger, echoing the President, said, "A growing number of law breakers jeopardize law-abiding people." Later that year the scene was repeated in London, where Burger again criticized "unprincipled" defense lawyers and then took a chair close by as Mitchell, at times quoting the Chief Justice, delivered his blunt and unprincipled attack on the Warren Court.

The appearance that Nixon, Mitchell, and Burger were engaged in a joint venture continued and even heightened through the summer and fall of 1971, as Black and Harlan left the Court and Nixon worked

*For example, the Law Enforcement Assistance Administration provided $163,950 for initial financing of the National Center for State Courts, the creation of which was proposed by Burger. LEAA, a part of the Justice Department, makes police assistance grants to the states and has discretionary funds for direct spending.

his way toward the nominations of Powell and Rehnquist. Burger allowed himself to be interviewed at length by the New York *Times*, and he expressed his and the President's conservative judicial philosophy when he said that "disappointments" may be in store for young men and women who believe "they can change the world by litigation in the courts."* He repeated the theme of constitutional restraint in a speech delivered at the dedication of the Georgetown University Law Center in Washington, saying that the courts, and by inference the Warren Court, have "given rise to the alluring prospect that our world can be changed in the courts. Those who would look to judges to innovate and reshape our society will do well" to look instead to the political process, Burger declared.** As he spoke, Georgetown students staged a counter-dedication, featuring as their speaker William Kunstler, one of the nation's best-known courtroom defenders of radicals. Burger later delivered a law and order speech at the Federal Bureau of Investigation and was the first Chief Justice in history to so honor the FBI and its director, J. Edgar Hoover; Nixon had addressed the FBI a few months earlier, saying, "The era of permissiveness with regard to law enforcement is at an end."† Burger and Blackmun took time out from their judicial and nonjudicial activities to recommend Herschel Friday to Mitchell and Nixon. The Chief Justice then resumed his speech making, addressing more than a dozen meetings of judges and lawyers across the nation and at the end of the year returning with Mitchell to the platform at Williamsburg. There, after a Black Panther named George Lester Jackson was killed inside San Quentin Prison in California and after the massacre of rebellious black inmates at Attica Correctional Facility in New York, the Chief Justice and the Attorney General addressed a national conference on prison reform that had been convened at the President's request.

Earl Warren, when he had sat as Chief Justice, had made some speeches. They were about the operational and procedural problems of the courts and, in the best judicial tradition, they were dry as dust.

*The interview was granted to Fred P. Graham, New York *Times*, July 4, 1971, pp. 1, 24.
**Speech entitled "A Generation of Change," delivered September 17, 1971.
†Nixon, who spoke on July 1, 1971, was not the first President to address a graduating class of the FBI National Academy. President Kennedy, who spoke there in 1962, was the first. Burger spoke November 3, 1971.

Warren Burger's speeches were livelier, more like Justice Douglas's writings. And again the editorialist took note in the ABA *Journal:* "Any President who seeks to lead the nation must communicate his policies and proposals to the people. Judges, however, are neither advocates nor partisans, nor can they properly be. Whenever judges take to the hustings, as it were, to discuss issues that have come or are likely to come before the Court, they are assuming a position at variance with the proper functioning of judges in a democracy. They are descending to the political forum and are to that extent giving a political tinge to determinations that above all else need to be absolutely free from even a suspicion of politics."[8]

The appearance then that Nixon's nominees went forth bearing presidential commissions was reaffirmed many times, and Burger and Blackmun proceeded to perform certain deeds of judicial transformation. The Supreme Court and its decisions began to change early in the Chief Justiceship of Warren Burger, as President Nixon had promised his political constituency they would change.

Burger was a kind of Chief Justice the nation had not seen for nearly half a century. Some of the fourteen Chief Justices who preceeded Burger are almost forgotten. A few, including Marshall, Taney, and Warren, are known for the strong decisions, right or wrong, that the Court handed down during constitutional crises of their times. A different few are remembered not as much for their leadership in the resolution of constitutional questions as for their accomplishments as court administrators. The talents required of a constitutional philosopher and a court administrator are different, but dedicated administrators are perhaps more capable than philosophers of changing the course of Supreme Court history.

William Howard Taft was the leading administrative Chief Justice, as well as the stoutest Chief Justice, in history. Taft had been a lawyer, judge, politician, and President. President Harding named Taft Chief Justice in 1921, and he served until 1930. He was an Ohio Republican, and a very staunch conservative. Ours is a "conservative government, strongly buttressed by written law, against the attacks of anarchy, socialism and communism," he wrote.[9] Taft as President was a "Stand-Patter" and he did not change as Chief Justice; he believed that the Court should not serve as an instrument of social progress.

Chief Justice Taft was an activist in the cause of court reform, and on behalf of his personal political ideology. He lunched at the White

House, with Harding and later with Calvin Coolidge. He telephoned congressional committee chairmen and talked with particular news-papermen he favored. He was a past president of the American Bar Association, and he actively solicited the support of the ABA for his projects as Chief Justice. He made many speeches and was the best lobbyist the Supreme Court had ever had, in terms of obtaining from the White House and Congress the appropriations and legislation required for his judicial projects. He obtained the necessary funds to begin construction of the Supreme Court's white marble building, the Court's first home of its own. The Judges Bill of 1925 was a legislative monument to his lobbying skills as well as his reforming zeal. The law, which gave the Supreme Court greater control over its then swollen docket and made other improvements in the machinery of the federal court system, still remained the major legislative enactment regarding court administration when Burger became Chief Justice forty-four years later.

However, then as now, the machinery of the courts was not un-related to the judicial product of the courts. Taft believed, according to one of his biographers, that reform of court administration, and particularly the greater control which the Supreme Court obtained over its own docket, could be used as tools, handy for keeping social issues and wild-eyed reformers out of the courts.[10] Similarly, Taft believed that the nomination of new Justices was not unrelated to the decisions the Court would hand down, and he played an active role in the selection of new members of the Court when Harding and Coolidge were in the White House. It was largely on Taft's recom-mendations that Harding nominated three extremely conservative Justices, George Sutherland, Pierce Butler, and Edward Terry San-ford. When Herbert Hoover succeeded Coolidge in 1929, Taft ex-pected to enjoy an equally cordial relationship with the new President. The 1920s, like the 1960s, had been years of affluence and high crime, and Hoover in his inaugural address struck themes that echoed the Chief Justice's words. Hoover spoke out against "disregard and disobedience of law," and called for "reform, reorganization and strengthening of our whole judicial and enforcement system."[11] But Hoover rather quickly showed that he was not entirely sympathetic toward Taft's ultra conservatism or his meddling, and Taft moodily complained of the President's "radical" tendencies. Taft was able to block the nomination of Cardozo as long as he remained Chief Justice, and Hoover named Cardozo after Taft died.

Taft also did not live to see the completion of his greatest monument, the Supreme Court's magnificent marble temple. The white marble for its exterior walls came from Vermont, marble from Georgia was used to wall the inner courtyards, and marbles from Spain and Italy graced the courtroom itself. The building was adorned with marble columns, bronze doors, and flowing fountains. The interior public areas were faced with marble, and the private offices throughout were paneled with solid oak. The total effect was Roman and opulent. It would have pleased Taft greatly but it did not please all of the Justices when the Court moved in in 1935. Harlan Fiske Stone called it "almost bombastically pretentious." Cardozo suggested that it would be appropriate for the Justices to ride to work on the backs of elephants. Apparently because the elegence was personally offensive to him, Brandeis refused to use his suite of offices in the building. For Brandeis and Cardozo, however, the memory of Taft also have made the structure less than inviting. Taft, in addition to blocking the nomination of Cardozo, had had an acid relationship with Brandeis and with Holmes.

In time the Court grew accustomed to its temple and for years little more was said or done about it. On his arrival in 1969, Warren Burger found it "a beautiful building but a marble mausoleum stark and unrelieved in its severity." So Burger decided to relieve its austerity, with touches of new opulence for the Court and its Justices. Burger, taking advantage of the prerogatives of an administrative Chief Justice, had large, artificial rubber plants placed in niches of the white marble interior that had been intended for statuary. He ordered begonias, planted in redwood tubs, placed on the marble plazas outside the building and bright lights installed at strategic exterior and interior locations. Pictures were hung on some of the marble walls inside. Then Burger obtained $8,600 from Congress and had the long, straight mahogany bench cut into three sections that were placed in the shape of a half-hexagon. The purpose of the new arrangement reportedly was to permit the nine Justices to see one another without stretching their necks. But from the public side of the bench, the half-hexagon seemed to disrupt the former equality of nine Justices, all sitting in a line. The new arrangement also tended to concentrate attention on the center section of the three, and on the Chief Justice who sat in the middle chair of the center section. The rearrangement of the bench necessitated the removal of the six tiny desks which had been immediately in front of the long straight bench, and at which

newspaper reporters had sat since 1935. Burger found room for the six
displaced reporters off to the side of the courtroom and some distance
from the triple-section bench. The Chief Justice also had furniture
moved and walls torn down, in order to enlarge the suites of offices
occupied by the Justices. And he requested of the White House and
Congress funds for eight new automobiles. He asked for eight sedans,
so that each Associate Justice could ride to work in his own auto and
there would be no further need for sharing the limousine assigned to
the Chief Justice.

"I would say," commented Professor Alexander Bickel of the Yale
Law School, "that Burger is modeling himself on the Chief Justiceship
of Taft."[12] Bickel, a well-known advocate of judicial restraint and
frequent critic of the Warren Court, approved of Burger and his
model. Many other legal scholars also recognized the striking similarities between the Chief Justiceships of Taft and Burger and approved
or disapproved. Philip B. Kurland, a professor at the University of
Chicago Law School, was not a constant admirer of the Warren Court
but became a severe critic of Burger. "As was the case with Taft,
Burger regards himself as more of a Lord Chancellor than a mere
Lord Chief Justice," Kurland wrote. Under the English system, so
much admired by Burger and Mitchell, the Lord Chancellor recom-
mends judicial appointments and he is a legislator and usually a
Cabinet officer, while the Lord Chief Justice holds office for life and
is confined to judicial tasks. "There is an inconsistency between the
judicial role and the political one that is recognized by the English
Constitution," Kurland continued. "The difference the Chief Justice
would seem to disregard as he assumes the woolsack of the Lord
Chancellor." Kurland did not argue with the need for reform, but
insisted that, under the American Constitution, the reform of court
administration should be left to Congress. Kurland added, "I would
suggest to anyone engaged as the Chief Justice is in improvement of
the administration of justice that it is the character and capacity of
the men administering the system far more than the system itself that
will determine the efficacy of a court of law. The shoemaker, even the
chief shoemaker, should stick to his last."[13]

Burger, however, did not find Kurland's advice to his liking, and
soon the comparison with Taft extended beyond the trappings of the
Lord Chancellor and into the courtroom. Taft's active and successful
solicitation of the White House on behalf of the nominations of Suth-

erland, Butler, and Sanford, and against the nomination of Cardozo, served more than the vanity of the Chief Justice; it served also to preserve and enhance Taft's command of a majority of votes on the Court and thus to ensure decisions which interpreted the Constitution narrowly indeed. Taft admittedly had more conservative votes to work with, initially. But Burger had Blackmun, at the very least. For his part, Harry Blackmun rarely came upon those cases and controversies that afforded the opportunity to fulfill the independent role he had promised at his confirmation hearing. When Senator Kennedy had asked the nominee about his lifetime friendship with Burger, Blackmun had replied, "I would have no hesitation whatsoever in disagreeing with him."[14] Nor did Justice Blackmun fulfill the role that Justice Douglas nobly forecast, when Douglas said that Blackmun "is what the mountain men I knew in the Far West would call a 'stout fellow.' "[15] To the contrary, Blackmun voted with Burger so often that they became known around the Court as the "Minnesota Twins."

The parallels between the Court over which Taft presided and the Court which Burger headed are not to be overdrawn. Taft reigned nearly nine years, and Burger came to office only in 1969. The ideological majority of which Taft was the prototype did not in its maturity practice judicial restraint, if that term is meant to describe a Court that defers as a matter of doctrine to other branches of government and refuses to hold unconstitutional any federal or state law or action. The conservative majority headed by Taft was so firmly dedicated to an ideology of stand-pattism, private property, and the privileges of wealth that it actively and repeatedly used its constitutional power to strike down state laws fixing minimum wages for women, state tax laws, a state standard-weight bread law to protect consumers from short weighting, and a New York law fixing the resale prices of theater tickets sold by scalpers. It was in 1930 that Professor Felix Frankfurter wrote, "Since 1920, the Court has invalidated more legislation than in fifty years preceding. Views that were antiquated twenty-five years ago have been resurrected." Later, after Taft's death, it was this same conservative majority that turned its judicial activism on federal social and economic legislation, nullifying as unconstitutional some of the most crucial New Deal legislation enacted by Congress in the early years of Franklin Roosevelt's Presidency.

Burger and Blackmun, in majority opinions or in dissents, did not urge that the Court use its constitutional authority to overturn social and economic legislation embodied in federal or state laws. The conservative judicial philosophy they represented stood for the more modest proposition that the Court should not use its power as final arbiter of the Constitution to initiate social, economic, and political reform and should defer to the initiative of executive and legislative bodies. The difference between Chief Justices Burger and Warren, of course, was that Earl Warren held that the Supreme Court should not, and constitutionally could not, defer, when the executive and legislative arms of government were unwilling or unable to respond to the legitimate and constitutional demands of large segments of the population.

Taft, then, took his judicial conservatism to considerably greater lengths than Burger would go, at least so long as Nixon represented executive authority. But all of this remained merely theoretical, in the beginning, because, as long as Hugo Black and John Harland remained on the Court, Burger did not command the certain numerical majority on which Taft relied. Burger and Blackmun were dissenters when the Court decided the big cases, and in the spring of 1971 when it decided the school busing case, the biggest of them all as it turned out, Nixon lost even Burger and Blackmun.

Still, Nixon in 1969, 1970, and 1971 did not lose them all. Even before Powell and Rehnquist became the third and fourth Justices named by Nixon, there were signs that Burger was moving the Court rightward, if slowly, with an inconstant majority and only on particular issues. After Powell and Rehnquist arrived, Nixon's ideological nominees began to consolidate as Justices, and there were new signs, indicating that the Supreme Court presided over by Warren Burger might yet, at some indefinite, post-Nixon time in the future, find in itself a capacity for judicial activism more closely paralleling the works of Chief Justice Taft.

The particular issues that first began to give way under Burger, prior to the arrival of Powell and Rehnquist, were those involving law and order. The Warren Court's decisions affirming the constitutional rights of persons accused by police of criminal offenses had been decided with less unanimity than its other major constitutional rulings, and they were thus more vulnerable to change. These were the decisions of the Warren Court that Nixon and Mitchell harped on endlessly. These also were the decisions that Burger had criticized when he was an appellate judge.

The Warren Court's criminal rights decisions, of course, were not suddenly reversed when Nixon addressed the Court and Burger was sworn in succeeding Warren. As Chief Justice, Burger was a vigorous dissenter when a majority of the members of the Court voted still to uphold or expand the rights of persons picked up and interrogated by police. In the *Whiteley* case, for instance, Burger and Black joined in their intemperate dissent, saying that such decisions "make many good people believe our Court enjoys frustrating justice."[16] In the *Bivens* case and a companion decision, Burger's dissent attacked the exclusionary doctrine itself, which for longer than half a century held that evidence unconstitutionally obtained by police could not be used to convict an accused individual.[17]

Some other law and order cases, however, commanded a different majority. They were not major cases and they represented no large victories for Burger and Blackmun, but they were victories nonetheless. One such case was a variation on the *Miranda* theme, the Warren Court's 1966 holding that an accused person is entitled to a lawyer and statements made by him while in police custody cannot be used against him, if not made in the presence of a lawyer. Nixon had been particularly critical of the *Miranda* ruling. In the new case the question was whether statements, inadmissible under the *Miranda* ruling in a defendant's direct testimony at trial, nonetheless could be used on cross-examination to impeach the credibility of his testimony. Chief Justice Burger, writing for the majority in the 5-to-4 decision, held that such statements could be used in cross-examination.[18] Voting with Burger were Justices Harlan, Stewart, White, and Blackmun; dissenting were the liberal Justices, Brennan, Douglas, and Marshall, plus the increasingly independent Justice Black.

By the same 5-to-4 lineup, the Court in another case held that the confrontation clause of the Sixth Amendment, as applied to the states by the Fourteenth Amendment, does not prevent the states from allowing hearsay evidence to be used in a criminal trial, even though the same evidence could not be used under rules applying to the federal courts.[19] Justice Stewart wrote the Court's opinion, in which Burger, White, and Blackmun joined. Justice Harlan wrote a separate opinion in which he concurred in the result but disagreed with Stewart's method of arriving there. Marshall's dissenting opinion, joined by Black, Douglas, and Brennan, asserted that "the majority reaches a result completely inconsistent with recent opinions of this Court."

Burger and Blackmun also were on the winning side in another, more dramatic and significant law and order decision. In this case, federal agents charged one James A. White with illegal transactions in narcotics. They obtained evidence against him by concealing a tiny radio transmitter in the clothing of a government informer, and, while the informer conversed with White at the informer's home, an agent hidden in a kitchen closet listened. White was convicted, and the question before the Supreme Court was whether evidence gathered by radio-equipped informers violates a criminal suspect's Fourth Amendment right to be secure from unreasonable searches and seizures. The majority opinion, by Justice White, was lengthy and legalistic but it arrived at the conclusion that testimony of federal agents that is based upon evidence so obtained does not violate a defendant's constitutional rights.[20] Burger, Blackmun, Stewart, Brennan, and Black concurred in the result. The dissenters were Douglas, Harlan, and Marshall. "The issue in this case is clouded and concealed by the very discussion of it in legalistic terms," Douglas's dissent asserted. "Electronic surveillance is the greatest leveler of human privacy ever known. How most forms of it can be held 'reasonable' within the meaning of the Fourth Amendment is a mystery."[21]

Chief Justice Burger's law and order successes on the Court were then not large. They were mixed with law and order decisions in other cases in which Burger and Blackmun were on the losing side, and the net results were not sufficiently encouraging to cause Nixon and Mitchell to stop making law and order speeches or to halt their criticism of the Warren Court. Still, Burger and Blackmun were winning some of the time on the law and order issue, and judicial conservatism prevailed in a number of other decisions in 1971, while Black and Harlan still were on the Court.

For example, there were two voting apportionment cases in which the majority, including Burger and Blackmun, declined to extend further the Warren Court's one man, one vote doctrine. In one case, brought by black voters living in the inner city area of Indianapolis, Indiana, a lower court had held that large, multi-member legislative districts, in which voters elected a dozen or so at-large state legislators, were unconstitutional because such voting apportionment schemes canceled out the voting strength of minority group voters. The Supreme Court, badly splintered with individual opinions that concurred in part and dissented in part, reversed the lower court and held that multi-member legislative districts do not inherently discriminate against black and other minority group voters.[22] In a second decision the Court upheld the constitutionality of state laws which require that proposals for municipal bond issues be approved not by a simple majority of voters, but by super-majorities of up to two-thirds of those voting. A lower court, in a case from West Virginia, had read the Warren Court's one man, one vote decisions to mean that super-majority requirements, applying to bond elections for construction of new schools, sewers, and other public facilities, were unconstitutional because a minority of voters could defeat a bond proposal. The Supreme Court held in a 7-to-2 decision that super-majority requirements were constitutional.[23] Chief Justice Burger wrote the Court's opinion, holding that such requirements do not single out any particular minority. Justices Brennan and Marshall alone dissented.

There were some other decisions in various areas of the law and of human affairs that, while again not earthshaking, suggested a turning away from the philosophy and indeed the compassion of the Warren Court. One such case was that of Rita Nell Vincent, a minor born in 1962 in Calcasieu Parish, Louisiana. The girl's father, Ezra Vincent, died in 1968 without a will and her guardian brought suit challenging the constitutionality of the Louisiana law that bars an illegitimate child from sharing equally with legitimate children in the father's estate. Erza Vincent had legally acknowledged himself to be Rita's father but, since he died intestate, she could not under state law share equally in the estate. The Supreme Court, in a decision by Justice Black, upheld the Louisiana law, saying it fell within a state's power to establish rules for the protection of family life and the disposition of property.[24] Black was joined by Burger, Harlan, Stewart, and Blackmun. The dissenters were Brennan, Douglas, White, and Marshall.

Another case posed this constitutional question: May the government send to prison, for draft evasion, a young man of unquestioned religious conviction who is a conscientious objector to the Vietnam war, but not necessarily to war in general? The draft law excuses any young man who, "by reason of religious training and belief, is conscientiously opposed to war in any form." The Supreme Court held that a young man, of sincere religious training and belief, cannot refuse to enter the armed forces if he claims objection only to the Vietnam war, and further held that the law does not violate the guarantee of religious freedom contained in the First Amendment.[25] The decision was reached by a lopsided 8-to-1 vote, with only Justice

Douglas dissenting. It reflected the majority's unwillingness to interfere directly and seriously with the President's Vietnam war effort, a reluctance that was most obvious in the Court's rejection of many cases in which it was asked to decide whether the war unconstitutionally transgressed upon the enumerated power of Congress to declare war.

The Court in the spring of 1971 decided three civil rights cases of substantial importance. The most significant was the school busing decision, which demonstrated the great force of constitutional precedent. The second decision, in which the Court also upheld the claims of blacks, involved statutory interpretation and no question of constitutional law. The third case raised a fundamental constitutional issue. The Court decided it against Southern blacks, and thereby turned away from the Warren Court's rulings in that area of constitutional law and human affairs which was most firmly fixed in precedent and most resistant to change.

The second case concerned an interpretation of the 1964 Civil Rights Act, which in part barred racial discrimination by employers and unions. The question before the Court was whether the act outlawed an employer's use of intelligence tests and educational requirements in hiring and promoting workers, where such tests and requirements are not directly related to job performance and operate to exclude blacks from employment opportunities. The Court held that the law bars the use of such requirements and tests.[26] The decision was unanimous and the Court's opinion was written by Chief Justice Burger.

A few weeks later the third civil rights case was decided, with a majority opinion that was truly startling and that seemed almost absurd, as a matter of constitutional law. The case of *Palmer* v. *Thompson* came from Jackson, Mississippi. The city of Jackson had desegregated its public recreational facilities, including its five public parks, as required by lower federal court orders. But the city council decided that it would close the swimming pools in the parks, rather than allow blacks to swim with whites. Black citizens went back to the lower courts to force the city to reopen the pools on a desegregated basis. The blacks cited as precedent Supreme Court decisions holding that Southern states constitutionally could not close their schools as an alternative to desegregating them. But now the Supreme Court, in a 5-to-4 decision, held that swimming pools were to be distinguished from schools.[27] Justice Black wrote the majority opinion, saying "Congress has passed no law" requiring cities to operate swimming pools and the Court must not "stretch" the Constitution to reach swimming pools. Black was joined by Burger, Harlan, Stewart, and Blackmun. The dissenters were Douglas, White, Brennan, and Marshall. "I had thought," Justice White wrote, that "official policies forbidding or discouraging joint use of public facilities by Negroes and whites were at war with the Equal Protection Clause."

Clearly, the Supreme Court was beginning to turn away from the philosophy and the humanism of the Warren Court, as President Nixon since 1968 had been promising, and even before the arrival of Justices Lewis Powell and William Rehnquist.

After Powell and Rehnquist, in January of 1972, took their seats at the mahogany bench Burger had severed into three pieces, the Court and the Constitution began to change more dramatically and drastically, and Nixon's campaign to exorcise the spirit of Earl Warren began to yield results, tangible and intangible.

The Minnesota Twins became the Nixon Quads and ideology divided the Supreme Court bench into three parts as palpably as had the carpenter's saw. Burger, Blackmun, Powell, and Rehnquist voted together with such frequency that the predictability of their position suggested a discipline more akin to politics than jurisprudence. Among Nixon's quadruplets, Powell alone seemed to demonstrate some capacity for independence and thoughtfulness. The second section of the ideologically divided bench was occupied by Douglas, Brennan, and Marshall, although this liberal trio was not quite as solidly unified as once it had been. At the third section sat Stewart and White, the less predictable and more independent members of the Warren Court, who now held the balance of power. Increasingly, one or both voted with the Nixon appointees and tipped the balance in favor of the change sought by the President.

Ideology did not divide the Court on all issues. There were some decisions, as on questions of income tax law, personal injury suits, and maritime liability, that were neither ideological nor predictable. There were a few others that, if predictable, were of no profound ideological consequence. The emerging conservative majority, for instance, threw out center fielder Curt Flood's antitrust suit against the big league baseball business.[28] The Supreme Court itself had conferred the antitrust exemption on organized baseball exactly 50 years earlier, when in 1922 it held that baseball was a local game of athletic skill, not to be defined as interstate commerce. Flood, represented by a lawyer now in private practice in Washington named Arthur J. Goldberg, argued that the 1922 decision should be reversed, not only because baseball now is big business but also because the Supreme Court in recent years had held organized football, basketball, and boxing subject to the antitrust statutes. But the Court, in a decision by Justice Blackmun, refused to hold baseball subject to the same laws. The Blackmun opinion did not distinguish baseball from other professional sports; to the contrary, it said that "professional baseball is a business and it is engaged in interstate commerce." The Court simply said, from its marble dugout, that, since the President and Congress had not by statute made baseball subject to antitrust, the Court should not either. The decision was one of the better examples of strict constuctionism, meaning deference to the majoritarian branches, and, as Blackmun conceded, it also was an "aberration" and an "anomaly" in antritrust law. The liberal trio dissented.

Few issues in American life, however, are as sacrosanct, in jurisprudence or politics, as the baseball business. Issues of individual rights and government powers, of racial equality and desegregation, are not immutable and to these the emerging conservative majority applied the doctrine of strict constructionism with ever more drastic and dramatic effect. In cases growing out of these crises of our times, the four Nixon appointees almost invariably voted as a bloc, in victory or defeat but more often in victory. The Court, in 1972, during the term in which Powell and Rehnquist took their seats, decided more than a half dozen major individual and civil rights cases growing out of citizen and political dissent to the Vietnam war and Nixon won all but one. The Court ruled on an approximately equal number of significant law and order controversies and the four Nixon appointees were the dissenters only once, which was when the Court decided the ultimate law and order question by holding the death penalty unconstitutional. The Court also decided two important racial controversies. Blacks lost the first. They won the second, but the victory cast a dark shadow on the future of racial desegregation in America; the four Nixon appointees dissented, and for the first time since the Supreme Court in 1954 first held school segregation unconstitutional, the Court was not unanimous in a constitutional decision requiring school desegregation.

The cases growing out of antiwar dissent and the Nixon Administration's efforts to repress that dissent brought the members of the
Court face-to-face with their President, continuing the classic confrontation of government power with the Bill of Rights that had begun
a year earlier with the Administration's effort to stop publication by
the New York *Times* and other newspapers of the secret Pentagon
Papers. The public disclosure of the Pentagon Papers, notwithstanding the late Justice Black's eloquent reaffirmation of the First Amendment, led to federal grand jury investigations in Los Angeles and
Boston, and to a decision by the Supreme Court holding that Senator
Mike Gravel, Democrat of Alaska, and his aides could be called
before a grand jury to testify concerning the source and disposition
of a copy of the Pentagon Papers that Gravel had obtained and made
public.[29] The Court's decision further held that members of Congress
can be required to testify before grand juries concerning activities
other than those that can be defined strictly as "legislative acts." The
decision therefore restricted the Speech and Debate Clause of Article
I, which says that members of Congress "shall not be questioned in
any other Place."

The same majority that decided the *Gravel* case, consisting of the
four Nixon appointees plus Byron White, held also that the First
Amendment does not stand in the way of grand jury subpoenas requiring Earl Caldwell of the New York *Times* and other newspaper
and television reporters to testify to knowledge gained from confidential news sources concerning the activities of antiwar dissenters, Black
Panthers, White Panthers, drug pushers, and assorted other targets
of federal and state prosecutors.[30] The majority opinion, by Justice
White, agreed with journalists that "the flow of news will be dimin-
ished by compelling reporters to aide the grand jury in a criminal
investigation." But White held that any such First Amendment values
must give way to "fair and effective law enforcement."

Again the same majority, with Chief Justice Burger writing the
majority opinion this time, upheld the constitutionality of surveillance
by the U.S. Army of Americans in America, including even senators
who did not wholeheartedly support the Vietnam war and anyone else
who, according to Burger, harbored "some potential for civil disorder."[31] The Army had established its computerized domestic intelligence in 1967, after President Johnson ordered troops into Detroit to
quell racial rioting, and the Army systematically and secretively had

snooped on blacks and whites. Burger could find in the Army surveillance no chilling effects on the First Amendment and disposed of the issue by holding that those snooped upon had demonstrated no real injury. In his dissent, Justice Douglas declared that "the act of turning the military loose on civilians, even if sactioned by Congress, which it hasn't been, would raise serious and profound constitutional questions."

And further, Nixon appointees plus White prevailed in a controversy that pitted the constitutional rights of dissenting citizens not against government authority but against the rights of private property.[32] The majority decision, by Justice Powell, held that owners of large suburban shopping centers can invoke state trespass laws to cause the arrest of individuals who peaceably are handing out antiwar and other leaflets in the public areas of shopping centers, even though such centers are otherwise open to the public at large and are integral parts of their communities. "It becomes harder and harder for citizens to find means to communicate with other citizens," Thurgood Marshall lamented in dissent.

In those and other constitutional decisions growing out of citizen dissent, White cast his lot with the solid bloc of Nixon appointees, while Justice Stewart dissented along with the three liberals. White plus the Nixon foursome similarly prevailed on a number of law and order issues.

In one such case, the five member majority held that the Constitution does not require a unamimous vote of jurors for conviction in most criminal trials in state courts.[33] The decision, written by White, was the most important criminal ruling handed down by the Court since Nixon became President; its purpose, White wrote, was to "facilitate" and "expedite" law enforcement. Its effect would be to secure more convictions for state prosecutors. In dissent, Stewart declared that "only a unanimous jury can minimize the potential bigotry of those who might convict on inadequate evidence." Marshall said the Court "cuts the heart out of two of the most important safeguards the Bill of Rights offers a criminal defendant: the right to a jury and the right of proof beyond a reasonable doubt." Douglas asserted that the majority had "discarded two centuries of American history," and Brennan agreed. On the same day, May 22, 1972, the Nixon bloc picked up the votes of both White and Stewart to render a six-to-three decision which further augmented the powers of prosecutors by giving them additional tools with which to force recalcitrant witnesses to talk. The majority interpreted the Fifth Amendment's guarantee against self-incrimination to mean that witnesses can be compelled to testify before grand juries, even though they later may be convicted on the basis of other evidence for the crimes they are forced to discuss.[34] When the Nixon bloc lost White, it picked up Stewart. The foursome plus Stewart held, for example, that criminal suspects normally are not entitled to legal counsel at police station lineups.[35] That decision deeply undercut the 1967 Warren Court decision which held that the right to counsel applied at the line up stage of police custody —a decision that Richard Nixon during the 1968 campaign denounced as "almost ridiculous."

The term that ended June 29, 1972, produced three decisions concerning the constitutional rights of ordinary criminal defendants and of political dissenters that did not fit the pattern of the other decisions of the emerging conservative majority. In each there seemed to be good reason why the decision did not fit the pattern. The first involved presidential overreaching in the use of electronic surveillance devices, so much in conflict with a recent law of Congress as well as with the Constitution that even the Nixon appointees could not defend their patron. In the next the Nixon appointees joined in extending a Warren Court doctrine concerning a constitutional right so basic that the doctrine was no longer politically controversial. In the third and most sensational decision, the Court held the death penalty to be unconstitutionally cruel and unusual punishment. And the four Nixon appointees responded with a chorus of dissent.

There were no dissents to the Court's decision which held that the Nixon Administration's enthusiasm for electronic surveillance of antiwar and political dissenters must acknowledge at least some bounds. Indeed, the Court's opinion was written by a Nixon appointee, Lewis Powell. The Warren Court, of course, had not held that all police and FBI surveillance of criminal suspects was unconstitutional. Congress in 1968 had passed the law, comporting with the Court's decisions, that explicitly sanctioned surveillance under carefully prescribed court warrant procedures; the law did not apply to not interfere with the President's power to spy on Russian agents and foreign enemies. After Nixon became President and replaced Ramsey Clark with John Mitchell, the Justice Department quickly utilized the authority to obtain warrants and eavesdrop on run-of-the-mill criminals. But Nixon and Mitchell looked upon antiwar and other political dissenters, for surveillance purposes anyway, not as ordinary criminals but as foreign agents. Therefore, the Nixon Administration admittedly and unabashedly used electronic "bugs" and wiretaps against such dissenters without first applying for court warrants and thus submitting to judicial control of the placement and duration of listening devices. Powell's opinion held that such warrantless surveillance violated both the 1968 law and the Fourth Amendment.[36] "History abundantly documents the tendency of government—however benevolent and benign its motives—to view with suspicion those who most fervently dispute its policies," the Powell opinion declared. The decision appeared to be at war with the Court's ruling that dismissed a challenge of warrantless Army surveillance; if there was a conflict, it went unresolved, possibly because military surveillance of American citizens was so novel that the warrant question was never reached. On the other hand, the Powell opinion did not stop Justice Department surveillance of dissenters, but only subjected FBI bugging and wiretapping to a warrant requirement which, Powell said, might be tailored to the special needs of internal security. Besides, Powell added, there really was no good reason for thinking that "the government's domestic surveillance powers will be impaired to any significant degree" by the decision.

There also were no dissents when a Warren Court doctrine was extended to its logical conclusion. The Warren Court in *Gideon v. Wainwright*—the case argued before the Court so long ago by a brilliant advocate, Abe Fortas—had held that the states were required by the Fourteenth Amendment to provide counsel to all indigent defendants charged with felonies. So basic and vital is the right to counsel, especially to poor and black defendants, that the American Bar Association supported the extension of the principle to lesser criminal offenses and the new Court's decision came as no surprise. The Court, in an opinion by Justice Douglas which drew some separate concurring opinions from the Nixon appointees but no dissents, held that the states must provide counsel to indigent defendants in all criminal prosecutions, including misdemeanors, before a jail sentence can be imposed.[37] And if this decision seemed in conflct with the majority decision refusing counsel to indigents in police lineups, the explanation was that the right to counsel is not absolute but neither is it to be denied absolutely in any criminal prosecution.

When the Court on the final day of the term came to its most sensational decision, it proved once more that in deciding the most

difficult issues in human affairs the members of the Court will find precious little guidance in history, precedent, or the intentions of the Founding Fathers. Each justice is on his own and the issues are resolved more in terms of judicial philosophy, personal ideology, and conscience. All of the five justices who had sat with Earl Warren—Douglas, Brennan, Marshall, Stewart, and White—agreed to hold the death penalty unconstitutional, as it was applied in 1972 under state and federal laws to murder, rape, treason, aircraft hijacking, and other capital offenses. Nixon's four—Burger, Blackmun, Powell, and Rehnquist—dissented.[38] Not one of the nine, however, reached his conclusion for precisely the same reasons as any other and the issue therefore produced nine separate opinions. Among the five concurring opinions, the opinion of Justice Brennan, a Catholic, rested most firmly on moral grounds. Brennan wrote that punishment "must not be degrading to human dignity" and in his view the abolition of capital punishment comported with "the evolving standards of decency that mark the progress of a maturing society." For Marshall, abolition was "a major milestone in the long road up from barbarism." For Douglas, the death penalty was unconstitutional because relatively more blacks than whites have been executed for murder and rape. Stewart said the penalty had been "wantonly and freakishly imposed" and White wrote that "where the penalty is so seldom invoked, it ceases to be the credible threat essential to influence the conduct of others."

Among the dissenters, Burger predictably based his opinion on his philosophy of judicial restraint: "Legislatures, not courts, are constituted to respond to the will and moral values of the people." Blackmun was filled with "abhorrence" of the death penalty, but also voted against its abolition because he was not a legislator. Rehnquist charged that the majority "encroaches upon the legislative branch, state and federal." Powell wrote the longest and in a sense the most illuminating exposition of the strict constructionist viewpoint. He agreed that the death penalty had been applied relatively more often to blacks than whites. However, he said, "The 'have-nots' in every society always have been subject to greater pressure to commit crimes than their more affluent citizens. This is a tragic byproduct of social and economic deprivation but it is not an argument of constitutional proportions. Nor could any society have a viable system of criminal justice if sanctions were abolished or ameliorated because most of those who commit crimes happen to be underprivileged."

The abolition of the death penalty in America easily rated as the most sensational Supreme Court decision of 1972, if for no reason other than that its immediate effect was to lift sentences of execution from approximately 600 prisoners who had collected in death row cells because no executions had been carried out in this country since 1967. Most of the sentences presumably were converted to life imprisonment. Until the Constitution is amended or perhaps until the membership of the Supreme Court undergoes further change, the decision resolved an issue almost as old as the United States that, like so many other issues in this nation, was burdened with racial overtones.

The two major cases decided in 1972 in which race was not an overtone but the dominant theme were less sensational in the scale of national values. But the pair of decisions may prove in the long run to have been more significant to the Court and the nation. In both, the Nixon appointees voted as a bloc against the constitutional claims put forward by Negroes. The blacks lost their first claim. They won the second, but in victory there was a loss.

The first case had been brought by a black, K. Leroy Irvis, against Moose Lodge No. 107 in Harrisburg, Pennsylvania. The lodge was located near the state capitol in Harrisburg and Irvis, the majority leader of the Pennsylvania house of representatives, had been taken to the lodge by a white member as his guest. The constitution of the Loyal Order of Moose limited membership in lodges to white males and Irvis was refused bar service because he was black. The lodge was a private club and Congress had exempted private clubs from the 1964 Civil Rights Act, which outlawed racial segregation in restaurants and other privately owned places of public accommodation. Irvis nonetheless sued Moose Lodge No. 107, basing his action not on the law but on the "state action" doctrine which the Supreme Court had begun to formulate before Earl Warren became Chief Justice. The doctrine held that the Fourteenth Amendment may reach private acts of racial discrimination, when such acts are carried out under color of state law. The Court thus held in 1948 that racially restrictive covenants in private real estate transactions could not be enforced under state law. In later decisions, the doctrine was broadened to embrace other types of race bias that previously had been considered to be private matters. The Court held in 1951, for instance, that a privately-owned restaurant that refused to serve Negroes violated the Fourteenth Amendment because it was located in a building owned by a public parking authority.

Irvis's suit alleged that a private club that served liquor under license of the state similarly was in violation of the Fourteenth Amendment when it refused to serve blacks. The allegation was no more novel than other elaborate legal constructions to which blacks have been forced for the purpose of clearing equally elaborate and legalistic racial barriers erected by whites. A federal district court judge so found, holding that state liquor licenses are invalid so long as the private clubs that hold them practice racial discrimination.

But in 1972 the new Supreme Court majority reversed the district court and refused to uphold the state action doctrine in the Irvis case.[39] The decision was six-to-three. The four Nixon appointees were joined by both Stewart and White and the Court's opinion was authored by Rehnquist, who had formerly been the President's lawyer's lawyer. Rehnquist, taking the narrowest view of the case, wrote a concise opinion that distinguished state liquor licensing from the prior cases in which the Court had found state action sufficiently implicated to strike down private racial bias. Although Pennsylvania had an extensive liquor regulation and licensing scheme, the state "cannot be said to in any way foster or encourage racial discrimination," Rehnquist concluded. Douglas, Brennan, and Marshall dissented. Brennan, joined by Marshall, wrote that the "vital flaw" in the Rehnquist opinion was its "complete disregard of the fundamental value underlying the 'state action' concept." Douglas, now writing more carefully and at times more eloquently than when he was a concurring member of the Warren Court, asserted that "Pennsylvania is putting the weight of its liquor license, a valued adjunct to a private club, behind racial discrimination." Douglas, however, also was careful not to tread on "the associational rights which permit all white, all black, all brown, and all yellow clubs to be formed."

The Court turned next to the school desegregation case. It came from a small town, Emporia, Virginia, and it did not directly involve busing, the issue that viscerally stirred the President. Both Stewart and White deserted the Nixon appointees to vote with the three who also had been members of the Warren Court, and the Nixon bloc lost. Blacks won and the majority opinion was more poignantly written by Justice Stewart than it could have been by any one of the predictably liberals. Yet, this was the first important school desegregation case decided since Nixon could count four of his appointees on the Court, and there were four dissents.

Emporia lies near the center of Greensville County, Virginia, a rural area near the North Carolina border. Emporia children had attended schools operated by the county school system. The elementary and high schools in the county still were racially segregated in 1969, when a federal district court ordered Greensville County to desegregate by pairing all-white and all-black schools. Two weeks later, Emporia announced its intention to withdraw from the county and establish its own school system. Its stated reason was to achieve "quality education" for Emporia children.

The Supreme Court majority found, as the district court had, that Emporia's withdrawal would frustrate school desegregation.[40] The Stewart opinion held that state and local governments cannot avoid desegregation by splintering school districts under the guise of quality education. The Warren Court, Stewart wrote, had "focused on the effect—not the purpose or motivation—of a school board's action. Only when it became clear—15 years after our decision in *Brown* v. *Board of Education*—that segregation in the county system was finally to be abolished, did Emporia attempt to take its children out of the county system."

The case concerned only Emporia, Virginia, and not the mighty issue of busing, but Burger assigned to himself the task of writing the dissenting opinion. Burger was willing and able to accept Emporia's professed reason for withdrawal from the county school system. The Chief Justice's words were strikingly similar to those of the President: "Local control is not only vital to continued public support of the schools, but is is of overriding importance from an educational standpoint as well," Burger asserted. "To put it in the simplest terms," he added, "the Court goes too far." Inasmuch as Nixon had arrived at that same conclusion concerning racial desegregation of America's schools, the words of the Chief Justice gave the appearance of puppets on an ideological string pulled by the President.

And thus, 18 years now after *Brown* v. *Board of Education,* the great weight of constitutional precedent was ignominiously shunted aside by Nixon's four justices. Thus was the unanimity of the Court broken in pressing forward the unfinished business of desegregating America's schools, the business begun in 1954 with the first and finest of the Warren Court's works. And thus did Richard Nixon lead the Court, the Bill of Rights and the Fourteenth Amendment into retreat.

# Epilogue

*Those who would give up essential Liberty, to purchase a little temporary
Safety, deserve neither Liberty nor Safety.*

> Letter of the Pennsylvania Assembly
> to Governor Robert Morris, 1755.

The battle for control of the Supreme Court was part and parcel
of the struggle for control of America's future, and it could not have
been less.

Political storms have thundered outside this quiet place before. The
passing of another strong Chief Justice, John Marshall, began a time
of political and constitutional turmoil in which the Senate refused to
confirm nominations by Presidents Tyler, Polk, Fillmore, and Buchanan, and the Court was deeply divided. At another time, President
Franklin Roosevelt attacked the Court with political fury unparal-
leled—until Richard Nixon.

In the turmoil following the Marshall Court, however, fate did not
give to any one President the opportunity to dominate the Court with
his nominees. That opportunity came to Roosevelt, but it came slowly
and his nominations were robbed of political drama and ideological
imperative. Besides, Roosevelt's party controlled the Senate.

Nixon came to the White House in a new era of turmoil not unlike
that following the Marshall Court and fate and Lyndon Johnson's
cronyism gave him the unique opportunity to dominate the Court,
and he made the most of it.

President Nixon's place in history is secure: Nixon politicized the
Supreme Court more dramatically than any President in history.

At a time when America's white majority feared again for its safety,
Nixon promised law and order. He led the majoritarian branches into
retreat from positions reluctantly taken on the abiding issues of liberty
and equality. As the Warren Court had ordered desegregation "now,"
Nixon demanded an end to school busing, "now."[1] He led the Court

and the Constitution into retreat, but this backward journey was longer and harder.

Under Nixon, the appearance of law and order was restored, and America paid with a little liberty. The payment was not high enough, however. If American history teaches no more, it teaches that racism is bound up in violence—sudden, unpredictable, insane violence of assassins' gunfire aimed at the political right, at George Wallace, as well as at the left.

Violence and anarchy are the anthithesis of Equal Justice Under Law, and, as Nixon said, "It would be a total repudiation of our constitutional system" if the Court agreed with the President on every issue.

Nixon was not that President; racism has not yet brought the nation again to the brink of consummate violence. Presidents come and go, Nixon also said, but justices who were their patrons remain and the constitutional decisions of the Court go on, next term, next year, and decades beyond.

This, then, is the hope and this is the danger.

The struggle between liberty and safety is centuries older than the United States. This nation was born in an age of rebellion and innocence, when it was believed possible for the people to create a government strong enough to assure them of safety from enemies foreign and domestic, and not strong enough to threaten their liberty.

Two centuries have passed, and the constitutional balance that was struck between liberty and safety has served most of the people reasonably well, thus far. The United States has survived thirty-seven Presidents, through Richard Nixon; an even one hundred Justices of the Supreme Court, through William Rehnquist, and roughly eleven thousand senators and representatives who have sat in ninety-two Congresses. Ultimate constitutional wisdom has never resided permanently in any one of the three branches, and the Founding Fathers probably did not expect it would. The Supreme Court, where such wisdom might be expected, if anywhere, helped to bring on the Civil War, among its other self-inflicted wounds.

From a certain optimistic point of view, the great battles won and lost between Presidents Johnson and Nixon and the Senate over the Supreme Court were the grandest evidence in recent history of the continuing survival capacity of the democratic system. In the long view of history, the executive always has been the most dangerous branch; the judiciary, the least dangerous, and so long as the legislative branch can defend the latter against the former, as occasion demands, the greatest danger to liberty would seem contained.

Certainly the spirit of liberty was resoundingly reaffirmed when the Supreme Court threw off the restraints Nixon tried to impose on publication of the Pentagon Papers, declaring, in the words of the late Justice Black, that the Constitution protected the press precisely "so that it could bare the secrets of government and inform the people."[2] Freedom reigned when the late Justice Harlan held that "one man's vulgarity is another's lyric," and therefore the state was not constitutionally permitted to make a criminal offense of "the simple public display of this four letter expletive" against the Vietnam war.[3] These and other contemporary interpretations of the constitutional powers of government and the liberties of the people were honored, even while Nixon and Congress fought over Supreme Court nominations. For instance, conservatives in Congress, who for a decade had seethed over the Warren Court's decisions that barred official sponsorship of prayers in public schools, thought late in 1971 that their time had come to surmount the difficulties of constitutional amendment. But the "school prayer amendment" intended by its sponsors to overturn the Court's decisions was defeated when it failed to receive the required two-thirds approval of the House of Representatives.[4]

The democratic system, then, remained reasonably intact. The President, Congress, and the Court, more often than not in harmony, responded to the crises in human affairs of these times. They handed down laws and decisions that were intended to reduce water and air pollution; they tried to curb inflation; they sought to implement birth control, and otherwise to liberate women. This is not to say that the responsiveness of government was complete or that the responses it made were entirely successful in solving the crises at hand. Still, the system demonstrated a sometimes remarkable capacity to respond, even to the crisis presented by a generation of long-haired, bearded young people, inscrutable to the older, more affluent generation that occupied the political ground known as middle America.

Young, white Americans who dissented against the Vietnam war were responsible in no small part for President Johnson's decision to take his reitrement in Texas. Nixon, even at the risk of alienating ultraconservatives in his own party, tried to accommodate to the demands of young whites by withdrawing most, if not all, American armed forces from Vietnam. The President, Congress, and the Court together made a further accomodation, by lowering the legal voting age to eighteen from twenty-one. Congress passed the Voting Rights Act Amendments of 1970, to lower the voting age in all federal, state, and local elections, and Nixon promptly signed it, even while expressing doubt that the voting age could be lowered by legislation, as opposed to constitutional amendment. The Supreme Court deftly managed the constitutional problem, by slicing it into two precise halves; Justice Black, the key figure in the accomplishment of this feat, spoke for the Court in ruling that Congress could lower the age to eighteen for voting in presidential and congressional elections, and that Congress could not by mere legislation extend the franchise to eighteen-year-olds in state and local elections.[5] Within six months therafter, Congress adopted and the necessary states ratified the Twenty-Sixth Amendment, extending the franchise to eighteen-year-olds in all elections. President Nixon celebrated its certification with a five hundred-voice youth choir.

The movement toward racial equality in America did not stop after Richard Nixon became President. Democratic processes are too inefficient to be stopped quickly and certainly, as an automobile traveling three or perhaps five miles an hour can be stopped. Desegregation still moved forward until finally, two days after Wallace won in Florida, the President, out of political frustration, proposed to Congress and the nation that the movement be thrown into reverse.

A racist can be elected governor of Alabama, but not President of the United States. Nixon was no racist. He was a politician who had campaigned for law and order and against the Warren Court. He would change the Court by appointing "strict constructionists," and he began by replacing Earl Warren with Warren Burger. His administration, the White House said, would stand for the proposition that the time had come for a policy of "benign neglect" toward black Americans. "Benign" meant that the executive branch would continue to file lawsuits against racial segragation in education, employment, and public accommodations, in quantities competitive with the exceedingly modest volume of suits initiated by the preceding Democratic administrations.* It meant, Mitchell said, that blacks should watch what the Nixon Administration did, rather than listen to what it said. Whites should listen and they were told that "neglect" meant that the executive branch no longer would threaten to cut off federal financial assistance to school districts that resisted desegregation orders. It meant that the Department of Justice no longer necessarily would stand shoulder to shoulder with black litigants in desegregations suits. It meant, "I am against busing," as Nixon said. It meant nomination of Southerners to the Supreme Court who were symbols of white resistance to the forward movement of school desegregation, and it meant Nixon's bitter denunciation of the Senate for its refusal to confirm Clement Haynsworth and Harrold Carswell. Nixon promised the South its day "will come on the High Court," and he delivered Lewis Powell of Virginia, even if the fulfillment did lose a bit of its luster to Mitchell's clumsy encounter with the American Bar Association.

Nixon and Mitchell "out-Wallaced Wallace," but only until the next presidential election season. Nixon's grasp of justice proved less than secure, and after the Court in 1971 unanimously held that busing was a constitutionally appropriate means of achieving school desegregation, he abandoned benignancy. He disavowed his own Administration's modest busing plan for Austin, Texas, schools and declared that now the executive branch would "work with school districts to hold busing to the minimum required by law."⁶ Chief Justice Burger attempted to come to Nixon's assistance with his injudicious explanation to the entire federal judiciary of what the Court's busing decision did not require. But Wallace was back, saying with scorn that he had "nothing but utter contempt for the courts of this land" and, with

*Civil rights litigation of the Justice Department, including cases initiated by the department and participation as intervenor or amicus in private litigation, by calendar years:

| | SCHOOL DESEGREGATION | VOTING | EMPLOYMENT | HOUSING | PUBLIC ACCOMMODATIONS |
|---|---|---|---|---|---|
| 1965 | 25 | 14 | — | — | 18 |
| 1966 | 64 | 7 | 8 | — | 29 |
| 1967 | 26 | 3 | 10 | — | 42 |
| 1968 | 24 | 2 | 27 | 2 | 32 |
| 1969 | 35 | 1 | 17 | 22 | 42 |
| 1970 | 27 | 8 | 10 | 37 | 15 |
| 1971 | 7 | 6 | 22 | 35 | 59 |

ridicule, that "every member Nixon put on the Supreme Court voted for busing."⁷ To which Nixon replied, as Wallace proved his racist mettle in Florida, "I propose that the Congress now accept the responsibility to put an immediate stop to further new busing orders by the federal courts." Out-Wallacing Wallace with new ardor and dash, Nixon proposed to "enlist the wisdom, the resources and the experience of Congress in the solution of the problems involved in desegregation policies that are true to the Constitution. Conscience and the Constitution," he declared, "both require that no child should be denied equal educational opportunity." He said that the process begun in 1954 of dismantling the old system of separate schools for whites and blacks "has now been substantially completed." He added, "It is essential that whatever we do to curb busing be done in a way that will not break the momentum of the drive for equal rights and set in motion a chain of reversals that would undo all the advances so painfully achieved in the past generation."⁸

Nixon already had broken the drive for equal rights. He had become President of the United States at that point in its constitutional history when, for the second time, white prejudice was receding and racial equality was moving forward. Conscience and the Constitution required that white prejudice give way to racial equality in education, employment, and housing, and it barely had begun to give way. The drive for racial equality in education could never be completed, or even substantially completed, if blacks in the cities were separated from whites in the suburbs by hoary political demarcations now become the new barriers behind which prejudice sought refuge from equality. The school bus could cross the barriers and school desegregation could move forward. The school bus was nothing more than a temporary tool of school desegregation, useful until such time as the equal employment and housing opportunities promised by the Constitution and by law became realities, and Americans worked, lived, and went to school together, regardless of "race, color, or previous condition of servitude." Skillfully, purposefully, and politically, Nixon converted the school bus from a symbol of equality into a symbol of racism. He proposed to amend conscience and the Constitution. He emphasized separate and de-emphasized equal. He moved to curb busing in a way that would set in motion a chain of reversals that would undo all the advances so painfully achieved in the past generation.

Nixon held no popular mandate from a majority of the American people; he had sought and found his plurality in the white South and the white suburbs. From the day he moved in, the White House no longer was that essential moral symbol of white acceptance of black equality. If Eisenhower, Kennedy, and Johnson did not invest large amounts of their political prestige in the cause of racial equality, Nixon invested nothing. He attempted to change the Constitution by changing the Supreme Court, and when time ran out, he met the challenge of another presidential election campaign and of George Wallace by investing his political prestige and his presidential leadership in a proposal that he and Congress change the Constitution and reverse the forward movement of racial equality in America.

The dichotomy of the American spirit and the Constitution is as old as the nation. The Constitution is color blind, the white American majority is not.

When the Constitution was tested against white racism in the crucible of civil war, the Constitution was upheld. When the Constitution was tested in the Warren Court, it again was upheld. The Constitution cannot be ignored, as Nixon made patently clear.

Still it remains true, as Nixon tried to make equally plain, that the politics and ideology of white prejudice have had more than the Constitution to say about black men's liberty and safety. The white majority has controlled America and will continue to do so. The Constitution means what men from time to time say it means, and ultimately it means what the white majority says it means. White racism and white conscience forever have been at war and the place assigned to blacks has been determined by the political resolution of that war. The politics of white racism is based on white fears (although there are Harvard "profs," available to Presidents, who claim evidence of biological bases) and on the political assumption that whites can have their liberty and safety while denying the same to blacks. The most virile strain of racism insists that white liberty and safety are dependent upon the denial of equality to blacks. For whites, the system has worked for nearly two hundred years because blacks have stayed in the places variously assigned to them by the white racial majority, and whites reasonably have retained their liberty and safety, at least insofar as blacks are concerned.

The assumptions that blacks will stay in their place and that whites need not fear for their liberty and safety may no longer be valid, however. Nixon's proposal notwithstanding, it may well be that the

Civil War and the Thirteenth, Fourteenth, and Fifteenth Amendments will control the aspirations of black Americans after all, and there can be no more turning back without violence—in which whites also will lose their safety and liberty. Slavery *was* abolished and blacks *were* accorded the full rights and privileges of American citizenship under the Constitution. If it took blacks many years to rediscover the Constitution, it cannot be assumed that they will abandon their discovery voluntarily. Blacks have made some gains, in education and in employment, and they have found an identity and a self-assurance. Times have changed. Black migration has trampled the line of geographic wrath that a century ago divided the North and South. Blacks will find a new leader to succeed Martin Luther King, Jr., and a new civil rights movement will be pressed forward in the cities of the North from which whites have fled as well as in the South. It is too late to turn back the clock, or to say to blacks, as John Mitchell did, that the laws are no more than "extravagant promises which could not be met."[9]

Black and white America are converging, and the safety and liberty of all are likely to move forward or backward together. There is no question but that the white majority will continue to control the country. The question is how. Constitutional accommodation, begun under Eisenhower, Kennedy, and Johnson, can continue. The law cannot wipe prejudice from men's minds nor can it provide blacks with education, jobs, and homes; it can change a few men's actions and appeal to many men's consciences and open to blacks equal opportunities for education, jobs, and homes. Or, accommodation can be refused and black demands for equality can be answered with white repression. White police forces, National Guardsmen, tear gas, and gunfire will be met with black sniper fire, arson, and guerrilla warfare. The escalation of violence already has begun. The unmilitant National Association for the Advancement of Colored People, after accusing the Nixon administration of being "anti-black," sponsored a commission which charged that "the criminal law is being used as the first line of defense" against blacks and the poor.[10] The uprising at Attica Correctional Facility in New York, which was suppressed in a bloody rain of police gunfire, was brought on by the "revolutionary tactics of militants," Governor Nelson Rockefeller charged.[11]

Effective repression, however, would be quite difficult under the democratic system, and if the inefficiencies of democracy cannot stand in the way of white safety, they also cannot stand in defense of white liberty. And there are precedents here, also. Wars, civil disturbances, and economic disasters have strained democracy throughout history. The enumerated war powers of Congress seem now in large part to have been taken by or given to the President. Modern communications and transportation have infused the enumerated power of Congress to regulate commerce with a soaring quality undreamed of by the Founding Fathers, and much of that power also has been transferred to the executive branch. The Great Depression, World War II, and the administration of Franklin Roosevelt set into motion a historic enlargement of presidential power that has never abated. The states long since have fallen as bulwarks against the powers of the central government, and the executive branch has invaded deeply the powers of the legislative branch. Sometimes the Supreme Court has had opportunities to halt an unconstitutional exercise of power, but it has not often taken advantage of its opportunities. The people look to the President for safety from their enemies, foreign and domestic, and place in him their hopes for full employment and full purchasing power, without grievous depression or inflation.

Times change and presidential power grows apace. The legacies of the age of Roosevelt included affluence for the working man, big government, big business, big unions, more wars, overproduction, overpopulation, pollution, and inflation. Finally, in the 1960's, a new generation of young, white, long-haired Americans rose in dissent against America's overabundance of militarism, statism, and materialism. The system responded, sometimes remarkably well, within the confines of the Constitution. But there also were responses of government that went beyond even the boundaries laid out by Roosevelt. Nixon pressed forward on the frontiers of presidential power more boldly certainly than any President since Roosevelt. Roosevelt had promised the people a measure of economic security in exchange for a measure of economic freedom. Nixon assumed control of wages and prices, occupying the constitutional ground Roosevelt had invaded, and went beyond with sorties into the field of civil liberties.

When Nixon tried to stop publication of the Pentagon Papers, he relied on what he claimed to be the inherent powers of the President to protect the nation's internal security. Nixon, his lawyer Mitchell, and his lawyer's lawyer Rehnquist claimed that it was within the inherent power of the President, and not the constitutionally enumerated power of the courts, to authorize government surveillance of white and black dissenters. In the name of internal security and presidential power, and no more, they ordered massive police sweeps of Washington streets in which demonstrators against the war and innocent bystanders bodily and indiscriminately were hauled off to detention centers. They insisted that newsmen who refused to testify before grand juries about black and white militants could be jailed for contempt, under certain circumstances, the First Amendment notwithstanding. They advocated preventive detention, and they proposed to suspend the constitutional rights of black children to equality of educational opportunity. "I am persuaded," Nixon asserted, "that Congress has the constitutional power" to amend the Constitution by legislation.[12]

The President did not obtain all he sought from Congress or the Court. Congress, however, enacted no major new civil rights legislation after 1968.* If control of the Court was in doubt, control of the Chief Justiceship was not. A few days after Nixon addressed Congress on the busing issue, Burger wrote in an opinion for himself that when the courts have "unjustifiably frustrated the executive branch, Congress may, of course, take any legislative action it deems necessary to make unmistakably clear its intentions, even to the point of limiting or prohibiting judicial review of its directives."[13]

A little temporary safety undoubtedly can be obtained, under this President or another, and liberty given in exchange. Arrogant power and politicized justice tear at the Constitution and the freedom of more than two hundred million Americans, only some twenty-two million of whom are black.

A greater wisdom was spoken seventy-five years ago by the first Justice, John Marshall Harlan:

> The white race deems itself to be the dominant race in this country. But in view of the Constitution, in the eye of the law, there is in this country no superior, dominant, ruling class of citizens.
>
> Sixty millions of whites are in no danger from the presence here of eight millions of blacks. The destinies of the two races are indissolubly linked. The sure guarantee of the peace and security of each race is the clear, distinct, unconditional recognition by our governments, National and State, of every right that inheres in civil freedom, and of the equality before the law of all citizens.[14]

*Congress in 1970 extended the Voting Rights Act of 1965 and in 1972 gave the Equal Employment Opportunity Commission certain enforcement authority, but denied the EEOC cease and desist powers.

# Notes

CHAPTER 1, THE BEGINNINGS OF A BATTLE

1. As quoted by Charles Warren, *The Supreme Court in United States History* (Boston: Little, Brown and Company, 1928), vol. II, p. 2.
2. New York *Times*, August 8, 1965, p. 40, "Fortas, High Court Nominee, Leaving Law Firm That Is a Capital Byword."
3. The exchange was retold by Abe Fortas in an issue of the *Yale Law Journal* which memorialized Thurman Arnold after his death. *Yale Law Journal*, vol. 79, no. 6 (May 1970), pp. 988, 994.
4. For a discussion of the litigation undertaken by the members of Arnold, Fortas & Porter during the McCarthy period, see Thurman Arnold, *Fair Fights and Foul* (New York: Harcourt, Brace & World, 1965).
5. Durham v. U.S., 214 F.2d 862 (1954).
6. Gideon v. Wainwright, 372 U.S. 335 (1963).
7. *Wall Street Journal*, March 23 and 24, 1964, p. 1.


CHAPTER 2, THE NATURE OF THE COURT

1. Paul A. Freund, "Constitutional Dilemmas," *Boston University Law Review*, vol. XLV, no. 1 (Winter 1965), pp. 13-23.
2. Paul A. Freund, *The Supreme Court of the United States* (Cleveland and New York: World Publishing Co., 1961), pp. 106–8.
3. Marbury v. Madison, 1 Cranch 137 (1803).
4. McCulloch v. Maryland, 4 Wheaton 316 (1819).
5. Gibbons v. Ogden, 9 Wheaton 1 (1824).
6. Gibbons v. Ogden, op. cit.
7. McCulloch V. Maryland, op. cit.
8. Gibbons v. Ogden, op. cit.
9. Boyce v. Anderson, 2 Peters 150 (1829).
10. Charles River Bridge Co. v. Warren Bridge Co., 11 Peters 420 (1837).
11. U.S. v. *The Amistad*, 15 Peters 518 (1841).
12. Scott v. Sanford, 60 U.S. 393 (1857).

CHAPTER 3, THE ABIDING ISSUE

1. Civil Rights Cases, 109 U.S. 3 (1883).
2. Plessy v. Ferguson, 163 U.S. 537 (1896).
3. U.S. v. E. C. Knight Co., 156 U.S. 1 (1895).
4. See, Standard Oil Co. of New Jersey v. U.S., 221 U.S. 1, and U.S. v. American Tobacco Co., 221 U.S. 106, both decided in 1911.
5. Pollock v. Farmers Loan & Trust Co., 157 U.S. 429, 158 U.S. 601 (1895).
6. Paul A. Freund, *The Supreme Court of the United States* (Cleveland and New York: World Publishing Co., 1961), p. 26.
7. Schecter v. U.S., 295 U.S. 495 (1935).
8. Korematsu v. U.S., 323 U.S. 214 (1944).
9. Youngstown Sheet & Tube Co. v. Sawyer, 343 U.S. 579 (1952).


CHAPTER 4, THE WARREN COURT LEADS

1. Sweatt v. Painter, 339 U.S. 629 (1950).
2. Abe Fortas, "Thurman Arnold and the Theatre of the Law," *Yale Law Journal,* vol. 79, no. 6 (May 1970), pp. 988, 999.
3. Paul A. Freund, *The Supreme Court of the United States* (Cleveland and New York: World Publishing Co., 1961), p. 188.
4. Flast v. Cohen, 392 U.S. 83 (1968).
5. Leon Friedman, editor, *Argument: The Oral Argument Before the Supreme Court in Brown v. Board of Education of Topeka, 1952–55* (New York: Chelsea House Publishers, 1969), pp. 243–44.
6. Brown v. Board of Education, 347 U.S. 483 (1954).
7. Brown v. Board of Education, 349 U.S. 294 (1955).
8. Anthony Lewis, *Portrait of a Decade: The Second American Revolution* (New York: Random House, 1964), pp. 126–28.
9. Harper v. Virginia Board of Elections, 383 U.S. 663 (1966).
10. Colegrove v. Green, 328 U.S. 549 (1946).
11. Baker v. Carr, 369 U.S. 186 (1962).
12. Gideon v. Wainwright, 372 U.S. 335 (1963).
13. Escobedo v. Illinois, 378 U.S. 478 (1964); Miranda v. Arizona, 384 U.S. 436 (1966).
14. Lewis, *Portrait,* pp. 114–15.
15. Jones v. Mayer, 392 U.S. 409 (1968).
16. Sullivan v. Little Hunting Park, Inc. 396 U.S. 229 (1969).


CHAPTER 5, THE BLACK SEAT

1. See Victor S. Navasky, *Kennedy Justice* (New York: Atheneum Publishers, 1971), pp. 6–27.

2. See *Report of the National Advisory Commission on Civil Disorders* (Washington: Government Printing Office, March 1, 1968), pp. 63–87.
3. William Raspberry, in the Washington *Post*, July 23, 1971, p. A23; Raspberry, a black columnist, was writing about comments Vice President Spiro T. Agnew had just made about black leaders in Africa, but Raspberry's remark is applicable to the rise of Justice Marshall also.
4. U.S., Congress, Senate, Committee on the Judiciary, *Nomination of Thurgood Marshall: Hearings*, 90th Cong., 1st Sess., July 13, 14, 18, 19 and 24, 1967.
5. Ibid., p. 163.
6. *Report of the National Advisory Commission on Civil Disorders*, op cit., pp. 115–141.
7. The discussion was reported in *The Exonian*, student newspaper of Phillips Exeter Academy, April 16, 1969, p. 3.

CHAPTER 6, THE PERILS OF CRONYISM

1. Theodore H. White, *The Making of the President 1968* (New York: Atheneum Publishers, 1969), pp. 105–6.
2. Clark, March 20, 1967, in testimony before a House Judiciary subcommittee.
3. White, *The Making of the President*, p. 80.
4. Ibid., pp. 112–13.
5. U.S., Congress, Senate, Committee on the Judiciary, *Nominations of Abe Fortas and Homer Thornberry: Hearings*, 90th Cong., 2d Sess., 11–13 July 1968, p. 106.
6. Ibid., pp. 104–5
7. Ibid., p. 124.
8. *Nixon Speaks Out: Major Speeches and Statements by Richard M. Nixon in the Presidential Campaign of 1968* (New York: Nixon-Agnew Campaign Committee, 1968), pp. 135–52.
9. Jones v. Mayer, 392 U.S. 409 (1968).
10. New York *Times*, June 24, 1968, p. 1, "Reagan Questions Motive for Warren's Retirement." Although the White House did not announce Warren's retirement plans until June 26, knowledge of the plans became widespread soon after the Court's adjournment on June 17.
11. *Nominations of Abe Fortas and Homer Thornberry: Hearings*, op. cit., p. 8.
12. Ibid., p. 103.
13. Ibid., pp. 105–6.
14. Ibid., p. 46.

## CHAPTER 7, INTO NIXON'S LAP

1. Oliver Wendell Holmes, *Collected Legal Papers* (New York: Harcourt, Brace and Co., 1921), p. 292.
2. Nixon's campaign statements are quoted in *Nixon on the Issues* (New York: Nixon-Agnew Campaign Committee, 1968), pp. 81, 83, 85–6.
3. New York *Times*, November 15, 1968, p. 1, article headed "Warren Firm on Retiring; Leaves Date Up to Nixon."
4. Ibid.
5. Theodore H. White, *The Making of the President 1968* (New York: Atheneum Publishers, 1969), p. 431.
6. Powell v. McCormack, 395 U.S. 486 (1969).
7. Hunter v. Erickson, 393 U.S. 385 (1969).
8. Gaston County, North Carolina, v. U.S., 395 U.S. 285 (1969).
9. Stanley v. Georgia, 394 U.S. 557 (1969).
10. White, *Making of the President*, p. 251.
11. *Time*, May 19, 1969, p. 95.
12. William Lambert, "The Justice and the Stock Manipulator," *Life*, May 9, 1969, pp. 32–37.
13. *Wall Street Journal*, April 22, 1969, p. 40.

## CHAPTER 8, NIXON RUNS WITH THE BALL

1. The statement was made July 1, 1969. There is no official transcript of Mitchell's comments in the Great Hall, but his statement as taken down by reporters was, "You'd be better informed if instead of listening to what we say, you watch what we do." Mitchell apparently was attempting to tell the blacks that they should watch what the Administration was doing in the civil rights area, instead of listening to critics of Administration policy. That, however, is not what he said, and the remark was widely accepted as an admission that the Administration's statements and actions were not at all times consistent.
2. New York *Times*, May 23, 1969, p. 1, article headed "G.O.P. Aware in Campaign of Fortas' Tie to Wolfson."
3. See, Charles D. Harris, "The Impeachment Trial of Samuel Chase," *American Bar Association Journal*, vol. 57, January 1971.
4. U.S., Congress, Senate, Committee on the Judiciary, *Nominations of Abe Fortas and Homer Thornberry: Hearings*, 90th Cong., 2d Sess., 11–13 July 1968, pp. 124–25.
5. See, for example, the New York *Times*, May 16, 1969, p. 20, article headed "The Fortas Shock Waves" and subheaded "Capital Takes Hard Look at the Ethics of Men and Balances of Government."
6. Peters v. Hobby, 349 U.S. 331 (1955).
7. An address before the Ohio Judicial Conference, in Columbus, Ohio, September 4, 1968.

8. Frazier v. U.S., No. 21,426, decided March 14, 1969.
9. Powell v. McCormack, 395 F. 2d, 577 (1968).
10. Powell v. McCormack, 395 U.S. 486 (1969).
11. Julius Duscha, "Chief Justice Burger Asks: 'If It Doesn't Make Good Sense, How Can it Make Good Law?' " *New York Times Magazine,* October 5, 1969, pp. 30–31.
12. The transcript of the press briefing was widely made available also to members of the press who had not attended: The White House, "Informal Meeting of the President with Members of the White House Press Corps" (The President's Office, May 22, 1969).
13. U.S., Congress, Senate, Committee on the Judiciary, *Nomination of Warren E. Burger: Hearings,* 91st Cong., 1st Sess., 3 June 1969.

## CHAPTER 9, NIXON SCORES IN COURT

1. "Informal Meeting of the President with Members of the White House Press Corps" (The President's Office, May 22, 1969).
2. *Roosevelt and Frankfurter, Their Correspondence 1928–1945,* annotated by Max Freedman (Boston: Little, Brown and Co., 1967).
3. The story of Franklin Roosevelt's battle with the Supreme Court was told by Robert H. Jackson in *The Struggle for Judicial Supremacy* (New York: A. A. Knopf, 1941). Jackson served the New Deal in various capacities, rising to Attorney General in 1940. Roosevelt named him as Associate Justice in 1941, and, except for service at the Nuremberg trials of Nazi war criminals, he remained on the Court until he died suddenly in 1954.
4. Gibbons v. Ogden, 9 Wheaton 1 (1824).
5. An address at the Milton S. Eisenhower Symposium, Johns Hopkins University, Baltimore, Maryland, November 13, 1970.
6. At the Association of the Bar of the City of New York, April 9, 1970.
7. At the Fiftieth Anniversary dinner of the American Civil Liberties Union, New York, December 8, 1970.
8. "Informal Meeting of the President with Members of the White House Press Corps."
9. Senator Ernest F. Hollings, a conservative Democrat from South Carolina, who was one of the chief supporters of the nomination of Judge Haynsworth, later commented that he had recommended the nominee to the President in May, 1969; U.S. Congress, Senate, Committee on the Judiciary, *Nomination of Clement F. Haynsworth, Jr.: Hearings,* 91st Cong., 1st Sess., 16–26 September 1969, p. 37. Hollings later also criticized Nixon for failing to begin soon enough to press for Haynsworth's confirmation, saying the White House initially made the nomination and left it "hanging on the clothesline."

CHAPTER 10, NIXON FUMBLES

1. Theodore H. White, *The Making of the President* 1968 (New York: Atheneum Publishers, 1969), pp. 171, 498–99. The states of the Old South were in 1968 and will be in 1972 of the utmost importance to the Republican Party in gaining a national plurality of votes. Senator Thurmond was consulted by Nixon even before Nixon won the Republican nomination for President in 1968, but Thurmond's major contribution to the Nixon campaign was that he was able to hold South Carolina for the Republicans and prevent its loss to George Wallace. It thus was no coincidence that Nixon, in filling the Supreme Court seat left vacant by Fortas, turned first to South Carolina rather than another Southern state.

2. U.S., Congress, Senate, Committee on the Judiciary, *Nomination of Clement F. Haynsworth, Jr.: Hearings,* 91st Cong., 1st Sess., 16–26 September 1969, pp. 40, 43.

3. Ibid., p. 74.

4. Ibid., p. 42.

5. Textile Workers v. Darlington Co., 380 U.S. 263 (1965).

6. *Haynsworth Hearings,* p. 43.

7. Ibid., pp. 270–86.

8. Ibid., pp. 314–32. The contesting positions relative to the future of the Supreme Court were ably stated in the dialogue between Representative Ryan, for the liberals, and Senator Sam J. Ervin, Jr., of North Carolina, for the conservatives.

9. Ibid., p. 314.

10. Griffin v. Board of Supervisors of Prince Edward County, 377 U.S. 218 (1964).

11. Bradley v. School Board of the City of Richmond, Va., 382 U.S. 103 (1965).

12. Green v. School Board of New Kent County, 391 U.S. 430 (1968).

13. *Haynsworth Hearings,* pp. 76, 463.

14. Ibid., p. 326.

CHAPTER II, NIXON FUMBLES AGAIN

1. In an interview with newsmen in his office in Greenville, South Carolina, November 21, 1969.

2. U.S., Congress, Senate, Committee on the Judiciary, *Nomination of George Harrold Carswell: Hearings,* 91st Cong., 2d Sess., 27 January–3 February 1970, p. 13–15.

3. Phillips v. Martin Marietta Corp., 400 U.S. 542, decided by the Supreme Court on January 25, 1971. The Supreme Court vacated the Fifth Circuit's decision and remanded the case for further proceedings. The High Court held, in an unsigned and rather brief opinion, that the Fifth Circuit panel had erred in summarily ruling that the Martin Marietta

policy did not discriminate by reason of sex. The High Court said the policy might be legal if an employer could demonstrate that the family obligations of women with children of pre-school were relevant to job performance. But the record in the case brought by Mrs. Phillips needed further examination concerning the job requirements, the Court concluded.

4. *Carswell Hearings,* pp. 21–23, full text of speech, as reported in the Irwinton, Georgia, *Bulletin,* August 13, 1948.
5. *Carswell Hearings,* pp. 56–57.
6. Ibid., p. 63.
7. Ibid., pp. 133–38.
8. Ibid., pp. 136, 138.
9. Ibid., p. 276.
10. Ibid., p. 141.
11. Ibid., p. 156.
12. Ibid., p. 127.
13. Ibid., pp. 238–54.
14. Ibid., pp. 31–32, 107–11, 254–66.
15. Nixon in letter dated April 1, 1970, to Senator William B. Saxbe, Republican of Ohio; copies were widely distributed to the press by the White House. The President's letter was in response to a letter in which Saxbe observed that White House support of the Carswell nomination seemed "less than wholehearted" and asked for the President's response.


CHAPTER 12, SOUTHERN POLITICS AND A NORTHERN JUSTICE

1. "Statement by the President Regarding the Supreme Court Nomination" (The President's Office, April 9, 1970).
2. As quoted in Earl Mazo and Stephen Hess, *Nixon, A Political Portrait* (New York, Evanston and London: Harper & Row, Publishers, 1968). pp. 278–82.
3. Joseph Foote, "Mr. Justice Blackmun, A Profile," *Harvard Law School Bulletin,* vol. 21, no. 5 (June 1970), pp. 18–20.
4. U.S., Congress, Senate, Committee on the Judiciary, *Nomination of Harry A. Blackmun: Hearing,* 91st Cong., 2d Sess., 29 April 1970.
5. New York *Times,* April 17, 1970, p. 20.
6. *Blackmun Hearing,* op. cit., p. 1
7. Ibid., p. 61.
8. Ibid., p. 15.
9. Ibid., p. 11.
10. 392 U.S. 409 (1968).
11. *Blackmun Hearing,* op. cit., p. 12.
12. Ibid., p. 56.
13. Ibid., pp. 39–40.
14. Ibid., pp. 38–39.
15. New York *Times,* November 22, 1969, p. 12.

## CHAPTER 13, RETRIBUTION AND RECKLESSNESS

1. *Evergreen,* no. 77 (April 1970), pp. 40–41.
2. For Representative Ford's charges, as well as a parallel statement contained in a House resolution introduced by Representative Louis C. Wyman, Republican of New Hampshire, see U.S., Congress, House, Committee on the Judiciary, Special Subcommittee, *Associate Justice William O. Douglas: Final Report on H.R. 920,* 91st Cong., 2d Sess., 1970, pp. 1–15, 357–63.
3. Art. II., sec. 1.
4. Art. I, Sec. 2.
5. Art. I, Sec. 3.
6. Ibid.,
7. Art. II, Sec. 4.
8. New York *Times,* April 21, 1970, p. 42.
9. *Douglas Final Report,* pp. 367–84 (including comment of certain other House members).
10. Ibid., p. 37.
11. Ibid., p. 349.
12. Ibid., p. 40. The figures were obtained by the Celler subcommittee staff from Douglas' income tax returns, supplied by the Internal Revenue Service.
13. Ibid., see p. 235. See also p. 236, where the agency is identified as the William Morris Agency, Inc.,
14. Ibid., p. 162.
15. Ibid., pp. 274–76.
16. Ibid., pp. 145–46.
17. Ibid., p. 110.
18. The Johnson foundation, set up in 1956, was first called the Lyndon B. Johnson Foundation and later its name was changed to the Johnson City Foundation; *Wall Street Journal,* June 30, 1964, p. 1. The Richard M. Nixon Foundation was established in 1969, apparently in anticipation of the creation of a Nixon presidential library as well as for other tax-exempt purposes; New York *Times,* May 13, 1969, p. 20.
19. *Douglas Final Report,* pp. 175–227, concerning Douglas's relationships with the Parvin Foundation and the Center for the Study of Democratic Institutions.
20. Ibid., p. 178, 267.
21. Ibid., pp. 89–90.
22. *New York Times,* May 24, 1969, p. 1.
23. Douglas's statement was delivered orally, Dec. 17, 1970.

CHAPTER 14, PROMISES AND THREATS

1. Bivens v. Six Unknown Named Agents of the Federal Bureau of Narcotics, 403 U.S. 388 (1971).
2. FBI *Law Enforcement Bulletin* (September 1971), p. 3,4.
3. Whiteley v. Warden, Wyoming State Penitentiary, 401 U.S. 560 (1971).
4. Cohen v. California, 403 U.S. 15 (1971).
5. Coleman v. Alabama, 399, U.S. 1 (1970).
6. Unser v. Luckenbach Overseas Corp., 400 U.S. 494 (1971).
7. 347 U.S. 483 (1954).
8. Brown II, 349 U.S. 294 (1955).
9. Griffin v. Board of Education, 377 U.S. 218 (1964).
10. Green v. County School Board, 391 U.S. 430 (1968).
11. Jones v. Mayer, 392 U.S. 409 (1968).
12. Swann v. Charlotte-Mecklenburg Board of Education, 402 U.S. 1 (1971). See also related cases, decided the same day, Davis v. Board of School Commissioners of Mobile County, 402 U.S. 33, and McDaniel v. Barresi, 402 U.S. 39.
13. *Wall Street Journal,* August 4, 1971, p. 2.
14. *Bombing in the United States,* a report released January 12, 1972, by the International Association of Police Chiefs, Gaithersburg, Maryland.
15. New York *Times* May 12, 1971, p. 38.
16. New York Times Co. v. U.S., decided with U.S. v. Washington Post Co., 403 U.S. 713 (1971).
17. Winston-Salem/Forsyth County Board of Education v. Scott, 404 U.S. 1221 (1971).

CHAPTER 15, POLITICS AND PROFESSIONALISM

1. Washington *Post,* September 29, 1971, p. A6.
2. *The Legal Profession in the United States,* Second Edition. Chicago: American Bar Foundation, 1970, p. 20.
3. Weaver, *Warren: The Man, The Court, The Era,* pp. 283–84.
4. Douglas, *Points of Rebellion,* p. 95.
5. Mitchell's agreement was contained in his letter of July 23, 1970, to Lawrence E. Walsh, chairman of the ABA Committee on the Federal Judiciary. Walsh's response to Mitchell was dated July 27, 1970.
6. American Bar Association, *Report of the Standing Committee on the Federal Judiciary,* February 5, 1972, pp. 4,5.
7. ABA, *Report of the Standing Committee on the Federal Judiciary,* October 31, 1971., p. 5.
8. *Cleveland Press,* October 6, 1971, p. 2.
9. *Chicago Tribune,* October 24, 1971, p. 1.

10. Clark v. Board of Directors of the Little Rock School District, 328 F. Supp. 1205 (1971).
11. ABA, *Report,* October 31, 1971, p. 6.
12. Ibid., p. 7.
13. See Jack Anderson, The Washington Merry-go-round, a syndicated column, Chicago *Daily News,* October 21, 1971, p. 16.
14. See, exchange of letters between Derek C. Bok, president of Harvard University, and Kleindienst. Bok's letter, signed also by Albert M. Sacks, dean of Harvard Law School, was dated November 19, 1971, and Kleindienst's reply was dated December 14, 1971. See also, Washington *Post,* December 25, 1971, p. 1, an article headed, "Harvard's Bok Claims FBI 'Intimidated' Law Professor."
15. ABA, *Report,* October 31, 1971, p. 8.
16. Ibid., p. 15.
17. The White House, Statement by the President, October 21, 1971.
18. The White House, Remarks of the President, Washington Hilton Hotel, October 22, 1971.
19. *The Challenge of Crime in a Free Society,* report of the Commission on Law Enforcement and Administration of Justice, 1967, pp. 303–08.
20. *Leadership and Responsibility on the Changing Campus,* papers presented at the Eighth Annual Meeting (Washington: American Association of State Colleges and Universities, 1969), p. 86.
21. Richmond *Times-Dispatch,* August 1, 1971, p. 1, an article titled "Civil Liberties Repression: Fact or Fiction."
22. *Report of Blue Ribbon Defense Panel,* supplemental statement dated September 30, 1970, p. vii.
23. Bok letter of November 19, 1971, and Kleindienst reply of December 14, 1971.
24. U.S., Congress, Senate, Committee on the Judiciary, *Nominations of William H. Rehnquist and Lewis F. Powell, Jr.: Hearings,* 92d Cong., 1st Sess., November 3–10, 1971, p. 7.
25. Ibid., p. 4.
26. Ibid., p. 203.
27. Ibid., p. 219.
28. New York *Times,* December 7, 1971, p. 1.
29. New York *Times,* March 11, 1970, p. 18.
30. *Rehnquist and Powell: Hearings,* p. 46.
31. Ibid., p. 441.

CHAPTER 16, OUT-WALLACING WALLACE

1. See, William F. Swindler, "The Politics of Advice and Consent," *American Bar Association Journal,* vol. 56 (June 1970), pp. 533–42.
2. In an interview on the "David Frost Show," taped April 1, 1971, for broadcast on April 8, 1971; transcript as released by the Justice Department.

3. American Bar Association, *Report of the Standing Committee on the Federal Judiciary,* October 31, 1971.
4. *American Bar Association Journal,* vol. 57, December 1971, pp. 1209–10.
5. Ibid., p. 1209.
6. The White House, Statement on Nationwide Television and Radio, in which Nixon announced the nominations of Powell and Rehnquist, October 21, 1971.
7. ABA *Journal* vol. 57, December 1971, p. 1209.
8. *American Bar Association Journal* vol. 55, November 1969, p. 1050.
9. Quoted by Leon Friedman and Fred L. Israel, editors, *The Justices of the United States Supreme Court 1789–1969* (New York and London: Chelsea House Publishers, in association with R.R. Bowker Company, 1969), vol. III, p. 2105. The biography of Taft, by Alpheus Thomas Mason, appears at vol. III, pp. 2103–2121.
10. Ibid., pp. 2119–20.
11. Ibid., p. 2111.
12. *Wall Street Journal,* October 28, 1971, p. 1.
13. Kurland, "The Lord Chancellor of the United States," *Trial* magazine, vol. 7, November/December 1971, pp. 11, 28. The magazine is published by the American Trial Lawyers Association.
14. U.S., Congress, Senate, Committee on the Judiciary, *Nomination of Harry A. Blackmun: Hearing,* 91st Cong., 2d Sess., April 29, 1970, p. 40.
15. Douglas, statement to the press, December 16, 1970.
16. 401 U.S. 560 (1971).
17. 403 U.S 388 (1971). The companion case was Coolidge v. New Hampshire, 403 U.S. 443 (1971).
18. Harris v. New York, 401 U.S. 222 (1971).
19. Dutton v. Evans, 400 U.S. 74 (1970).
20. U.S. v. White, 401 U.S. 745 (1971).
21. Ibid., at 756.
22. Witcomb, Governor of Indiana, v. Chavis, 403 U.S. 124 (1971).
23. Gordon v. Lance, 403 U.S. 1 (1971).
24. Labine v. Vincent, 401 U.S. 532 (1971).
25. Gillette v. U.S., 401 U.S. 437 (1971).
26. Griggs v. Duke Power Co., 401 U.S. 424 (1971).
27. Palmer v. Thompson, Mayor of the City of Jackson, 403 U.S. 217 (1971).

EPILOGUE

1. White House, Message to Congress, March 17, 1972.
2. 403 U.S. 713 (1971).
3. 403 U.S. 15 (1971).
4. See *New York Times*, November 9, 1971.
5. Oregon v. Mitchell, 400 U.S. 112 (1970).
6. White House, Statement by the President, August 3, 1971.
7. *New York Times*, August 27, 1971, p. 14.
8. White House, Message to Congress, March 17, 1972.
9. U.S. Department of Justice, Statement of the Attorney General, March 1, 1972.
10. *New York Times*, August 1, 1971, p. 33.
11. *New York Times*, September 14, 1971, p. 1.
12. White House, Message to Congress, March 17, 1972.
13. The statement was made in an opinion by Burger, in which no other members of the Court joined, when *certiorari* was denied in Volpe v. D.C. Federation of Civic Associations, Per Curiam, March 27, 1972. The comment was made in a case that did not involve busing. However, coming ten days following the President's busing message, it could not be considered irrelevant to the constitutionality of Nixon's proposal. See *New York Times*, April 3, 1972, p. 36, an editorial, "The Chief Oversteps."
14. 163 U.S. 537 (1896).

# Index